# Out
### of
# Faith

# Out
of
# Faith

*a mother,
a sect,
and a
journey
to freedom*

# MARIA COMPTON

**BLINK**
bringing you closer

First published in the UK by Blink Publishing
An imprint of The Zaffre Publishing Group
A Bonnier Books UK Company
4th Floor, Victoria House,
Bloomsbury Square,
London, WC1B 4DA

Owned by Bonnier Books
Sveavägen 56, Stockholm, Sweden

Instagram: @blinkpublishing
X: @blinkpublishing

First published in 2024 by Blink Publishing

Hardback ISBN: 978-1-78512-182-1
Ebook ISBN: 978-1-78512-185-2
Audiobook ISBN: 978-1-78512-186-9

British Library Cataloguing-in-Publication Data:
A CIP catalogue record for this book is available from the British Library.

Printed and bound in Great Britain by Clays Ltd, Elcograf S.p.A

1 3 5 7 9 10 8 6 4 2

MIX
Paper | Supporting
responsible forestry
FSC
www.fsc.org
FSC® C018072

Blink Publishing is an imprint of Bonnier Books UK
www.bonnierbooks.co.uk

*To my precious children,*

*Even though we are torn apart; a place where hugs and conversations are a distant memory, know that my love for you hasn't changed.*

*This memoir is a voice filled with hope, a beacon of light, a constant reminder that you are in my thoughts and that I will never give up on bringing us back together.*

*I love you forever and am here for you.*

*Until the day when we are together again,*

*Mum*

# CONTENTS

# PROLOGUE

## *16 February 2021*

The day begins like any other Tuesday: I drive to my nanny job for a 7 a.m. start. Dawn is breaking and the cold northern air mists my windscreen. I look forward to my work. I'm good at it. It brings me a sense of belonging. I look after three school-age children – two boys and a girl. They're great kids. I've grown to love them. Their parents, my employers, make me feel a part of the family.

They know that I'm in my fifties, that I'm estranged from all six of my own children, and that I'll never see them or any of my grandchildren or my parents or siblings again. We talked about it at the interview. I explained about the Plymouth Brethren Christian Church as best I could. I told them that my people had been called the Exclusive Brethren for a hundred years, but that in 2013 they'd changed their name to the Plymouth Brethren Christian Church. I went on to tell them how things used to operate if you chose to part company with them.

'If you left them, they closed their doors to you completely,' I said at interview, trying to find ways to make it simple. 'They pulled up the drawbridge. They didn't like you speaking to anyone inside again, not even your own children.'

I could see them wince, then lean in. I saw the tears brim in their eyes. I saw them imagining what it might feel like to lose their children.

'Probably best not to talk to your children about my past,' I said a few minutes later when we agreed I'd take the job.

They nodded.

'Too difficult to explain,' I said.

1

They nodded again.

'How do you cope?' the mother asked suddenly, gripping her husband's hand, wiping away tears.

'I get on with my life,' I said. 'Best to keep looking forward. I'm glad to be out. I try not to look back.'

After dropping my charges at school for 9 a.m., I drive to my next job where I'm a housekeeper for a busy family of six. I love this job too, and this second family. When I'm busy juggling the housekeeping in this house, it's easy to remember some of the good things from my old life: raising six children, cooking, cleaning, keeping on top of everything.

I'm making beds, tidying bedrooms and dusting furniture when my phone rings. I glance at the number. It's my friend Barry. I don't pick up. I don't like to answer personal calls during work hours. Instead I text him to say I'm working but that I hope everything is OK and I'll call him back when I get home.

'Ring me straight away,' he texts back immediately. 'I have some urgent news.'

Barry is ex-Brethren like me. Sometimes he sends me news about things happening inside. He has a secret Brethren 'contact'. Sometimes, via this secret contact, Barry passes on snippets of precious news of my family to me. What news could be urgent? I ask myself now. Has someone in my family died? Is one of my children seriously ill? Is it my parents?

I ring him straight away. Barry answers the phone immediately.

'Are you sitting down?' he asks. I can hear how nervous he is. I can hear that he's battling with himself. I take the bedroom chair next to the row of family photos that I've just polished.

'I'm sitting,' I say, bracing myself. 'Tell me.'

'Juliet is getting married today,' he says. 'Did someone let you know? Tell me someone got in touch to tell you.'

Juliet is my fifth child, my only daughter. I haven't seen her in five years. She's the one I've been holding my breath for. She's the one I hope might still have the strength and the will to get out.

'No,' I say, my voice breaking, trying to keep calm for Barry's sake. 'No one told me.'

No one has died but still I cry out in anguish. Marriage in the Plymouth Brethren Christian Church can be like a living death for some women. I'll never get Juliet out now. Once she has children she'll be trapped for life, especially if her husband wants to rule over her. She'll never have autonomy. Not unless she knows, like I came to know, that she has to choose between staying with her children and going mad.

'How could she not tell me?' I ask through my tears, but I know the answer. I know the kind of things they say about women who leave. Barry struggles to reply and I can hear the emotion in his voice too.

'Maria,' he says, 'I don't know what to say. I'm so sorry to be the one to tell you.'

'Who is she marrying?' I ask, taking a breath. 'Is it someone I know?'

'A young man from Northampton called Nathan,' he says, no doubt relieved that we are getting to specifics. It turns out that I know some of his family, but I've never heard of Nathan. I tell Barry that I need a little time to take this all in.

'Ring me back,' he says. 'I'm here. We all are.'

As soon as I ring off, I put my head in my hands and sob. What if Juliet had called me? What would I have said? What was there to say?

I hear my therapist's voice. She's good. She's been working on finding ways of helping me keep the children in my heart, of not cutting them off as they have been encouraged to cut me off.

'How do you feel?' she asked me in our first session, after I'd given her the outline of my story.

'Torn,' I said. 'Torn.'

'Yes,' she said, making a note.

'I wish I could talk to them,' I said. 'Tell them what I feel.'

'Tell me instead,' she said. 'Keep talking to me. I won't hang up on you. I won't walk away.'

Now, still reeling from the news, hunched up in the chair in someone else's house, I can hear her voice inside my head: *What would you want to say to Juliet if she was here now?*

'Did you feel this was your only option?' I begin and, once I have begun, it's hard to know where to stop. There are so many things I want to tell Juliet, so many things I want to ask her. 'Brethren marriage is so final,' I hear myself saying. 'You'll never be able to leave. And your children may choose to stay in the Brethren, giving up contact with both you and the "evil" world outside.'

But I want to tell her that I understand too, because I'd done exactly as she had done. When I was eighteen I made the decision to marry a man I barely knew, thinking that once I was married I'd be in charge of my own home, that I'd have a car, status, respect, children, a house to decorate, a garden to grow things in, a husband who would be master of my house but who would also respect me.

'Of course you want those things,' I want to say to Juliet. 'You can't imagine any other future, can you? But do you actually know this man you're marrying? Have you spent any time alone with him? Have they let you?' I think of how little I knew about my husband on my wedding day. I'd never been alone with him. I'd never been allowed to. I had no idea who he was.

The bedroom is silent apart from the sound of sobbing. I must pull myself together. I can't fall apart like this at work. I want to go home and bury my head under the bed covers until this pain goes away.

I hear voices downstairs. My employers, Ali and Gemma, are in the house. My eyes are swollen and red. I'll have to explain. But they know so little of my history; I skirted around it in their interview, and I've only sketched a little of it since. I'm embarrassed.

When I walk into the kitchen, Gemma sees my swollen face.

'Maria, what on earth is the matter?' she says. 'Has something happened?'

'I've just heard that Juliet, my daughter, is getting married today,' I say, my voice breaking.

'What?' she exclaims. 'You've just *heard*? She didn't tell you?'

The sobbing starts again. I can't seem to stop. Gemma leads me to the sofa, sits me down next to her and puts her arms around me. I lean into her, trying to catch my breath. Ali hands me a cup of sweet tea. I feel their kindness and

4

love calm me. I'll be OK, I tell myself. There are so many people that care in my new world. So much kindness. So much understanding.

'I'm so sorry,' I tell them. 'I shouldn't be bringing this to work.'

They answer in unison, in kindness: 'Never, ever feel you have to apologise,' they say. 'We're always here for you.'

Gemma suggests I go home for the afternoon, but I tell her that I'd prefer to keep busy. I won't be beaten. But as I clean and cook and tidy that afternoon, images go round in my head. Juliet will be wearing a pure white dress. No bridesmaids, no wedding party, just a simple meal with one or two family members. Then she'll be whisked off by her new husband to their home in Northampton. No honeymoon. I don't care how simple the celebrations are though. Like all mothers I just want to see my daughter marry a man she loves – a man who loves her. I try to picture her in my mind's eye in her pure white wedding dress walking into the simple Plymouth Brethren Christian Church meeting room but it's so difficult. The last time I'd spoken with Juliet she'd been sixteen years old. I know she looks beautiful. I hope her husband will be kind to her.

That evening, I have a conversation on Zoom with my therapist – whom I shall call Esther. The entire session focuses on the news of Juliet's marriage and how I feel about it. Esther has experience of working with survivors of forced marriages. She talks to me about something called 'coercive control' – a term I'm not familiar with.

She explains how domestic abuse doesn't have to be about bruises and punches, but can be about using fear, brainwashing, humiliation and isolation to get control over someone's mind completely. It's against the law now, she says.

I'm still overwhelmed by the news I've had today. I tell Esther how Juliet, just like me and most Brethren women, will have had very limited communication with her husband before her actual marriage day. I tell her how she will have been forbidden to tell me about her marriage because I'm an outsider now, and because I might have tried to persuade her out of it.

'You could write it all down,' she says. 'Maybe that will help. You could explain your life to your daughter in the form of a memoir. You could write it for all the women like you – like her.'

I've often dreamt that one day Juliet might go looking for me; that she might be curious about or longing for her mother, or because – dare I imagine it? – she might be ready to sever ties with the organisation.

Esther allows me to imagine a space where I can speak directly to Juliet. She asks me what I would say. I focus on my computer screen and reply:

'Juliet, all I wish for is your happiness, but if for any reason you're ever not happy, please, please, don't be afraid to walk away. If your mum could do it in her forties, you can too. I love you always and forever. I'll be waiting.'

In voicing those words, it's like a message in a bottle nudged out to sea.

# PART ONE

# ONE

## The North of England, 1960s

The Plymouth Brethren Christian Church doesn't recruit their followers. It never has. Instead, Brethren families have large numbers of children and raise them in Brethren ways and with Brethren rules and Brethren beliefs from day one. Married couples are expected to produce as many children as they can – it's a badge of honour. Contraception was forbidden back in the 1960s, so if Brethren women wanted to control the number of children they had, they had to persuade their husbands to abstain from sex during ovulation – if they could.

My mother kept a careful eye on her cycles, but her fifth pregnancy came as a shock. Her fourth child, Brian, was just one year old. He was a slow developer. They were already testing him for disabilities. He took up a lot of her time. Then she fell pregnant again – with me. After giving birth, my mother had a day or two of rest in hospital then returned to her Brethren home with me all wrapped up against the cold. Like so many Brethren mothers, she now had multiple children under eight years old.

The addition of another child into an already busy home can't have been easy for either of my parents, with the daily meetings all families were obliged to attend, all the entertaining and – for my mother – the constant washing, ironing, meals and housekeeping. She would have had sleepless nights feeding me, worrying about Brian, and then she'd have to drag herself out of bed before dawn to wake and dress all her other children for the 5 a.m. Breaking of Bread meeting on Sunday, the day we called the Lord's Day. At this time, a Brethren wife was not allowed to do any paid work, but was expected to keep a tidy home, and endlessly host and entertain other Brethren families between the eleven meetings of the week. All this being done whilst appearing well-dressed and respectful, which meant always having our heads covered by headscarves when at meetings or in public.

At just eight days old I was baptised in faith by my parents in the family bathtub, so that I would never waver from the path on which God had put me. My parents believed me to be special, chosen by God Himself to be a part of the most privileged people on this earth: the Plymouth Brethren Christian Church – God's people. This was God's plan for me. Nothing was my choice. It was all God's choice, and I must grow up to accept that without question.

As I begin my story, as I look back, I see many happy times: family picnics, endless summer days on the beach in our pretty seaside town, laughing with Brethren friends and family, playing games with other Brethren children, but a shadow seems to be cast across those memories – a shadow of fear, of foreboding and confusion. The biggest of those fears, the one that stayed with me even beyond my eventual breakaway from the Brethren, was the fear of 'the Rapture': a time when, according to the Brethren doctrine, Jesus would come to take His bride, the Brethren, to be with him in Heaven. But he would only take us if we were ready. If we weren't ready, we'd be left behind to face the horrors of the Tribulation.

It was a warm Sunday afternoon a few months before my fifth birthday when I heard about 'the Rapture' for the first time. That afternoon I had my first experience with fear: a fear that has stayed with me for a lifetime.

It was the fourth and last meeting of the day. This was a gospel preaching, held in our small local meeting hall, with its closed curtained windows to keep the world out and its creaky floor with threadbare green carpet. I was tired and irritable and didn't want to sit in a stuffy meeting hall to listen to the drone of the preacher. I wanted to get out of my scratchy Crimplene smocked dress and play in the sunshine with my friends. My head hurt from wearing my headscarf for so long and the tight knot at the nape of my neck was pulling on my hair. The day had, as usual, been filled with meetings, interspersed with periods of entertainment and meals served by the Brethren women.

Today, like every Lord's Day, I had been awoken from a deep sleep at 5.15 a.m. Mum had dressed me in the dark before dawn while I was still half asleep and then Dad had carried me to our old blue Austin 1600 and, because there was no room in the back seat next to my four sleepy siblings, he had lowered me as usual into the footwell at Mum's feet. Resting my head against Mum's stockinged legs, I had done my best to stay asleep. Then we'd driven the short journey across town to our local meeting for the Breaking of Bread.

Now, almost twelve hours later, I was back at that same meeting hall and, although I'd caught catnaps throughout the day, I was grumpy, restless and overtired. Mum must have had enough of my fidgeting because she had asked Dad if I could sit next to him. Normally, the sisters and the girl children sat behind the men, the brothers, in the meetings but sometimes the very little girls were allowed to sit upfront next to their daddies.

I liked sitting next to Dad because he would usually take me on his knee, and I would cuddle up to him and doze. I liked laying my head against his crisp white shirt that smelt of starch and Old Spice. But I didn't like being so close to all those other men dressed in their crisp white shirts and navy trousers. Sometimes they'd pat my leg and wink at me. Some of the Brethren preachers were soft-spoken, nervous and boring, and that meant I'd be able to doze and wake up full of beans, as Mum called it, and be ready to play tag with my friends later in the meeting hall car park. But most of the ministering brothers shouted a lot. I didn't like being so close to the preacher who would stand and shout on the shiny wooden platform of that tiny, cramped meeting hall.

We sang the hymn, and Dad's leg jigged along in time so that I bobbed up and down in rhythm to the well-known tune. As the hymn ended, old Mr Gillespe got up from his seat, walked to the platform and took his place facing us behind the microphone stand. Mr Gillespe was a tall, rangy man with a shock of white hair and half-rimmed glasses. He wore a pocket watch tucked into his pinstripe waistcoat. He was one of the few Brethren men who still wore a suit. Since Mr Taylor, the Man of God (head of the Brethren church worldwide), had decreed in the 1960s that ties stopped the Spirit from speaking freely, most of the men now wore cardigans over their crisp white shirts, but not Mr Gillespe. He had stopped wearing the tie but kept wearing his three-piece suit regardless. He always had a twinkle in his eye, a smile on his face, and would miraculously produce a peppermint from his jacket pocket if any of us children passed him.

Settling into the crook of Dad's arm, I lean my head against his chest while my little legs dangle between his long legs. Thin shafts of light shine through the thinly curtained windows, casting dusty sunbeams around the room. After Mr Gillespe has prayed, he opens his large worn leather Bible and, licking his thumb, turns the thin crinkly pages to verses in Matthew 25. He begins reading the verses softly in his sing-song voice:

'Then shall the kingdom of heaven be made like to ten virgins that having taken their torches, went forth to meet the bridegroom. And five of them were prudent and five foolish. They that were foolish took their torches and did not take oil with them; but the prudent took oil in their vessels with the torches. Now the bridegroom tarrying, they all grew heavy and slept.'

His voice is so soporific that I'm soon nodding off. Suddenly Mr Gillespe's voice changes as he almost shouts the next part of the scripture: 'But in the middle of the night there was a cry, "Behold, the bridegroom; go forth to meet him."'

Lowering his voice again, Mr Gillespe goes on. I've heard this story before. Five of those virgins, the foolish ones, had no oil left in their lamps after the long wait for the bridegroom, so they had to go and buy more oil. While they were out buying oil, the bridegroom came. He took the five virgins who had brought enough oil with them – the wise ones – to the wedding. When the remaining five came home they found the house empty and the door locked against them.

'Keep awake therefore,' Mr Gillespe roars now, 'for you know not the day nor the hour!'

I wake with another jolt. Why do I need to keep awake?

'Are you awake?' Mr Gillespe shouts. 'Are you ready? Are you ready for the Lord Jesus to come for us? Are you ready for the Rapture? The Lord is coming soon but only those who are ready will be gathered with him and taken up on a cloud to Heaven to be with him forever! All the others will have the door shut against them. Shut. *Forever.*'

I shiver. What has happened to smiling Mr Gillespe? Why does he need to shout? How will I know if I'm ready? What will happen to me if I'm not ready and I get left behind?

My heart is thumping.

I glance up at Dad. He is smiling and nodding. The men around me are all 'Mmmming' and 'Ahhhing'. They must be sure they are ready. Am I the only one who isn't ready? Is Mr Gillespe talking to me? I look straight at him, trying to be brave. His eyes, peering over those half-rimmed glasses, are looking straight at me. I almost fall off Dad's knee with fright as he booms out his next words and stabs the air with his spindly fingers.

'Oh, sinner, be sure of your sins forgiven! Be sure of your link with the Lord Jesus! Be sure that you are filled with the Holy Spirit! Be sure that you will be on that cloud that goes up to Heaven at the Rapture!'

Putting my hands over my ears, I hear the words going round and round in my head. I am not ready, and Mr Gillespe knows it. Dad looks down at me and seems amused to see my hands over my ears.

Taking one hand away for a minute, he whispers in my ear, 'He is shouting a bit loudly today, isn't he?'

But it isn't the shouting that's scaring me. It's the words. I can't tell Dad that I'm not ready. I am Brethren and Brethren are expected to be ready.

That night, as I kneel next to my bed, I pray that I'll be ready for the Rapture and that I will not be left behind. As Mum tucks me up for the night, pulling the cosy flowery eiderdown up around me and kissing me, I put my arms around her neck, hold her tight and give her an extra-long kiss, terrified that it might be the last time.

'You know not the day nor the hour,' I hear Mr Gillespe roar, stabbing his fingers in the air.

13

I hardly slept that night, nor for many nights after. Through the darkest hours I lay staring at the ceiling, listening for the sounds of my parents and siblings in the silent house, terrified that they'd all disappear before morning, leaving me alone in the empty house to face what the Bible calls the Tribulation – the floods, the falling stars, the rising seas, the evil that would sweep over this whole earth and the wars that would follow.

After a few weeks, my parents began to worry about the number of times I visited their bedroom in the early hours of the morning. I was just checking to see if they were still there, of course, but I couldn't tell them that. They bought a set of bunk beds and moved my older sister Claire into my bedroom for company. I slept on the bottom with Claire above me. Having my sister there helped calm my fears a little when I awoke in the night from one of my nightmares.

In these dreams about the Rapture I was always running, running to catch up with my family, but my legs were heavy as lead, too heavy to lift. I remained stuck to the ground as I watched my family disappear on a cloud up into the sky further and further away from me until they were just a tiny dot, like a lost balloon. I would wake up with a jump and in a sweat. Then, by lying very still and listening for Claire's gentle breathing above me, I would eventually go back to sleep.

Once you turn twelve within the Brethren you are considered more responsible. You should be conscious that your sins are forgiven by Jesus. You should be sure that you are saved and that you will have eternal life in Heaven. You should be ready for the Rapture. If you aren't sure of these things, then, the preacher told us, it was urgent to get a 'settlement in your soul'. I didn't know what 'settlement' meant, nor did I really understand what was 'me' and what was my 'soul'. I never seemed sure of anything. I didn't understand many of the Bible teachings, and I understood even less of the Brethren teachings, but I didn't dare ask for fear of exposing my doubts.

I was almost a teenager and had spent the last six years attending a school where I was supposed to witness how worldly children lived and come to despise them. But, in the dark of the night when I was alone in my bed, I fantasised about what life would be like if I hadn't been born inside the Plymouth Brethren Christian Church. I fantasised about having a boyfriend. I dreamt of what life with a television would be like. Even though I knew these fantasies were a sin in the eyes of the Brethren, I couldn't seem to make them go away and, for that reason, I was still certain that I wasn't ready for the Rapture. One day all my family and everyone I had ever known in the Brethren world was going to be raptured up into Heaven and I was going to be left alone in this world, left to survive the Tribulation alone.

It's April. I come out of school at 3.30 p.m. and take the ten-minute walk home alone as usual. As I walk along the flag-stoned pavement, with the park on one side of the road and the rows of terraced houses on the other, I peep in the windows and wonder what sort of lives the people who live there have. I can see a television flickering in some of the rooms, and families smiling and laughing. What would it be like to not have to go to meetings every day but instead to live in a family that would sit around the television watching the latest programmes?

As I walk up our steep tarmac driveway towards the back door, I do my best to push those wicked thoughts away again. I turn my thoughts to the comfort of my own life and what will greet me when I walk through our back door. I know my older siblings and Dad will be at college or work until later, but Mum, Brian and my little sister Chloe will be home. Chloe is only nine months old. I'll play with her and forget these sinful thoughts. And then there will be Grandma (Dad's mum), sitting in her armchair by the front bay window of her little annexe within our home, with her long white scraggly hair tied back and hanging over her shoulder. Grandma is always there when I come home from school.

On reaching the back door I find that it is locked. I never come home to a locked door. If Mum isn't at home, I remind myself, then Grandma will be there. Going to the shed, I find the spare key hidden under the paint pot on the shelf. I unlock the back door and enter a silent house. Where is everyone? There is no one in our kitchen or lounge. I run into Grandma's living room. She'll be sitting there in that funny way she does, with her legs curled under her and her head dropped onto her chest gently snoring, or maybe she'll be reading the Bible.

I turn the old wooden doorknob and enter the musty room, but there is no Grandma, no gentle snoring, no open Bible – just an empty room. Maybe she is in her bedroom praying? Grandma is always praying, especially since Grandpa died four years earlier. I run to the bedroom and gently open the half-closed door, but no Grandma is kneeling by the bed. When I call her and I call Mum, all I hear is the echo of my voice within the walls of our Victorian detached house.

I go up to my bedroom, sit on my bed and tell myself to keep calm. Someone will be home soon. I remember that Brian is at work experience this week, so he won't be home until later. I go back downstairs and help myself to a glass of milk and some biscuits. Then, after emptying my schoolbooks onto our large dining-room table, I do my best to get started on my homework. I can't concentrate. I keep worrying about all those wicked thoughts I had earlier.

Then a new thought hits me: has the Rapture come at last? Have I been left behind because I'm not ready? Have I been left behind because of my evil thoughts and fantasies about television and boyfriends?

As I make my way back upstairs to my bedroom every floorboard creaks under my feet. I'm scared of this house when it's empty. It had been Grandpa and Grandma's house before we moved in to look after Grandma when Grandpa had died in 1976. Grandpa's parents had lived in it before that, so it has been in the Brethren for many years. I often think of all the Brethren men and women who have lived and died here. I wonder if they watch me. In the dead of the night, all sorts of shadows and noises seem to come out of its walls. I think of Grandpa, his face waxy white, laid out for days in his coffin in our hallway. Is he watching me now? Is he lurking in the walls of this house?

It's only four o'clock in the afternoon, but it seems like a terrible darkness has fallen over the whole house. I shiver.

I'm struggling to breathe. My skin feels cold, then hot. I think of praying but then I realise there is no point. It's too late. The door is shut. I can hear Mr Gillespe shouting that word again: 'Shut!' I am a sinner. I have been left alone to face the horrors of the Tribulation. Mr Gillespe's voice echoes around the walls: 'Are you ready? Are you ready for when the Lord comes to take us up with him to Heaven? Be ready for you know not the day nor the hour!'

I sit down on the low wooden bedroom chair by the window, so that I can watch the corner of the building and the little path that we use as a shortcut from the main road to our house. If I just sit here and keep my eye on that spot and keep breathing, I think, then I will see Mum the second she comes around the corner.

*She will come.*

*She must come.*

As I sit there, I lose all sense of time. It seems like forever. I think of the virgins and their lamps. Then I see – first the wheels of Chloe's pushchair and then the figure of Mum comes around that corner.

I begin to sob. The Rapture hasn't happened after all. I still have time to get ready. I run downstairs and into the kitchen as Mum comes through the back door.

'Where have you been?' I ask, trying to sound calm.

'Oh, I got delayed in the bank,' she says, taking off her coat and starting to unload the bags from the back of the pushchair. 'There was such a long queue and then I had to go shopping. You're a big girl now. I thought you would be fine on your own for a bit.' She lifts Chloe out of the pushchair and sets her down on the kitchen rug.

'Grandma has gone out for a little walk. She'll be back shortly. Are you all right? Has something happened?'

Keeping my head down so that she won't notice my tear-stained face, I grunt something in reply. I lift Chloe from the rug and hug her tight. I want to hug Mum tight too, but I know if I do that she will guess that something is wrong, and I don't want to tell her how frightened I've been. I can't tell her about my evil thoughts and fantasies and that I don't think I am ready for the Rapture. That will have to stay *my* secret.

# TWO

Before I was old enough to attend school I was mostly happy. My life was filled with meetings, playing with my Brethren cousins and sitting around our dining table surrounded by my family and friends. For me that was normal. I thought very little about how people in the outside world lived. My family and everyone else I knew called everyone who lived outside our fellowship the 'worldly people' or the 'worldlies'. The worldlies were ruled by Satan. They might not know it, but Satan controlled everything they did. They were all going to be left behind when the Rapture came. They'd all die, drown, burn, suffocate in the Tribulation, but you weren't allowed to tell them that.

Despite home life being protective and cosy, I'd never been comfortable around Brethren men. The men I knew, even my father, whom I loved, shouted a lot. They were unpredictable. They'd be friendly sometimes but they could turn. For instance, our town leader was serious and pious in the meetings but, once he'd downed a few whiskeys at home or in our lounge, he became the class clown. I didn't understand some of the jokes he told but, as I got older, I realised that many of them were 'near the knuckle'. He frightened me. But Grandpa Compton *terrified* me. I was always on tenterhooks around him.

Brethren boys were different. I played games with the boys in Brethren car parks and gardens rather than the girls. I was very close to my older brother Brian, not only in age but temperamentally. The other Brethren boys often bullied him because of his learning difficulties. They would laugh at him when he spent his time after the meetings chatting with our spinster babysitter, Miss Parker. They'd say things like, 'Here comes Miss Parker's boyfriend.' Or they'd purposely trip him up and laugh when he fell over. I felt I had a duty to look after him, mothering him even though he was older than me.

With television banned, and very few children's books allowed, Brian and I played games of let's pretend. Brian would sit on the lower stair while I sat behind him exactly as we did in the Brethren meetings: brothers at the front and sisters behind. I didn't own a doll in those days, so I'd fill a hot water bottle, dress it up in baby clothes, wrap it in a shawl and pretend it was my baby. Brian and I would place our hymn books and Bibles on our knees, then, just like the sisters did in the meetings, I would announce a hymn and we would both sing it enthusiastically. Then Brian would pray like the brothers did, and then read from the Bible. Sometimes he'd put on a very serious gruff voice as he mimicked old Mr James, or he'd copy Uncle Jack, talking very deep and low and clearing his throat with every other word. That would make me giggle when I was supposed to be sitting silently as the sisters should and then Brian would reprimand me.

When I was just five years old I took a fancy to a young Brethren boy called Kenneth. Kenneth and his family went to the same local meeting hall where we attended the Breaking of Bread meeting, the Monday Prayer meeting and the occasional Sunday afternoon Preaching. We weren't allowed to play or even talk to each other after the Breaking of Bread meeting, but Brian, Kenneth and I often played tag together after the Monday night meeting. I liked Kenneth; he was kind and didn't bully Brian as some of the other boys did. He was fun to be around.

Even at five years old I was aware that, as a Brethren girl, my future was marriage. The thought of ending up not married, like Miss Parker and many of the Brethren spinsters, scared me. I wanted what Mum and Dad had: love, happiness and children. Perhaps, I hoped, one day Kenneth would ask me to marry him. I dreamt of the wedding day, the children we'd have and how we'd live happily ever after.

One Sunday evening in winter, in the early 1970s, Kenneth and his family came to our house for tea. It was too cold and dark to play in the garden, so, after tea, once Mum had cleared the big dining table and sat down in the lounge with the other Brethren, I whispered to Kenneth, who was sitting crossed-legged on the thick-pile carpet next to me, 'Shall we go into another room and play a game?'

Even at only five years old I knew it was wrong for us to be alone; I knew that a Brethren boy and girl were not allowed to be alone in a room together. I knew we'd be breaking the rules but this time I didn't care. This time I wanted Kenneth to myself. He nodded and grinned. Getting down on all fours, we crawled out of the noisy lounge. Once in the hallway, we ran into the empty dining room. Having closed the door quietly, I dragged a dining chair over to the door and placed it firmly against it so that no one could come in. I wanted to be sure that we didn't get caught.

We sat on the floor playing dominos, our knees touching, looking up occasionally to smile at each other, laughing quietly. Suddenly there was a rattle and a pushing at the door. The chair I'd wedged against the door fell to the floor. Kenneth and I jumped up guiltily. My brother Edward stepped into the room. Looking at us quizzically, he asked in an amused voice,

'What are you two doing in here alone? Naughty children.'

I felt my cheeks flush hot. I put my head down and ran from the room with Kenneth following close behind. As we made our separate ways into the lounge, I heard Edward let out a wolf whistle and a laugh.

That night forged a friendship between Kenneth and me that lasted for eight years. Every year from the age of six I pushed an anonymous Valentine's card through his door. I did it until the year I was thirteen. It was our secret.

When we were both thirteen, I sent him a card with a rather saucy Valentine's verse written in it. This time I signed it with my name and lots of kisses. But things were already changing between us. I know now that like all teenage Brethren boys, Kenneth would have been feeling pressure to preach, to show himself to be an obedient Brethren boy in every way. There'd be no future for him inside the Brethren unless he proved himself.

That year Kenneth showed my Valentine's card to his dad. I was mortified that Kenneth's father had read the card I'd sent. I was shamed and punished by my parents. But it was the betrayal that was most painful. I wasn't sure I could ever forgive Kenneth for what he had done. I should have known that our secrets and our loyalty to each other couldn't last into adulthood. After all, as Kenneth grew up and became a good Brethren boy, he was expected to be vigilant and to expose the sins of others, especially those he loved.

# THREE

Jim Symington, a pig farmer from a small town in America, was the Brethren Man of God, or Elect Vessel, when I was growing up. He ruled over the 47,000 Exclusive Brethren around the world. He preached that it was important for Brethren children to 'rub shoulders with the world' as it would teach us to get a hatred of it. So, like many young Brethren children, I was sent to a worldly primary school. I walked the school corridors of the worldly people in a state of constant fear and awe that these children and our teachers must be very bad people if we were expected to hate them so much.

When I started school I entered a whole new world. How quickly was I supposed to hate these worldly people? Would it happen all at once, or slowly? Would I get into trouble if I never learnt to hate them? Standing there in the classroom on the first day, I recognised the little boy who lived in the big white house across the road from us. He was busy playing with the sand. He seemed happy to be in school. Maybe that was because his parents always seemed to be arguing.

I didn't recognise anyone else in the classroom. I was the only new Brethren child starting Wellfleet Primary School that year, and standing there alone in that unfamiliar classroom, unsure whether to approach the worldly children or cower from them, I was overwhelmed. I dropped my head to my chest, screwed my eyes up and cried. My worldly teacher, Mrs Stephenson, was by my side in an instant.

'Come on, Maria,' she said cheerfully, 'let's go and find someone for you to play with.' She led me towards a boy and girl who were busy playing at the water trough.

'Maria, this is Danielle and Darren,' Mrs Stephenson said kindly. 'They're twins. Danielle and Darren, you look after Maria for me. Show her the water toys.' She let go of my hand and headed back to the front of the classroom to comfort another crying child as we started chattering, shyly at first. Lost in spinning water wheels, sponges and water pipes, I'd soon forgotten Mr Symington and how I was supposed to get a hatred of these worldly children.

But it wasn't long before Mrs Stephenson announced that it was time to have morning assembly. Mum had given me strict instructions about morning assembly. I was supposed to sit outside the assembly hall and wait there with the other Brethren children from other year groups. But did my teacher know that? And what would I say to Danielle and Darren and any of the other children if they asked me why I was sitting out there?

Mrs Stephenson lined us all up in pairs at the classroom door. She put me next to a chubby little boy and told us to take our partner's hand as she led us towards the hall. I didn't want to hold hands with a worldly boy, but he took my hand in his and we followed the rest of the class out the door. Just as I thought I was going to burst with terror, I saw my brother Edward sitting outside the hall. I let go of the boy's hand and ran to join Edward. As several generations of Brethren children had gone through her school Mrs Stephenson knew the Brethren rules and had probably long given up questioning them.

Edward, who had been given our dad's name, was eleven and in his last year of primary school. He was tall for his age. I was glad to have him as my protector. Soon my two other siblings, Claire and Brian, and my four cousins joined us on the bench. When cousin Elaine came and took the spare seat next to me, I started chattering, but Edward gave me a sharp nudge, telling me we must sit in silence. Sitting silent was something we Brethren children were used to. We spent hours doing it in the daily meetings. Elaine had a book about animals with her, so she laid it across both our knees and began to turn the pages quietly.

To the other children and the teachers we must have looked quaint sitting there silently in a row in our Brethren clothes.

Most of the girls in my class wore trousers. Brethren girls and women weren't allowed to wear trousers, as it was believed that trousers were called 'men's apparel' in the scriptures. Even at five years old I envied the worldly girls in school, dressed in their trendy tartan trousers while I wore boring plain skirts and tops. As the fifth child and third girl in my family I usually wore hand-me-downs from my older sisters, which I detested. Mum handmade most of our clothes because it was hard to buy suitable ones. She was a great seamstress and did her best to make us look acceptable. But the biggest difference that marked Brethren girls from the worldly children was our long hair. In the 1960s, the Man of God had decreed that it was sinful for a woman or girl to cut her hair. Since then, all the Brethren women had to wear their hair long and sometimes loose, even the old women. Mum did her best to make my hair look nice by plaiting it for school, but, despite myself, I longed to have the short, fringed styles of the worldly girls.

As the years went on I did get a hatred of school, but it wasn't a hatred of the worldly children or teachers. I learnt to hate sitting outside of the morning assembly; I learnt to hate that we were separated from the other children; I learnt to hate being seen as different.

We didn't just have to sit out of assembly. Brethren banned religious education lessons too. I had only been attending school for a few days when our class had their first R.E. lesson.

'OK, children,' the teacher said, 'we're going to read a Bible story. So, everyone, except Maria Compton, come and sit on the reading mat. Maria, I've put a chair outside the classroom door for you to sit on. Take your reading book with you and I'll come and get you when we're finished.'

I pushed my chair back from my desk, picked up my 'Dick and Dora' reading book and walked towards the classroom door with my head bent in embarrassment and my cheeks burning. I could feel all the other children's eyes on me again as I opened the door as quietly as I could and stepped out into the empty corridor.

Once I was on the chair, I glanced both ways down the corridor. There was no one there but me. I did my best to make myself comfortable. I remember shivering. Whether it was from the cold or from the feeling of being alone, I couldn't tell you. And I couldn't understand why I'd been sent out. Why couldn't I listen to the Bible story? Was there something wrong with the school's Bible? Didn't every Bible have the same stories?

There were so many rules and prohibitions for us Brethren children while at school. No one explained these rules to us at home or at school, and we were not allowed to ask questions. Asking questions got you into trouble. You just had to do what you were told.

Sometimes I wonder now how my teachers felt about putting us Brethren children out there alone. I know they were acting under orders from the principal of the school, and they'd have been used to doing this for other Brethren children. But did they feel it was wrong? Did they do it against their better judgement? Did they worry about how tired and grey the faces of some of the Brethren mothers were, or wince when they heard the bullying, hectoring voices of some of the Brethren fathers? Did they worry for us growing up among these people? I guess, if they had a moment of doubt, they'd have told themselves that they were doing the right thing – being respectful of other religious faiths.

At lunchtimes we were expected to keep separate from the world in every sense. Back in the early 1960s, the previous Brethren Man of God decreed that the Brethren were not to eat with worldly people. He used the scripture in 2 Timothy 2 to support this doctrine, especially verse 19, where it says, 'The Lord knows those that are his; and, Let everyone that names the name of the Lord withdraw from iniquity.'

*Iniquity.* The word seems so old-fashioned to me now, and a word that certainly no one at school would have understood, yet it was a word we Brethren children heard most days. To the Brethren, iniquity meant evil, corruption and sinfulness. Iniquity was everything outside our fellowship, everything we weren't. This meant that we must never eat or drink with anyone outside of the Brethren or we might catch their iniquity, like catching chickenpox or lice. So, though we small Brethren children were supposed to 'rub shoulders with the world' to 'get a hatred of it', we were not supposed to rub shoulders with the world when we were eating. At morning snack time we had to stand or sit separately from our worldly peers and not engage in conversation with them. We had to go home for our lunch. By the time I had walked home, had lunch and returned, there was no time for me to play in the playground with the other children. This further segregated me from the rest of the school.

Of course, I was a weirdo to my peers. A boy in school shouted 'heathen' at me once. I had no idea what he meant at the time, but now I understand that he was from a Protestant family in Northern Ireland. He must have thought that because I sat out of school assembly and religious education that I was an unbeliever or, as his family would call it, a 'heathen'. He didn't understand that we were actually a great deal more hard-line 'Protestant' than his own family.

We Brethren children stood out in so many ways. By keeping separate from the other children at lunchtimes, by leaving the classroom again and again, by wearing our demure clothes and not cutting out hair, we must have seemed holier-than-thou. But we were just obeying orders. If anyone had asked me why we left the room or went home for lunch or didn't cut our hair, I'd have probably just shrugged.

All these Brethren rules we lived by came from the Men of God, the Brethren leaders. This meant that new rules came in as each new Man of God received 'new light' and decreed new sets of rules. Sometimes several new rules came in a single week, and we'd be reeling from the effects of them, trying to catch up.

For instance, there was one evening in the mid-1970s. I was about seven years old and was looking forward to attending the local swimming pool with my class for my first-ever swimming lesson. Mum had bought me a lovely bright-blue swimming costume and a matching blue swim cap to keep my long hair dry. We had just finished dinner and Dad had taken the comfy armchair in front of the Rayburn in our kitchen while Mum washed up and my siblings and I finished our pudding. Dad was reading the new ministry booklet (the most up-to-date word of the Man of God) that had arrived the previous evening. As leader of our meeting, he would use the time after dinner to prepare for the evening meeting. He'd scan the ministry booklet to look for any new light that might have come through that he'd need to explain to the local Brethren. Suddenly, he put down the booklet and said casually, as if it were of no special consequence, 'Mr Symington says that school swimming lessons aren't necessary.'

For Dad, this new rule might have been of little consequence. But not for me. I would be singled out from the rest of my class yet again. I was already forbidden to do any school sports, apart from the compulsory P.E. lessons, and now swimming lessons were going to be banned too. 'Aren't necessary'? What did that mean? We were supposed to accept each new rule as it came. I knew my father would say that the Man of God got his messages straight from God, so who was I to question God if He had said something about swimming lessons?

'Dad,' I said, carefully, my eyes full of tears, 'what does Mr Symington say is the reason for us not being allowed to go to swimming lessons?' The room fell silent as Dad shut the little white booklet and looked up at me surprised.

'Mr Symington feels,' he said firmly, 'that it is unseemly for children to be undressing and wearing swimwear in front of their worldly peers. He is protecting you and keeping you pure for the Lord.' He went back to his reading. There was nothing more to be said. No discussion to be had. New light was new light. Mum went back to her washing up and my siblings continued with their chatter.

I went up to my bedroom and shut the door. The lovely blue swimsuit that I had laid neatly on my bed with the swim cap beside it had lost its sheen. I scrunched it up and threw it into the bottom of my wardrobe, followed by the blue swim cap.

For three years, while my class peers went off for swimming lessons each week, I sat in the school corridor filling out my worksheets.

Brethren rules were rules, but new rules sometimes wiped out old rules. Three years later, when I had sat out of hundreds of swimming lessons and survived scores of uncomfortable conversations in school corridors about why we Brethren children didn't go to swimming lessons, Dad told us that Mr Symington had received new light on the matter of children's swimming lessons. Now we were allowed to go. People would say that the Lord had 'turned a corner' or 'moved on'. I didn't care what the reason was. I was thrilled. The trouble for me now was that my peers could swim but I could not.

When I lined up with my class peers for the first time to make the short walk to the local swimming baths, I was trembling with excitement. I did my best to act as though this was nothing new for me and tried to follow exactly what the other children were doing. In the changing room I slowly undressed out of my school clothes under the protection of the large towel Mum had packed. I eased on my brand-new navy swimsuit and pulled my blue swim cap over my plaited waist-long hair, checked myself in the full-length mirror and followed the other girls in my class out to the poolside.

The first thing that struck me was the smell. Chlorine was a new smell to me.

'OK, everyone, sit by the poolside!' our instructor Mrs Appleby bellowed. All thirty children complied obediently. Soon we were all sitting alongside the edge of the clear blue water, with steam rising invitingly from it. Sitting down alongside the other children, I let my legs dangle in the warm pool water as I listened to the excited chatter. Once we were all seated, Mrs Appleby ordered us in. I slowly turned myself around and lowered my body into the water, copying the others around me.

I am tall for my age, so the water only comes up to my waist. I am distracted by how warm the water is, the way our arms and legs make strange shapes under the surface.

'Everyone face me!' Mrs Appleby shouts. 'Today we're going to do the backstroke. You learnt this last year, remember?'

Mrs Appleby shouts a lot. I don't dare tell her that I wasn't at last year's lessons, and the teachers don't seem to have told her. So, I decide that I'll follow what everyone else is doing. I tell myself to keep calm and do exactly what I am told.

Out of the corner of my eye I watch the other children as they hold onto the side of the pool and curl their legs up in front of them so their feet are on the wall as they wait for Mrs Appleby to shout 'go'. Posing myself in that position I too wait for the command.

'Go!' shouts Mrs Appleby.

Pushing my legs away from the wall, I let go of the side of the pool. I feel my body catapult across the water but quickly realise I have no idea what to do next. I panic. Flailing my arms and legs wildly, I feel the water engulf me as I sink to the bottom of the pool. The water isn't deep, but my feet don't seem to be able to find the floor. I come up for air, splashing and waving my arms around, but it's no good. I sink to the bottom of the pool once more. In my panic I can hear the muffled voice of Mrs Appleby, somewhere in the distance.

'Maria, grab hold of the pole!'

Then I see it – a red pole with a ring on the end, just below the surface of the water. I grab hold of the ring and seconds later I am being dragged out of the water by a very wet and very angry Mrs Appleby.

'What on earth were you doing?' she asks. 'Don't you remember how to do backstroke?'

Through my coughing and spluttering I manage to tell her that this is my first swimming lesson and that I have no idea what I'm doing. Mrs Appleby looks puzzled and reprimands me severely for not telling her before the lesson began. She offers no comfort or sympathy.

I sit out the rest of that first lesson, and for every lesson afterwards I keep to the shallow end of the pool. I never again dare to lift my feet off the swimming pool floor. Neither Mrs Appleby nor any other swimming instructor through my school years ever manages to teach me to swim. Despite numerous swimming lessons throughout my adult life, I still can't swim unaided.

As I entered an all-girls high school in the late 1970s, school life became harder. The then Man of God was continually getting new light about what Brethren children were supposed to do in school. In the 1970s, many schools had started to use television in lessons but, as Brethren, we were forbidden to attend these lessons. Mr Symington said that television was 'of the Devil' and must not be watched under any circumstances. This meant leaving the classroom again and sitting in the school corridor working alone. When a new rule banning school trips came in, I'd watch the rest of the class climbing excitedly onto buses with their packed lunches while I sat for the whole day in yet another unfamiliar classroom or corridor.

The girls in my new school didn't understand. How could they? To them we must have seemed high and mighty, weird, different. I did my best to fit in where I could, but it was getting harder to fit in with worldly ways while sticking to the Brethren rules. I would try to find ways to wear my long hair in as trendy a style as possible even though I had always to wear a ribbon or token to show that I belonged to the Lord. I would make a thin hairband with a piece of ribbon and en route to school would backcomb my hair into something of a quiff so that the ribbon became barely noticeable. Each morning as I left the house, I'd hitch my skirt up as short as I dared to try to look like the other girls while hoping I wouldn't be spotted by any of the Brethren driving to work.

I had nothing in common with the other girls in my class, no shared experience of radio or pop music or television. As a teenager I would sit in my form room in the mornings doing my best to be invisible so I could listen in to the conversations of the other girls about going to the disco on Saturday night, or how they'd kissed a boy. I'd stand in the background, as they'd rave about the latest pop band or television programme. I longed to be able to join in the conversation and be one of them, and ask questions, but I wasn't even allowed to walk home with these girls, let alone enter into their worlds.

When I was fourteen years old something astonishing happened that changed my life at school for the better. Our English teacher, Mrs Hill, staged a singing competition for our class. I loved singing and had recently started playing the guitar, but did I have the confidence to stand in front of my whole class and sing? I decided I had little to lose. I didn't tell my parents or siblings about the competition in case they forbade me from entering. It was my secret.

The day of the competition arrived. Only twelve of my class had put themselves forward. The rest of the class and our teacher, Mrs Franks, would be the judges. I was to be up third and, as I listened to the two other girls sing, I realised that maybe I had made a mistake. My hands were sweating. I felt sick. I wanted to run out of the classroom there and then. I had never performed anything in front of my school peers. I had not been allowed to be in any of the school plays, yet here I was about to sing in front of thirty worldly girls.

'Maria, your turn,' I heard Mrs Franks announce.

I made my way to the front of the class, took a deep breath and did what I always do when I sing: I put myself into the lyrics, into another world, and sang my heart out. The song I chose was 'Pamela Brown'. The Brethren have always favoured country music. I'm not sure why – maybe it's because three of the Men of God were from America. Many country music songs would be played and sung when we entertained in each other's homes. At fourteen, I probably didn't understand the lyrics of the song but there was a sort of worldliness about it that I liked.

My voice comes out loud and clear but with a slight quiver of nervousness. I use the nervousness to feel the emotions in the song. I make actions with my hands to add to the expression of the sad words. I am enjoying myself. As I get near the end of the song I put all my passion and feelings into the last verse and chorus. I sway with the tune and the lyrics as I sing.

As I finish the last line, all I can hear is clapping and cheering. Still clapping, Mrs Franks gets up from her chair, gives my arm a little squeeze and says, 'That was beautiful, Maria. Well done.'

I walk back to my desk with my head held high. I've done it, and maybe, just maybe, I will win. After everyone has sung, Mrs Franks chats to the other judges and then announces the decision. 'And the winner is . . . Maria Compton. Well done and congratulations! Please come to the front of the class to receive your prize.'

Shyly, I walk to the front of the class while all around me I hear claps and cheers. As Mrs Franks hands me a wrapped

31

gift, all the girls start chanting, 'Encore, encore!' Mrs Franks looks at me with a smile. 'Would you be able to sing your song for us one more time?'

So, for the second time that day, I sang 'Pamela Brown' for my class.

After the singing competition the other girls treated me differently. One, Leanne, even did her best to befriend me. She lived close to our house and walked the same route home from school as me. Leanne was very worldly, but I admired her a lot. She seemed to live an exciting life: going to discos, having boyfriends and even smoking. Her parents let her do whatever she wanted, and I longed to have the freedom she had. She would often ask me to walk home with her and, occasionally, I'd agree, but I insisted that we walk the long way through the local park where I was sure no Brethren would see us. I couldn't be seen walking with a worldly girl like Leanne.

But I yearned for Leanne to like me almost as much as I feared the repercussions of breaking the Brethren's rules. I found ways of persuading her to meet me at the local park entrance, where we'd walk along the tree-lined paths hidden from the road so we couldn't be spotted by anyone driving by. I planned the route carefully so that when we reached the road we could immediately separate.

One day as we walked in that park, Leanne started asking me questions.

'Maria, are you going to stay in that weird religion of yours? Don't you miss TV and music?'

I was startled. Before replying, I glanced over my shoulder and, leaning in close to her, I answered very quietly: 'I don't know.'

At that moment I didn't know what I believed or what I wanted to do with my life. I longed to tell her that, although I didn't exactly miss TV or popular music, because I'd never had them, I would love to experience them. But I couldn't voice those thoughts out loud. I knew that even if the Brethren couldn't hear me, God could. So, instead I told her that if a Brethren boy asked me to marry him within the next few years, then I'd stay. She looked at me, puzzled.

'I couldn't do it,' she said. 'I couldn't live under the control you live under. I'd explode.'

'I know,' I said, my voice no more than a whisper now, 'but if I leave, I'll lose everything, all my family, everything.'

Leanne nodded in sympathy, but I knew she'd never understand what it would be like to leave the Brethren. It was a juddering moment. I knew I could never explain, and, in that second, I could see the gulf between Leanne and me – and all the other worldly girls – widening. I could see that one day the gap might become too great for me to ever cross.

It wasn't long after this conversation that, at the age of fifteen and in my last year of school, I seriously considered for the first time leaving the Brethren. I know now that I had reached the classic teenage phase of testing boundaries, but unlike normal teens where testing boundaries might result in getting grounded at worst, I was risking so much more.

My best Brethren friend Linda, my Brethren cousin Charlie and I had some serious discussions that year. Charlie, at sixteen, was a year older than Linda and me, and had just finished his last year of school. I admired him and loved him like a brother even though he was a cousin. He was funny and daring and often broke the Brethren rules. He had no fear of anyone, and I loved that about him.

The three of us would often sneak up the lane at the back of the meeting hall where no one could see us. Sometimes other rebellious teenage boys and girls would join us, and we would spend time laughing, flirting and joking, pretending that we were the same as our 'worldly' school peers. But we never dared go beyond winks, laughs and the fluttering of eyes. If we were found stepping over that line, the consequences would be severe. Because of the no mixing of boys and girls rule, Charlie and I met secretly one afternoon in the local park so as not to be seen by any Brethren driving by.

'Maria, let's run away together,' he said suddenly and earnestly. My eyes grew wide. I turned to look at him.

'What? Just you and me?' I asked, unsure if he was just messing about.

'And Linda,' he said. 'We'll all go together. What do you think? I love Linda and want to marry her one day, but I want to be free from the Brethren so that I can date her first like a normal boyfriend should. None of us is free within the Brethren. We need to get away. We need to make a plan.'

I couldn't believe what he was saying. Could we *really* get free? If there were three of us, then maybe we could.

'Seriously?' I asked. 'How? Where will we live? How will we live?'

'Don't worry,' he said. 'I've got ideas. I've been thinking about this for a while. Meet me here again this time next week and I'll tell you.'

For the next week, all sorts of ideas went through my head. Other teenagers had run away. I'd heard of a fifteen-year-old Brethren boy who had made a bolt for freedom. His parents had found him living with his worldly girlfriend's family and he had been thrown out of his home there and then. If he had found a kind, worldly family to live with and show him how to get by in the world, then why not me?

Linda and I didn't get to talk to Charlie much that week, but from time to time he and I would give a knowing wink to each other across the meeting room, hoping that no one would notice. We used winks and smiles to acknowledge our secret was safe. All week I imagined what it would be like to be free. Free to have a television. Free to listen to music on tapes and the radio. Free to cut my hair. Free to wear worldly clothes. Free to go on holiday. Free to have a boyfriend.

Then, after a week of sleepless nights, reality hit home. Of course I couldn't go free. Freedom meant I'd be shunned forever by my family and the only people I'd ever known. It would break my family's heart. Most of all, I couldn't bear to break my mother's heart. And, more difficult still, I would need money to be free. I had no money; I was still in school. It would be difficult to get work once I left school, as none of us had been encouraged to work hard. Charlie had no qualifications and was relying on his dad's very successful business to survive. If he left the Brethren, he'd be disowned and thrown out of the family business forever. He'd be destitute. We'd all be destitute.

Linda and Charlie were losing their nerve too. Linda's mum was pregnant with her seventh child, and, she said, it would break her parents' hearts if she left. It would shame them. The three of us met in the local park again, heavy-hearted. Charlie said he'd looked at all our options and had even gone to the estate agents to see what was available to rent but, in the end, it was the same for all three of us: even if we could face losing and shaming our family, we couldn't figure out a way to earn a living and survive in the outside world.

From now on I knew my only option was to marry, settle down and have children within the Brethren.

A few months before I turned sixteen, I left school with a handful of CSE passes. Back then, Brethren teenagers weren't permitted to attend university, but we were still allowed to attend college or to seek employment within a worldly firm. It wasn't long before those doors closed too.

The last thing I wanted to do upon leaving school was to become part of Dad's photocopier business but, as I knew they would, my parents told me that a secretarial position was available for me there if I wanted it. I resisted at first, telling them that we saw enough of each other as a family without working together every day. I tried to get a place as a trainee dental nurse but was turned down because I didn't have good enough grades. I signed on the dole for three months while I looked for work, but I finally had to accept that I had no choice but to work for Dad. Now I can understand why doing well at school was discouraged. The leaders knew that if poorly educated Brethren young people couldn't get jobs in the outside world they'd have to rely on the Brethren for employment. I started my first job as a receptionist in Dad's business. I was sixteen.

# FOUR

When I was growing up, the Brethren practised an extreme kind of separation. That meant, the Men of God said, that anyone who questioned the Brethren rules or didn't comply with them absolutely had to be withdrawn from, exiled, cut off, in order to maintain the purity of the fellowship. The Brethren called this 'withdrawal'. If you lived in the Brethren you watched many people, even family members, being withdrawn from. People you loved, people who were part of your everyday life – uncles, aunts, cousins – people who you saw every day or visited several times a month could disappear at any moment, withdrawn from, banished, never to be seen again, and often that meant all their children were banished too.

Uncle Matthew, Auntie Grace (Mum's sister) and their six children, our cousins, lived only a short distance from us, so we were often in each other's houses. I loved all my cousins, but Elaine was my favourite. Before I owned a doll of my own, Elaine would bring her dolls and we'd dress them up. She'd make funny faces behind the boys' backs to make me laugh.

On the Lord's Day I'd make sure to sit next to Elaine at our huge dining room table when the two families gathered for a meal at our house. The smell of roast beef, roast potatoes, vegetables and Yorkshire puddings filled the air. While Dad gave thanks to God for the meal, I'd squeeze Elaine's hand under the table.

'God and Father, we thank thee for this food and the company of one another. We thank thee for the fellowship and pray that thou wilt keep thy hand over each one of us. In the name of the Lord Jesus. Amen.' There was a chorus of 'amens' around the table and the meal began.

A few days later in a Brethren meeting, Uncle Matthew disagreed with something one of the Man of God's right-hand men had said. Uncle Matthew, Aunt Grace and all the children were immediately withdrawn from. I remember Mum's tears. Grace was her favourite sister. Even though I was only five years old at the time, I knew that we'd never be allowed to talk to any of them again unless Uncle Matthew repented and they returned to the Brethren.

In those early weeks and months I saw Elaine in the playground at school every day but I always looked away. I was scared my siblings would see me looking longingly at her. I knew I'd get into trouble if I so much as smiled at her. As we weren't allowed worldly friends, Elaine had been the only person I had played with in the school playground. Now I stood with my back against the school wall watching her play with the worldly girls. I felt so alone. Elaine looked happy.

Although I was only five years old, I was often allowed to take the short walk to school alone. It was a Wednesday morning when I left our house as normal and headed up the hill. As I got to the crossroads, I noticed Elaine walking in my direction. She smiled and waved at me. My resolve broke and I smiled back. I waited on the corner for her to catch up. I knew I shouldn't do that, but I'd missed her, and it was clear she missed me too.

Over the next few weeks, when I knew it was safe to do so, I'd wait at the crossroads for Elaine and we'd walk to school together. I knew I was doing wrong but I didn't seem to be able to help myself. Every time I did this forbidden act, I felt a mixture of fear and excitement. Elaine wanted to know how all her old Brethren friends were. I wanted to know what life on the outside was like. Had they got a TV? Did she go to worldly people's houses? Did they go to church? She told me that her mum and dad had taken them to a different Brethren meeting which wasn't as strict. They were allowed to have anyone in their home and could play with friends from school.

Our walk to school took us past the home of two elderly Brethren spinster sisters who lived around the corner from us. They were twins. We called them Auntie Edith and Auntie Betty. Like our Brethren spinster babysitter, Miss Parker, they would often come to our house to help my busy mum with the housework or babysit us while Mum did the shopping.

When I walked past their house, I'd see Auntie Betty sitting in a big armchair by the window of their front room reading a book or knitting. Auntie Betty seemed to read endless amounts of books. Sometimes I'd hear Auntie Edith complain to Mum about how Auntie Betty was filling her head with useless novels. As I passed their house while going to school, she would often give me a wave.

Elaine and I had to find a way of getting past their house without being seen. Elaine didn't worry as she no longer belonged to the Brethren, but for me, I could not be seen walking to school with my now worldly cousin or there'd be consequences. So, we'd crouch down on the pavement hidden by the privet hedge and crawl past.

We got caught a few months later, on a beautiful spring day. I'd met Elaine on the corner as usual. We'd managed to pass the old sisters' house without being seen and made our way up the steep hill of Chesterfield Avenue. At the top of the hill there was a busy crossroads and, to be safe, we always used the pedestrian crossing. Once across the busy road we only had the short walk up another hill to our primary school.

That morning, as we approach the crossroads near school, my grandparents turn the corner towards us and I almost bump right into them. This time I have nowhere to hide. Here I am, walking to school with my excommunicated cousin. I am so ashamed of myself that I can't even look them in the eye. I can't even bring myself to greet them. I seem to be frozen to the spot before I hear the green man on the pedestrian crossing bleeping its familiar sound. Without a word to my grandparents, I run past them and across the road. I run the rest of the way to school with tears rolling down my face.

What will happen to me? I'm a sinner. How will I be punished? I spend the whole day in school feeling sick with the fear of what will happen to me when I get home. I hide my tears from the teacher and the other children. How could I even begin to explain why I am so upset? No one will understand.

Grandpa is one of our local Brethren leaders. As a family, we have something to live up to. Have I ruined my family's standing by sinning? Grandma will be so disappointed in me too. She is a very religious woman and can often be heard whispering 'amens' during daily Brethren meetings. Unlike many of the women, she always keeps her eyes tight shut during the prayers. How ashamed they must both feel of their granddaughter.

I struggle through the morning, unable to concentrate on my schoolwork. During the morning break I keep well away from Elaine. I must never look at or speak to her again.

Mum picks me up from school as normal and, although she says nothing, I know my grandparents will have told her by now what I have done. Taking my hand in hers as normal, I feel the warmth of it around mine, and it comforts me. I know Grandpa will be sitting in our living room when we get home.

I've heard what happens to Brethren who mix with ex-Brethren. I've witnessed Brethren being thrown out for this sin. I am only five years old but, in my young mind, I still think this could be my punishment. How will I look after myself? Will my parents be in trouble too? Will they be withdrawn from?

Still holding tight to Mum's hand, I hide behind her skirt as we walk through our back door. As Mum leads me through to the living room, there is Grandpa with his tall frame folded into his favourite armchair. I do my best to keep hidden behind Mum. I am terrified; Grandpa has the power to punish me how he wishes. I run from behind Mum and head straight for the stairs as fast as my little legs will take me, but Grandpa is having none of it. As I run past him his long arm reaches out and his strong gnarled hand grabs a hold of my arm.

'Not so fast, girl,' he says, his face like thunder.

Standing before him trembling, with my head bent, I feel tears run down my face and watch them drip onto my shoes. Grandpa puts one long bony finger under my chin, lifting my head and forcing me to look at him. Giving me a long, hard, stern look, he shakes his head but says nothing. I know what that look means. It means 'don't ever do that again'. Pulling myself free from his grip, I wipe my tears with the back of my hand, mumble a sorry and run to the safety of my bedroom as fast as I can.

Nothing more was ever said of my walking to school with Elaine. That night I knelt by my bed and asked Jesus to forgive me for my sin. I knew that I had got off very lightly, but I also knew that I would never dare to do anything like that again. From that day on, if I ever saw any defected Exclusive Brethren members in the street, I would always cast my eyes down and keep walking. And I did. Elaine and I went through primary and secondary school just a year apart but, from that day, I have absolutely no memory of interacting with her or even seeing her again.

More than forty years later, in 2019, several years after I found my way out, I went to find my lost cousins. Elaine and I are both in our fifties now, but we have never forgotten each other. When we were reunited, we hugged, cried and just held each other. So many lost years, yet here we were, both away from the Brethren. We talked about the forbidden walks to school as little girls. We were both shocked to discover that neither of us had any memory of seeing each other. We *must* have passed in the corridors. Had we erased each other in our minds?

I often wonder how my children cope with my disappearance and what mental strategies they have used, knowing that while I remain outside the Brethren they will be discouraged from contacting me. Have they simply erased me from their minds as Elaine and I did all those years ago? Have they not *allowed* themselves to think of me? Have they cut me out of their memories and family stories?

Today, this might be called 'ghosting', but in the Brethren at that time it was called 'cutting off'. We were taught that we had to 'cut off' people who had sinned and been withdrawn from, even if they were close family members.

# FIVE

I think now of the many people I have been made to cut off over my forty-four years in the Brethren; the people who were there one day and gone the next – the aunts, uncles, cousins, people you'd seen every week in meetings; old ladies who had baked your birthday cakes or young men who had helped fix the roof. These were people who you'd never hear mentioned again; people you'd have to pretend had never existed to show that you put the Lord before 'natural ties'. Everyone in the Brethren has relatives who've been cut off. Everyone has wounds like that. Sometimes individuals disappeared. Other times it was whole families like Elaine's family or like Dad's only sister, Auntie Frances, who disappeared with her husband and my six cousins a few years after Elaine.

I was seven years old and sitting in an After Meeting. After Meetings were gatherings where the Brethren elders and the local leader of our fellowship considered matters of 'assembly discipline'. It was where sinners were dealt with.

Usually, I didn't listen that attentively, but that evening I distinctly remember hearing Auntie Frances' name so I listened more carefully. It came again, Frances Boyle. Had the elders perhaps got mixed up? Had they got the wrong Frances? I glanced at Dad down in the front circle of brothers, his face tight and red. I listened harder.

They were saying that Auntie Frances had got angry with old Mrs Boyle, her mother-in-law, and had pulled her hair in frustration. As a seven-year-old listening to the discussion, it sounded funny. I could easily imagine my redheaded, hot-headed Auntie Frances doing such a thing. I'd seen her clip her children around the ear when they misbehaved. Why were they talking about such a trivial sin in the After Meeting? In the After Meeting, the elders usually talked about people caught smoking, or having a radio, not something as trivial as a woman pulling another woman's hair. But that day the elders decided it was a sin that needed to be punished. So, to my amazement, they declared that Auntie Frances, along with her husband and their six children, were to be 'shut up'. Being shut up was like the first stage before being withdrawn from. It was a time when you were meant to shut yourself away with God and seek forgiveness for your sin so that you wouldn't be withdrawn from. During that time you couldn't attend any meetings and could only have contact with the elders, your priests. It was a great shame for any family members.

Sitting forward, I looked down through the rows of seats to the circle of brothers at the front. I looked at Dad sitting next to Grandpa as he always did. I couldn't read their faces as both were sitting with their heads down. Grandpa was our leader; why wasn't he saying anything? Why wasn't he defending his daughter? Why didn't Dad say something to stop this from happening? After all, he was an elder too. If he disagreed with this decision, wouldn't the Brethren listen to him? But neither Grandpa nor Dad spoke up to defend my Auntie Frances that day.

I'll never forget watching Auntie Frances walk out of the room with her head bent in shame and embarrassment, her three little girls, my cousins, following close on her heels, almost tripping over each other in their hurry to keep up.

A few weeks later, Auntie Frances and Uncle Robert's names came up again in an After Meeting. Apparently, while they'd been shut up, they had bought a caravan and had gone on holiday. To do this when you were meant to be shutting yourself up with God was a very grave sin. Now the elders declared that the whole family were to be withdrawn from. That meant they would be cut off from us forever just like Uncle Matthew and Auntie Grace had been.

I linked my arm through Mum's and rested my head against her. As I held onto her tight, I felt her body shake with silent tears. I glanced at Grandma, who sat on the other side of me, expecting to see her tears too, but her mouth was just a cold hard line. This was her only daughter. Why wasn't she upset?

I was soon distracted by a commotion among the brothers in the front circle. I strained my little neck to see what it was all about and could see the bent head of Grandpa. His head was almost touching his knees as his body shook uncontrollably. What was wrong? Was Grandpa ill? Suddenly he stood up. His tall frame seemed to have shrunk as he walked slowly from the silent meeting room with his head bent, dabbing his eyes with his large white handkerchief. That was when I realised that, for the first time in my life, I was watching Grandpa cry; big heart-wrenching tears had overcome him at the loss of his only daughter and grandchildren. Grandpa wasn't meant to cry. He was our leader; he was strong and important and so fierce and strict sometimes that he frightened me.

No one followed him out of the meeting room. No one went to comfort him. Eventually, Grandma got up from her seat and, squeezing her way past the legs of the sisters on our row, she followed Grandpa out of the room.

After that night I didn't see Grandpa and Grandma for six weeks. On the Friday evening meeting after my aunt and her family's withdrawal we had yet another After Meeting and I heard those dreaded words again:

'We feel we need to shut up our brother and sister, Mr Matthew Compton and his wife Grace,' an elder announced to a shocked congregation.

For the next six weeks I heard whisperings between my parents. I could tell they were shocked and upset not only by what had happened to Auntie Frances and her family but what was now also happening to Grandpa.

In the car on our daily fifteen-mile journey to and from the meeting, sitting squashed between my siblings, I would lean forward so I could hear the quiet conversations between my parents sitting in the front seats. I learnt that the reason Grandpa had been shut up was that he had shown how upset he was with the Brethren's decision to withdraw from his daughter and her family. The other elders thought this meant he didn't agree with the decision. They wanted to teach him a lesson by shutting him away with God and seeking forgiveness from the priests and God. This must have been a terrible time for not only my grandparents but also my parents. In a matter of weeks, Dad had lost his entire family.

Six weeks later, Mr Symington, the Man of God, intervened. Letters went backwards and forwards. There were phone calls. Mr Symington said that he was very angry that Grandpa, a much-respected and important Brethren leader, had been treated in such a manner. My grandparents were allowed back among the Brethren but Grandpa was never reinstated to local leadership. As an already frail man with ill health, he never really recovered. A few months later, at the age of seventy-two, he died very suddenly in hospital. Mr Symington preached that Grandpa had died because the Brethren didn't want him.

It was a very strange time. I had never experienced death so close before. We had just moved into Grandpa and Grandma's big old house to help care for them during Grandpa's illness, but now Grandpa was lying in an open coffin shrouded with white satin lace, in the tiny hallway of their annexe, his face all waxy. Brethren were travelling from all over the north of England to look at him in his coffin. They walked in single file around the beautiful oak coffin, stopping as they took time to study his face. There was an eerie silence through the whole house, broken only by the crying of the women and the occasional blowing of noses of the men.

Yet try as I might, I could not shed a single tear for the death of Grandpa. Was it because I was frightened of him? Was I one of the people who hadn't wanted him? Was it partly my fault too?

Over those strange two days, while Grandpa lay dead in our house, more Brethren came through our door than in all the ten years that I lived there – Brethren women in head-scarves and Brethren men clutching Bibles. Everyone seemed united in grief for a man who had stood by Brethren principles all his life; a man who had travelled as far as New Zealand to spread the gospel of the Brethren.

The local sisters joined together to help Mum and Grandma provide an endless supply of food for everyone. They had made trays and trays of neat little sandwiches, Victoria sponge cakes and tray bakes. The visitors stood talking in hushed tones, quietly eating the food set out on our big dining table. The men stood with a whiskey glass in one hand and a sandwich in the other, while some of the women held a glass of sherry and nibbled on slices of the cake.

It was a few months after Grandpa's death, when I was making my daily visit to Grandma's annexe to keep her company, that I found her sitting in her armchair in front of the gas fire, surrounded by piles of old family photo albums. As I entered the room, Grandma greeted me with a flustered 'hello' while quickly shutting the album on her lap. As she went off to the kitchen to get me my usual milk and biscuits, I started idly leafing through the old album she had set on top of the pile. I loved leafing through these books, studying the faces of people from long ago. The albums were full of beautiful photos that had mostly been taken by Grandpa. He had been a wonderful photographer. Before we moved into the house, he had used one of the upstairs bedrooms as a darkroom, where he had lovingly developed each photograph himself. These weren't just any old photos; they were taken and developed with skill then beautifully mounted into quality binders.

The album Grandma had been looking at was my favourite. It was full of photos of Dad and Auntie Frances as children. Each photo was a full A4 size and filled the page it had been carefully mounted on. There was the photo of Dad as a little boy riding a donkey and the one of him playing with his train set. Then there was the beautiful one of Auntie Frances as a young teenager sitting at her desk studying, her hair loose down her back, catching the light. The picture I liked best was the one of Dad as a child of around four or five years old, kneeling beside a chair where Auntie Frances sat with a large book on her knee, reading him a story. I loved the contented expression on Dad's face as his big sister read to him. Grandpa had captured the closeness between them even though they were seven years apart in age.

I turn the page to the one of Auntie Frances studying but it's blank. All that remains are the four little mounts that have held the photo in place. I hurriedly turn to the page where Auntie Frances sits reading to Dad and I almost drop the album in shock. Someone has carefully removed the photo, cut out Auntie Frances all around her edges and replaced the photo in the album. All that remains is Dad sitting alone next to a hole.

In a bewildered panic I turn each page. All the photos of Auntie Frances have either been removed or neatly cut out. I pick up another album and quickly turn the pages only to discover that this one is the same. Any trace of Auntie Frances has been taken out of every photo album.

I stand up ready to run to Grandma in the kitchen to tell her what I've discovered, when I notice the winter sun glinting on something on the worn arm of Grandma's chair. It's her silver sewing scissors. Next to her chair, hidden in the corner, is a wastepaper bin. The bin is full of those cut-up photos of Auntie Frances; every one of them has been ruined beyond repair.

I jump up from the floor and run from Grandma's room before she has time to return with my milk and biscuits. I can't face her. Auntie Frances has been gone from our lives for more than a year. Why has Grandma waited until now to do this awful thing? If Grandpa had seen his beautiful photographs being cut up like that he would have been so angry. But now that he was gone, he would never know. Was that why Grandma had waited? Did she blame Auntie Frances for Grandpa's death? Now Grandma has cut Auntie Frances off literally. Now she has been erased.

As I sit here today, writing these words, my eyes are drawn to the photos of *my* children lined up along the back of my desk. As Grandma was forbidden to ever see her daughter again, did removing every photo of Auntie Frances help to dispel every memory of her? Had this been her way of coping with the loss of her daughter? Is this how my children are coping with not being allowed to have any contact with me? Have they cut me out of old photos? Have they done everything in their power to cut me out of their memory? Has *my* mum cut me out of every photo in the old family photo albums?

I can't help but wonder how my family and my old Brethren friends who are still in the Brethren *really* feel about those that have been cast out or have decided to leave. Are they heartbroken at losing their family members and age-old friends? Or have they no feelings left for others? Then I remember that I was once one of them. There was a time when I would have done exactly as they do. There was a time when I lived in fear of breaking the rules, when I kept my mouth shut for fear of being withdrawn from. I don't feel anger towards them now. They are still my family, and I am still theirs.

# SIX

In 1981, Mr Symington told the Brethren that he had received important new light from God. The reason that the Rapture had not yet come, he told them, was because too many Brethren members had unconfessed or unforgiven sins that needed to be settled. Mr Symington decreed that the Assembly (the Brethren) needed to be cleansed. All Brethren aged sixteen and over had to look back on their lives and think about whether they had ever done anything impure or unclean and then confess it. Depending on the severity of the sin, the person would need to be either shut up or withdrawn from for seven days. It was up to local leaders to make judgements. The scripture that Symington used to endorse this was Numbers 12, verse 15, where Miriam is shut out from the camp for seven days to be cleansed from the leprosy that God has sent to her as punishment for speaking ill of the prophet Moses. If you were fully repentant after the seven days, as Miriam had been, then you would be purified and could return to the Brethren.

Dad was the local leader in our district at that time. With so much cleansing to be done, judgements to make and discipline to be imposed, we saw very little of him in the spring and summer of 1981. Every evening, after each daily meeting, he was either on priestly visits listening to confessions or on the telephone to Brethren who had found something in their past or present that could be classed as unclean or impure. Every Tuesday evening we were expected to attend the After Meetings where judgements were made. The priests would tell the whole local congregation in detail what each new person's unclean sin was and then they were either shut up or withdrawn from for seven days. Mostly the sinner would be present to hear the verdict and then would have to leave the hall in shame.

There were so many words and phrases I heard in these After Meetings which made no sense to me as a naive young teenager: words like 'masturbation', 'fondling', 'sodomy' and 'fornication'; phrases like 'unclean acts' and 'skin-to-skin touching'. I've heard that in some towns the priests went into extreme graphic detail of every sinful act that had been confessed. Dad spared my family and the Brethren the embarrassment of the detail but he often shouted down the mic in anger.

Holding the microphone close to his mouth one time, he had yelled, 'No homosexuality in the Assembly!' A local brother had confessed to having a brief sexual encounter with a worldly man. That poor man was promptly withdrawn from, never to be heard of again. Seven days was regarded as not long enough for him to repent of so grave a sin.

It was a bewildering time, but it was also gripping, not just for me but also for everyone in our fellowship. It gave the Brethren plenty to gossip and 'ooh' and 'ah' about. Looking back, it must have been especially humiliating for those who returned after their seven days, knowing that their dirty laundry had been aired in public. Some of these Brethren had already confessed these sins back in the '60s and '70s and had been absolved, but now Mr Symington's new light required them to re-confess so they could be properly clean. Now they had to expose these so-called sins all over again in front of children and teenagers and everyone they knew.

Meanwhile, outside our assembly, on 29 July 1981, the world stopped to watch the fairytale wedding of Prince Charles and Lady Diana. The Brethren have always been intrigued by the Royal Family but, as we didn't own or watch television, we would have to wait until we saw the newspapers, which were still allowed at that time, to catch a glimpse of what this glorious wedding had looked like.

Some Brethren were more daring than others and, as it was a national holiday, these more daring Brethren decided to take a sneak peek on television on the big day. Back in the 1980s, televisions were often displayed and running in the windows of local television shops. If you happened to be in town that day, you most likely would have seen Brethren standing staring wide-eyed at the window of such shops in a bid to get a glimpse of the wedding of a lifetime. But being so daring on that day had been a big mistake. When Symington got word of what had gone on and how Brethren had dared to defy the rule of no television, he was very angry. He instructed the elders of each locality to take to task any members of their congregation who had watched the Royal Wedding and shut them up. He decreed that each sinner should be shut up so that they would repent of their sins before God and the Brethren.

A special After Meeting was arranged for the following Tuesday in the large local meeting room. I had sat through many such local meetings that year and had listened to many Brethren being shut up over the last few weeks and months as part of Mr Symington's new light. I had watched as they had been told to leave the meeting, maybe to never be seen again. So far my immediate family seemed to have escaped the purge, but that was about to come to an end.

On arriving at the local hall that evening, Dad takes his seat in the front row as usual, while Mum, my three sisters and I sit with the other sisters in the circular rows behind the brothers. The room is almost full, with a congregation of around 300 Brethren. The first part of the meeting is a blur to me as my main interest is in the After Meeting – the confession meeting. Who will be the sinners this time? I ask myself, as I look around the full meeting hall. As the local leader Dad conducts the proceedings again. He takes the microphone and asks for anyone who has watched the Royal Wedding on television to speak up and confess.

One by one people begin to confess their sin. The brothers speak either for themselves or for female members of their family because sisters aren't permitted to speak in the meetings. Some brothers as young as fifteen or sixteen confess. One by one Dad shuts up each sinner, and with heads bent in embarrassment and shame, they leave the hall. We are halfway through these proceedings when suddenly an old sister shouts to Dad from the back row where we sisters are sitting.

'Edward Compton, I saw your daughter Claire watching the television through the window of Woolworths!'

Dad looks flustered. His face reddens with embarrassment. His own daughter is being denounced as a sinner. Quickly recovering himself, he promptly shuts up my sister, his daughter. In humiliation, seventeen-year-old Claire leaves the hall escorted by Mum.

The rest of the After Meeting blurs. I sit in shock listening to Dad continue his shutting up of sinful Brethren. By the time the meeting is finished, he has shut up around fifty of his community.

Apart from the sound of Claire and Mum sobbing, the car journey home is silent. No one dares to speak. I am conflicted. I'm angry with Claire. How could she do this to our family? I'm sorry for her too. She probably didn't think she'd get caught. Did she even think she was sinning?

They call it shutting up as you're being 'shut up with God', but it is so much worse than that. When we get home that evening, Claire is promptly sent to her bedroom and the door is closed. We are instructed not to speak to her until she is repentant and free again. While she is shut up, not only must we not speak to her, but she also mustn't leave her bedroom apart from using the bathroom. Mum prepares her meals and leaves them on a tray outside her bedroom door. Now that I know the true meaning of being shut up, now that it has come into our house, I am petrified it might happen to me. My sister is trapped in her room in our home, forbidden any contact with anyone, even her own family.

My bedroom is next to Claire's and, as I lie in bed each night, I hear her weeping. I know she is feeling alone and scared. I want to go and comfort her, hold her in my arms.

A week later, Mr Symington decided that those who were repentant could return to the fellowship. Thankfully my sister passed that test, but I don't think she ever really recovered from the shock and shame. I remember her talking to me about it many years later when she told me she felt it was good that God had taught her a lesson about sinning, that it had stopped her from ever being disobedient to the Man of God again.

Some of those who had been shut up for the sin of watching the Royal Wedding on television decided that this was the last straw, an opportunity to walk away, and they never returned to the Brethren. We never saw or mentioned them again.

That whole incident left me, and probably most of the people in our fellowship, petrified of ever breaking the Brethren rules. From then on, I did my best to toe the line, but the purge wasn't over yet.

It's only a few weeks after Claire had been shut up. I come home to see two of the local elders' cars in our drive. With my school bag slung over my shoulder, I enter the house through the back door and walk into our kitchen as normal. I stop in the doorway of the lounge. Mr James and Mr Turner are sitting in the two armchairs while Mum and Dad sit opposite them on our big corner settee. They seem to be in some serious discussion. Mum is crying. Dad's complexion is grey and drawn. As I enter the room, they all fall silent.

Mum gets up from the settee, comes towards me, and, putting her arm around my shoulders, she whispers tearfully in my ear, 'You'll be going to stay with the Jameses for a few days, love. I've put a suitcase in your room ready for you to pack. Hurry along now,' she adds as she opens the lounge door and gently pushes me through it.

I make my way upstairs to my bedroom and, after closing the door, I lean my back against it as I try to make sense of what is happening. Has Dad sinned? Has Mum sinned? Are my parents going to be shut up, or worse, withdrawn from? Am I ever going to see them again? Though confused, I know that now is not the time to ask questions.

I open the door of the old walnut wardrobe and begin pulling clothes off hangers and shoving them into the suitcase Mum has left out for me. How many outfits do I need? How many school shirts? How long am I going away for? I empty the drawers of my dressing table, throwing all my knickers, bras, socks and tights into the suitcase. I open my headscarf drawer and throw them all in too.

I hear voices on the landing outside my bedroom door. I hear Claire pleading with Mum at the bottom of the stairs, asking her to tell her what is going on. I hear my brothers, Edward and Brian, going into their bedroom and closing the door. Are my siblings coming to the Jameses with me? What will happen to our little sister, two-year-old Chloe? She's too young to be taken from our parents. Will Grandma be allowed to stay in her annexe, or will she have to move out too? Sitting on the over-full suitcase, forcing it shut, I click the metal clasps into place. As I stay sitting on it for a moment, wondering what to do next, there's a knock on my bedroom door and Dad calls out, 'Maria, are you ready? I'll carry your suitcase down if you are.'

I open my bedroom door, look up at Dad with a watery smile, and say, 'I'm ready.' As he carries my suitcase down the stairs and puts it into the boot of Mr James's big estate car, I ask myself, *am* I ready? Am I ready to be separated from my parents?

While Mr James and Mr Turner wait in their cars, Mum and Dad gather us all together in the lounge. Dad can't look us in the eye. He looks defeated.

'Mum and I are going to be shut up for a few days,' he says, his voice breaking, 'so you are all going away. It's best this way. You can still go to the meetings and enjoy the company of the Brethren while we get matters sorted.'

What 'matters'? I want to ask. But I know I can't ask questions. I know I need to do as I'm told. If I'm obedient, then God will make everything better. Each of us hugs our parents. I can't even cry. I'm still in shock at what's happening.

As Mum hugs me tight, she whispers in my ear: 'I'm so sorry. It won't be for long and soon we'll all be back together again.' Letting go of me, she gives me a weak smile and says, 'Bye bye, Maria. Do your best to enjoy yourself and be good.'

We each file out of the back door, not daring to look back. Deb, Claire and I get into Mr James's car. Edward and Brian get into Mr Turner's car. As we reverse out of our driveway, I long to take a last look at our house, but instead, I rest my head in my hands and close my eyes tight.

———

At the evening meeting Mr James picks up the mic and announces, 'It is felt that we need to shut up Edward and Joan Compton.'

He says that all their children apart from Chloe will be staying with other Brethren families until their parents' release. Mr Turner confirms the decision, and everyone says 'amen'. I am relieved that the details of my parents' sins aren't discussed in public, but I also long to know what they are.

Claire is crying beside me. Mrs James fumbles in her handbag for a hanky and hands it to her. My sister Deb lays a hand on Claire's arm for comfort. I keep my head down in shame. We are in disgrace. I look along the row of sisters to where Grandma is sitting. Her hands are clasped tightly in her lap as she stares pale and stony-faced in front of her. She has been allowed to stay in her annexe if she agrees to lock the interlinking door and doesn't converse with my parents.

When we got back to the Jameses' chalet-bungalow that night, Mrs James made up beds for us three girls in their daughters' bedroom. Their two daughters set up camp beds in the cupboard within the eaves. If the situation hadn't been so sad, it would have been an exciting adventure for us all. But as I lay awake, long after everyone else was asleep, I let the tears come. I longed to be in my own bed with Chloe in her cot next to me, and my parents just across the hallway. I lay there thinking about Mum and Dad and wondering how they were feeling. I'd never seen Dad cry, but I could imagine that he'd be crying now. I hoped they'd be able to comfort each other. I thought of little Chloe and how bewildered she would be in the empty house. It was early morning before I managed to close my eyes and get some sleep. Those days and nights were hard. Although the Jameses were so kind to us, I was homesick. I cried myself to sleep most nights.

It was three weeks before my parents were restored back to the Brethren. I can remember the day like it was yesterday. To this day I've no idea why they were kept in this state of limbo and imprisonment for longer than the assigned seven days.

Tuesdays came and went. Everything happened in those Tuesday After Meetings. Shutting up on a Tuesday, withdrawing from on a Tuesday, confessions on a Tuesday; even weddings had to be on a Tuesday. So, that Tuesday evening we had yet another After Meeting and Mr James announced that Mum and Dad could be restored back among the Brethren. Everyone said, 'amen'. Mr James and Mr Turner rushed off straight after the meeting to deliver the good news to them.

It is after nine o'clock before we are dropped off at our home with our suitcases. I am so excited to see Mum, Dad and Chloe again. We all rush through the back door together, almost tripping over each other as we step into our warm, familiar kitchen. Mum is crying, but this time I know it's tears of joy as she hugs us all in turn. Dad has already got a glass of whiskey in his hand as he fusses around us all, patting the boys on their backs, giving me a peck on the cheek, hugging us. We sit on the high bar stools in the kitchen, some of us on the arm of Dad's favourite armchair, little Chloe sitting on Deb's knee, her eyes wide. It feels wonderful for us all to be together again. Mum suddenly clears her throat and says:

'We honestly thought we'd never see you again after what Mr Symington said about Dad and after what I did. It's time to tell you what my sin was. You need to know.'

But before she can tell us what I am dying to know, Dad puts his hand on her arm and says, 'Let's not talk about that now, love. Let's celebrate us all being together again.'

With that, he goes to the drinks cupboard in the lounge and returns with a bottle of whiskey in one hand while carrying as many of our best glasses as he can in the other. He sets the glasses down on the breakfast bar and pours seven neat whiskeys with ice.

At thirteen years old, I had never tasted alcohol apart from the fortified wine at the Lord's Supper every Lord's Day morning. I take the glass Dad hands me but I'm unsure what to do. In his excitement has he made a mistake? Aren't I too young? Looking around at my older siblings, I see that each has a glass of whiskey just like mine. It's a bonding moment for us. Sharing this grown-up drink with Dad, Mum and my older siblings makes me feel for the first time that I am being treated as an adult. They all look unperturbed as they bring the amber liquid to their lips, so, following their example, I do the same. It's so strong that I almost choke on the first sip. Then there's a warm feeling as it passes my lips and slips down my throat. There's a warm feeling in the room as well – one of relief. The sheer relief that our family are all back together again as we should be.

# SEVEN

I was seventeen, working as a receptionist for my dad's business and doing my best to look attractive without breaking any Brethren rules. Since Linda, Charlie and I had abandoned the escape plan, I had tried my best to toe the Brethren line and be a good Brethren girl. I was ready to settle down and do whatever was expected of me.

I received my first invitation to a three-day meeting. This was proof that I was now trusted to travel away from home by myself. A three-day meeting was special. Brethren travel from all around the world to gather in a designated city to have Bible readings and instruction from an important Brethren elder. Sometimes even the Man of God attended and gave instruction and teaching. It was also, of course, an important way for the young men and women to mix with Brethren from other parts of the UK, so that when new marriages came about there wouldn't be too much unhealthy inbreeding. This one was to be held in the southeast of England. Apart from an occasional one-day fellowship meeting in Bristol, I had never left the north of England before.

About six months before this I'd made a new pact with God that I'd be a good Brethren young woman from now on. I promised Him that I'd listen in the meetings, I'd say my prayers morning and evening, I'd stop flirting with the young Brethren men, I'd stop reading novels, I'd respect the Brethren system and stop having doubts about its truth, I'd stop fantasising about what life in the outside world would be like – and so the list of good deeds went on.

What had made me decide to change? Two things. The first was that I thought if I promised God all these things, then He would provide me with a husband. I really wanted to settle down, get married and have children. That was what Brethren girls did and, in those days, if you got to eighteen and weren't married you were classed as on the shelf. I was fast approaching eighteen and certainly didn't want that. I prayed that God would provide a husband for me soon.

The second reason was that a close friend of mine who, at seventeen years old had decided to leave the Brethren with her new husband, had repented and returned. There had been great rejoicing when a married couple called Jayne and Mike returned from being out in the world for two years. They were accepted back like heroes. Having tried worldly life, they had decided it wasn't for them. In my mind that meant that the world was just as bad as we'd been told. It wasn't a place for good people like the Brethren. It was evil. No one could be trusted in the outside world. There was no love there. Real love was only among the Brethren. The fact that my friend had tried it and then returned must mean it was all true. It was time for me to accept where I was in life and commit myself to the Brethren lifestyle wholeheartedly.

Now I convinced myself that God was sending me to the meeting as a reward for my compliance, and an answer to my prayers. I had a deep-down hope that He'd show me my future husband while I was there.

Fifteen Brethren from my local area climbed into a minibus that freezing November morning to make the long journey south for a weekend of meetings, eating, drinking and 'mixing' with new Brethren. I was nervous but excited.

Jayne and Mike were on the bus too. I made sure to sit next to Jayne on the back row of seats; I had questions I wanted to ask her about life outside. As the minibus wound its way across the British countryside, Jayne told me about their travels. She described how all the time they were out in the world she'd pleaded with God to show her what to do. She was certain, she said, that He had led them back to the Brethren. Jayne's father had died a few months before her marriage. While she was in the outside world, she said, she felt her father was looking down on her in disapproval and disappointment. She had felt crippled by guilt. Although she and Mike both had siblings in the outside world who had left the Brethren in earlier years, they both missed their parents painfully. Jayne worried constantly about her grieving mother. The guilt and loneliness had an impact on their young marriage, and they decided that if they didn't return to the Brethren, they were going to lose each other. So, like a prodigal son and daughter, they had returned.

This long bus conversation with Jayne strengthened my resolve to commit fully to the Brethren way of life. Over the coming years, until I finally made the break, I would often go over that conversation with Jayne in my head, trying to recover the resolve and commitment to the Brethren that I'd had back then.

Although the meetings were in the Southeast that weekend, I had been allocated accommodation with a Brethren family approximately twenty miles away from where we would all gather. As we piled out of the minibus, tired and weary, we were greeted by a group of southern brothers. These were our hosts. I was tired but giddy with anticipation.

My host, Greg Wright's house was a buzz of activity. Evelyn, Greg's wife, greeted me briefly and nervously. Samantha, one of their four teenage daughters, showed me to my bedroom. It was small, simple and neat with flowery wallpaper, a wardrobe in one corner and a dressing table in the other, one single bed and two camp beds neatly set out next to each other. The single bed, Samantha explained, was mine. Samantha and Sonya would sleep on the camp beds and Philippa and her other sister Jess in their parents' bedroom. She showed me the space they had made in the wardrobe and left me to unpack.

I'd brought a suitcase full of new clothes on which I'd spent a month's earnings. There were tailored skirts, bright silk headscarves, handbags and shoes, all carefully colour co-ordinated. I wanted to look the part for these meetings. Each outfit had to pass my father's inspection: nothing too revealing, nothing too bright and long skirts to keep my legs well hidden from view. I was excited to hang my new winter coat in the wardrobe: a full-length, double-breasted, navy wool coat with large gold buttons. Mum thought the gold buttons added sophistication.

We were supposed to spend the first evening in spiritual preparation so we would be alert and well rested for the many reading meetings and preachings we'd be attending over the next three days. On Friday and Saturday, we would attend at least three meetings each day and on Sunday there'd be at least four meetings including the Lord's Supper. It wasn't supposed to feel like a holiday but it felt like one to me – a holiday from my mundane life back home.

I was the youngest guest staying at the Wrights. There were four couples and two young men in their twenties staying there too, on camp beds and in spare rooms. They all seemed friendly enough, but the conversation seemed very reserved in comparison to the lively northern chatter I was used to.

For the hosts this was a very busy few days. Evelyn had been preparing for weeks, baking, cooking and filling the freezer. She looked exhausted. I'm sure her daughters helped where they could, but they were young and it rested on Evelyn to get it right. Food had to be excellent, bedrooms comfortable and the whole house would have had a spring clean.

When I got downstairs and into the kitchen, I found Evelyn rushing from one job to the other. She was obviously struggling. I buttered rolls, prepared salad and did what I could to ease her burden. I was used to this – Mum gave each of us girls tasks when we hosted other Brethren families.

As the man of the house, Greg's job was to make sure all his guests were at ease and comfortable. He was also responsible for serving the alcohol. I was thankful to see that he was restrained in how much he served. Dad was also restrained, especially with the younger Brethren guests, but I'd been in many households where the men of the house handed out huge glasses of whiskey or sherry, pressing it on you. Drinking alcohol had become a macho thing among the Brethren since the days when Jim Taylor had been the Man of God in the late 1950s. He had introduced a drinking culture as a way of masking his own alcoholism.

He died of an alcohol-related illness in 1970. I was thankful for the restraint in this house. Drunkenness frightened me.

I was anxious about my long straggly hair, so I was glad when the meal was over and I had time to start my preparations for the next day. Part of my nightly routine was to divide my damp hair into twelve sections and plait it. I then put a roller on the end of each plait. It took time and effort but the result in the morning was worth it, as it gave me an almost permed look, very fashionable in the '80s. As I wasn't permitted to go to a hairdresser or even put scissors to my hair, this was the next best thing. But as I sat on the edge of the bed plaiting my hair, the girls looked at each other and sniggered.

'Do you do that every night?' Sonya asked.

I nodded, embarrassed. I'd have to take care they didn't see the makeup I'd managed to sneak into my suitcase. Makeup was forbidden in the Brethren, but I couldn't bring myself to comply with this rule for the occasional special event, so had dared to go out and buy myself light foundation, blusher and pressed powder.

The girls rose at six to help their mother prepare breakfast. I had the bedroom to myself to dress, do my hair and apply my secret but discreet makeup. I laid out the plum jumper with its scooped neck and puffy sleeves which came tight at the cuffs that I had assigned for this first meeting. I'd wear it with a long, beige A-line cord skirt that sat neatly on my slim waist. Once dressed, I eased on my sheer tan tights before undoing my curlers and plaits. Running my fingers through my curled hair, so as not to make it frizzy, I finished off my look by applying a little foundation, blusher and pressed powder to my face, then tied on the silk headscarf and checked myself in the mirror. There would be more than a thousand people in this meeting hall – more Brethren in one place than I had ever seen before. My future husband would be there, I was certain of it. The Lord was going to bring him to me.

Once we'd got through the queues and scrambled to our assigned seats in the hall, I sat down to enjoy the scene and scan the room. A long queue of young brothers waited to take their seats just below where I was sitting. My eyes were suddenly drawn to a young man. He was tall, stocky and very handsome.

'That's Kevin White,' Philippa said, smiling at my blushes. 'He's older than he looks,' she added laughing.

'How old?' I asked.

'He must be eighteen, I think. I'm crazy about his brother, Harry,' she whispered, her cheeks flushing too.

'Where is he from?' I was trying hard to sound casual.

'Oh, he's local – his family live right beside this meeting hall.'

Silence fell as Mr Simmons, who had been assigned to lead these meetings, entered. As usual, we started with a hymn. I always enjoyed singing the hymns, and here the acoustics and volume from the combined voices in the hall were amazing. I joined in with all my heart and voice as we sang.

After the hymn Mr Simmons led the long and interminable prayer. The older Brethren always kept their eyes closed through these prayers. The young people, not so much. I put a hand over my eyes so that I could peek through at everyone around me. I spotted Kevin White sitting a few rows below me to my left. He had his head bent but his eyes weren't closed. He was definitely handsome, his skin tanned. From where I was sitting I could even see the hairs from his chest peeping over his shirt. When he looked towards me, perhaps aware of my eyes on him, I looked away, embarrassed.

The meeting started but I soon grew bored and distracted by the constant monotone voices of the brothers. I knew that as a good sister I should listen but, much as I tried, my mind continued to wander. When I dared to glance at Kevin for a second time, he was not only looking at me, but he was smiling. Then he winked. Naughty boy, I thought to myself as I smiled back. He *was* cute.

I scribbled a few questions in my notebook and passed it to Philippa. Has Kevin White got a girlfriend? I wrote daringly. Has he got a house? How many siblings has he got? Is he friendly? Philippa smiled and gave me a nudge when she read the note. She started to write her replies, but her mum saw what she was doing and gave her a sharp poke in the ribs, nodding for her to listen to the meeting. Shrugging her shoulders, she smiled and mouthed the word 'later'.

Once the morning meeting was over, we all filed outside into the cold November air. The Wright girls went off to talk to their friends and I tagged along behind, but quickly tired of their gossip. Standing alone with my back against the wall, I watched the little groups of Brethren dotted around the car park – groups of young unmarried sisters, groups of young unmarried brothers, groups of couples and older people.

Drifting back into the warm foyer, I was overwhelmed by the sound of hundreds of people in conversation. When I spotted Kevin standing by the coat pegs, talking to another young brother, I took the initiative and approached them. He and his friend looked up in surprise. I could see a hint of amusement in both of their faces. This wasn't what they were used to. It was the men who were supposed to approach the women, not the other way around. I could see other eyes on me but I kept my nerve. This was my chance.

'Hello,' I said, my voice tight. 'I'm Maria.'

'We've met somewhere before, haven't we?' Kevin said, with a wide smile.

'Yes, I was thinking that too,' I said.

Kevin introduced me to his Australian friend, who'd travelled all the way from Sydney and was staying with Kevin's family. The three of us were soon at ease with each other. Kevin and I chatted easily about where we might have met before. Now that I was up close to him, I could see the bulge of his muscles under his shirt. His face was clean-shaven but he had dark stubble on his chin as though he'd been shaving for many years. He had swarthy skin, a wonderful smile, and big dark brown eyes.

I tried to look him in the eye while we talked. From talking to Kenneth, flirting with other teenage boys and watching how young married couples behaved, I'd learnt that men liked that. They liked to think you were hanging onto every word they were saying. My strategy worked. Kevin began to hang onto every word I said too.

The three of us laughed and joked about our different accents. Kevin said he loved my Northern accent. That was a good start. We chatted briefly about our families and our work. He was one of four children and he worked for his dad as a mechanic. When Kevin's Australian friend decided he wanted to go outside and talk to others, the conversation was cut short because it would not have been right for Kevin and me to remain talking alone. Kevin gave me a wink as he walked away. I smiled and fluttered my eyelashes at him.

When I found Philippa again in the car park she immediately started to tease me about Kevin. Someone had already told her that I had been seen talking to him. I laughed it off, telling her there was nothing to get excited about.

That afternoon I was delighted to discover that our allocated seats would stay the same all weekend. This meant I could feast my eyes on Kevin. As the meeting progressed, he seemed to be observing me as much as I was watching him. Every time I looked in his direction, he was looking at me. This was exciting. I'd never had a boy show me so much attention before.

Friday slipped into Saturday in a blur of ministries and scriptures. Kevin and I were still making constant eye contact during the meetings, and I longed for a chance to talk to him again before I went home on Sunday. The Wright family continued to tease me about Kevin but I brushed it off. They had noticed our winks and smiles during the meetings. Winks and smiles were often the butt of jokes but crossing the line into one-to-one chatting would not be acceptable. The Wrights spoke highly of the White family and the girls said that from what they knew of Kevin, he seemed a nice person. Why wouldn't he be a nice person? After all, I told myself, he'd been brought up as Brethren the same as me. I could trust him. We were like one big family.

Sunday arrived. My outfit for that day was a purple and green tartan gathered skirt with a matching purple cowl-neck jumper, a purple headscarf and black, high-heeled court shoes. My hair was curled to perfection and my secret makeup made my skin look almost perfect. When I looked in the long wardrobe mirror for about the tenth time that morning, I had a good feeling. I had a spring in my step.

After an early Lord's Supper held in the Wrights' house at dawn, after breakfast, after packing all my belongings into my case, I took one last look in the mirror to make sure I looked my best.

On entering the foyer, we were hit by a wall of bodies. The noise of constant conversation mixed with the sound of crying babies and children was deafening. Unlike the rest of the weekend, the babies and their carers attend on Sunday; it's the Lord's Day, and no one can miss the Lord's Day. Parents were busy trying to get their families in order so they could enter the hall quietly. Once we'd scrambled into our allocated seats, I watched amazed as a mother walked in with six little girls in tow. They all looked close in age, ranging from seven down to a baby in her arms.

'That's the Goddard family,' Philippa whispered, seeing me stare. 'Thirteen children,' she added, raising her eyebrows.

With all the extras, and all the squashing up on the rows of seats that day, Kevin ended up sitting further away from me, but we could still see each other. Although he still smiled at me occasionally, he looked tense. Had his parents noticed what we were up to and reprimanded him? Worse still, had I imagined his attention to mean more than it actually did?

The meeting seemed to go on forever. By the time we'd listened to the reading meeting and six preachers, two hours had passed. I knew there'd only be an hour after the meeting before I had to join the rest of the northern Brethren in the minibus to make our way back home. Time was running out.

In the crush after the meeting I couldn't see Kevin. He'd probably gone home to help his parents get dinner ready, I told myself, trying to quell a panicky sense of disappointment. I joined the long queue of people in front of me making their way out of the hall and into the noisy foyer. Suddenly Philippa was beside me grinning. She handed me a note.

'It's from Kevin,' she whispered before disappearing into the crowd. My hands were sweating as I unfolded the paper. In large uppercase letters were the words: MEET ME ROUND THE LEFT-HAND SIDE OF THE MEETING ROOM BY THE DOUBLE DOORS.

My heart was pounding now. I looked at my watch: I had exactly forty-five minutes before I had to leave. I was standing on the right-hand side of the room. What was my quickest route to get to the left? Edging my way out of the queue, excusing myself and apologising as I went, my mouth dry, I managed to get out into the car park and almost ran to the other side of the hall.

Finally, I reached the double doors, and there was Kevin stood waiting for me, alone. Was it safe for us to stand here alone where people might see us? I didn't care. I wanted to talk to him. I wanted to be close to him. I'd risk getting reprimanded for that. As I approached, Kevin stepped forward with a look of both relief and nervousness.

'I wasn't sure you'd come,' he said quietly.

I longed to be able to hug him to reassure him but that wasn't allowed, so instead, remembering to look into his eyes, I moved in closer and gave him a shy smile. I could see that he longed to touch me too, but he kept his hands in his pockets as he stood with his back against the wall, while I stood as close as I dared. I was so close now I could smell his aftershave. I asked him if he had worn the scent to attract girls.

He laughed. We both laughed.

I told him that I didn't have much time before I had to leave, so whatever we needed to say we didn't have long to say it. We talked about our families. He pointed out his sister in the distance. He said if his dad caught us talking, he wouldn't be pleased. His dad wanted him to be at least nineteen before he got married and he'd only just turned eighteen. I asked him if he had a house. He said that he was looking for one but hadn't found anything yet. A young brother had to have a house before talking about marriage to a young sister.

As we talked, we moved closer and closer to each other. As our arms touched, I felt a tingle go through my body. I could see that he felt it too. When it was time for me to leave, I didn't want to go. I wanted to stand and talk all day.

'Will you write?' I asked.

'Yes, of course,' he said. 'Look – I have something for you.' He opened the front cover of his Bible and took out a neatly folded ten-pound note. Next, he took a pen out of his coat pocket, unfolded the note and, leaning on his Bible, he wrote across the top. He slowly folded the ten-pound note back up and handed it to me, smiling.

As I took it, our hands touched, and I felt that thrill go through me again. I unfolded the note. Across the top he had written, Love You, Always and Forever! Kevin xx

'Don't you ever forget that,' he said.

'I won't,' I replied in a shaky voice. 'Thank you.'

I longed to kiss him then, but we wouldn't be allowed to kiss until we were married. We quickly exchanged addresses. I glanced at my watch, struggling to breathe. I was ten minutes late for the bus; the others would be looking everywhere for me. We said our goodbyes. Leaning in closer to him, I felt his body against mine for a brief moment.

'Goodbye, Kevin,' I whispered, afraid I might faint. 'I hope we see each other again very soon.'

Turning away quickly so as not to break any more rules, I made my way to the minibus, my legs trembling. I was giddy with excitement, but I mustn't let anyone know. Apart from telling my family, it would need to be our secret until the various conditions all Brethren marriages were subject to had been met.

# EIGHT

By the time I got home I was so exhausted all I wanted to do was go to my bedroom, collapse on my bed and catch up on some sleep. I headed upstairs with Mum and Dad close on my heels.

I stepped into my bedroom and froze in shock by the open door. While I'd been away my parents had redecorated my bedroom: there was trendy new wallpaper on one wall in bright blue with red, yellow and green splashes across it. They'd installed a washbasin. I was stunned. My parents had been busy all weekend doing this for *me*. They must have worked so hard.

'Well, do you like it?' Mum asked, her face flushed with pride.

'Mum, I love it!'

If we were a normal family, I probably would have thrown my arms around both my parents and kissed them, but we weren't a normal family. We didn't show physical affection. It's not the Brethren way.

'I'm getting married,' I blurted out, suddenly overcome with emotion. 'I've met my future husband.'

Mum laughed nervously. 'Who to?'

'His name's Kevin White. He's from the south of England,' I told them, remembering that nothing could be official until Mr Symington had been consulted. Nothing happened without Mr Symington's say so, even who we could or couldn't marry.

Dad looked concerned.

'Here we are making your bedroom all nice for you,' Mum said, 'and you come home and tell us you're going to leave us to get married!'

We all laughed. My heart was full.

Mum had so many questions, but I needed to get some sleep. My head was in a whirl. Now that I was home, and the excitement was wearing off, all sorts of questions were going around in my head. Was I being too hasty? Did I *really* want to marry a stranger? Was this what God wanted for me? Did I care for Kevin enough to learn to love him?

I flopped down on my bed in exhaustion as Mum drew the curtains – new curtains that matched the wallpaper and my quilt cover. Dad kissed me lightly on my forehead as Mum pulled the new covers over me.

'Mum and I will support you in whatever you do,' he whispered. 'God will guide you.'

I closed my eyes and slept.

When I woke, the winter sun was peeping through the bright-blue curtains. The numbers on the new digital clock on the bedside table read 2 p.m. I had been asleep for hours. I lay looking around me at my new bedroom and smiled. Life felt good. I jumped out of bed, got on my knees and prayed.

'God and Father, thank you for showing me your love. Thank you for the love of my parents and the love of Kevin towards me. Guide me, Lord. Keep me pure. Keep your hand over Kevin and help us to grow together in love. In the name of Our Lord Jesus Christ, amen.'

I took the precious ten-pound note from my dressing table, read Kevin's message again and slipped it into my pocket before heading downstairs.

I stood in the doorway to take in the scene for a moment. There was Mum standing over the Rayburn preparing the evening meal – Lord's Day leftovers, a lamb hotpot. She'd serve it with fresh homemade bread spread thick with butter. Mum was always in the kitchen, cooking and baking for us and filling the freezer with food for entertaining our Brethren friends at the weekends. By this time, my sister Deb and my brother Edward had married, so she also helped with the care of her four young grandchildren. Our house was always full of bustle and noise. I loved this home. Leaving all this behind wouldn't be easy. Was I ready to be a housewife, a wife, a mother?

Looking up from her cooking, Mum turned and smiled at me.

'How're you feeling?'

'Good,' I said, sitting myself down on the comfy armchair near the warm Rayburn.

'So, tell me about this young man, then. How do you know he's serious about you?'

Taking the ten-pound note out of my denim skirt pocket, I carefully unfolded it and handed it to her.

'Ooh!' she exclaimed. 'He is serious! Well, the question is, Maria, do you *like* him?'

'Mum, I *really* think I do,' I said. 'He's very good-looking. Cute.'

'Cute?' she said, laughing. 'Are you sure that's enough?' Then her tone turned serious. 'Marriage is about finding someone who will love and respect you. Someone you can trust. Someone who knows how to bring up a family under the guidance of God, the Lord and the Brethren. Someone who is obedient to whatever the Man of God tells us. Those are all the things that matter, Maria.'

I nodded. 'But how will I know those things, Mum,' I said, 'if I don't know him?'

'You just know,' she said. 'And, by the look in your eyes, I think you know already.'

I felt myself relax. Hadn't God sent me to the three-day meeting? Hadn't He shown me the man I was to marry? I was certain that this was all in God's will and plan for me.

Mum reminded me that until Kevin had a house and had got the final stamp of approval from Mr Symington, my 'arrangement' with him must be kept a family secret. Nothing was set in stone at this point.

I went to my room and wrote my first letter to Kevin. I told him of my feelings and how I felt God had provided him for me. How I was sure that this was God's will. I signed it with lots of kisses and a P.S. saying I couldn't wait to hear back from him. I popped a recent photo of myself in the envelope too – I wanted him to be able to look at it every day until we met again.

For a long week I waited for the postman to put a letter through the door. Every day I asked myself the same questions, over and over. Why was he not replying? Had he changed his mind? Was this God's way of testing me? With every day that went by my family began to doubt Kevin's intentions more and more. My best friend teased me. She asked if Kevin might be a fabrication of my imagination. I couldn't sleep. I couldn't concentrate on my work. I carried that precious ten-pound note around with me. I took it out of my pocket to look at it again and again. Until I had a reply, my life was on hold.

Then, just when I'd given up all hope, a letter arrived addressed to me in Kevin's handwriting. I sat nervously on the edge of my bed while I ripped open the envelope. This, I hoped, would be the first of many love letters.

It wasn't a long letter; just one sheet of paper neatly folded with a photograph of a smiling Kevin tucked inside. I'd thought about him so much since our meeting but my memory of what he looked like was fading, so it was good to get a photograph. What wasn't so good, however, was some of the content of the letter. Kevin explained that his father had forbidden him to contact me until he was in a position to buy a house and prove he could support a wife and family. Kevin had pleaded with his father to be allowed to write this one brief letter, as he feared I'd think he didn't love me. But he was allowed no further contact with me until he had enough money for a deposit on a house. Kevin's father had told him he couldn't marry until he turned nineteen, which was ten months away. The letter closed with Kevin expressing his belief that the Lord would allow this to happen if we prayed fervently for a house to become available that he could afford. He signed off with love and kisses.

After all the pent-up feelings of the previous week, I was disappointed. I had wanted to at least be allowed to write to Kevin. Why were the Brethren's rules in his area so much stricter than the Brethren's rules in the North? I knelt by my bed, covered my head with a clean white hanky and I asked the Lord for strength and guidance in the months ahead. As I got up from my knees, I felt a new sense of purpose and determination.

'Well?' Mum said. 'So, what did young Kevin have to say? I hope he sent a photo so we can see what he looks like.'

She wiped her hands on her apron and took the photo from me.

'Wow,' she said, 'he's very handsome.'

I passed her the letter. She read it, folded it up and passed it back to me.

'Well,' she said, 'at least he's being obedient to his father. That says a lot about the type of person he is. I know this will be hard for you, Maria, but as Kevin says, it's the Lord's way of testing your love for each other and the main thing is, he loves you.' Then she gave my arm a little squeeze. 'Chin up, girl, you can do this.'

'Yes, Mum, I can,' I said, as I slipped the letter and photo back into my skirt pocket. 'I'll use this time to earn some money and fill my bottom drawer.'

The next four months were difficult. Every chance I got, I studied that photo, looking at Kevin's muscular arms bulging through his tight jumper and imagining those arms around me, holding me tightly but gently. I peered at the dark hair on his chest showing at his open shirt neck. I stared at his dark eyes. During the day the photo was pinned to my office wall. During the night it was stuck to my bed. During the meetings, it was tucked into the front of my Bible. I longed to know more about the man behind that face. Who was he?

On Valentine's Day, exactly three months after my first letter from Kevin, my mother burst into my bedroom when I was dressing for work to thrust a thick pink envelope into my hand.

'It must be from him! I'll leave you to open it in peace,' she added with a wink, as she left my bedroom and closed the door. I pulled out the most beautiful, romantic, gaudy Valentine's card. After I'd lingered over the sentimental words on the front and opened it to read the words inside, a beautiful love song played. Kevin had sprayed the card with his aftershave. The scent brought me back to our first meeting and how close we'd stood together as we hid out of view at the back of the meeting hall.

But what was written inside the card was what excited me most. Kevin wrote that he'd managed to find a house and he was finalising the mortgage, so very soon we would be able to have some contact. The wait was almost over. Soon we could be together. When I ran downstairs, bursting to share the news with my family, Dad put his hand on my shoulder.

'You have been patient and obedient to the Lord and He shall reward you.'

'Well,' Mum said, smiling, 'we'd better start planning for the big day and think about that wedding dress.'

I laughed. 'But Mum,' I said, remembering, 'we can't get married until he's nineteen and we've got Mr Symington's permission.'

'I'm sure it'll all be fine,' Mum said. 'The seven months until Kevin's birthday are going to fly by.'

Seven months seemed a long way off to me. My older sister, Claire, was less enthusiastic about the impending marriage. 'Why on earth would you want to move to a strange place?' she sneered as she left the room. 'Rather you than me.'

Since I'd come back from the Southeast, Claire had been consistently negative about Kevin. I put her comments down to jealousy and chose to ignore them: she was now twenty years old and had no sign of interest yet from a man. I knew that, like me, she was bored with work and longed for marriage.

Three weeks later, Kevin telephoned. Mum took the call and told me to use the phone in their bedroom for privacy.

'I've got the house!' he announced excitedly. 'And not only that but I asked David Johnston [the local leader] if we can meet at the next Bristol fellowship meeting in two weeks. He's agreed to add our names to the invitation list.'

Every month there was a special meeting in Bristol, which Brethren from all around the world attended. It was a privilege to get your name on the invitation list. I couldn't believe it. I was going to see Kevin in person, in the flesh, in two weeks' time. There was so much I wanted to say and ask, but now that he was on the phone, I struggled to find words.

'How are you?' he asked.

'I'm good,' I said. 'I'm so happy,' I added as I took a deep breath, trying to calm myself. I was thankful when Kevin started telling me about the house and all the renovations that he wanted to do. Soon the conversation began to flow, and it seemed no time until I heard a knock on my parents' bedroom door and Dad announced that our hour was up and it was time to say goodbye. An hour was all we were allowed. I told him that I had to go but would write to him every day. He told me how much he loved me, and we kissed down the phone as we said our goodbyes.

A few days after this phone call, Kevin rang Mr Symington in America and asked for his permission to marry me. After many questions, we were given the go-ahead and our courtship was made public. We were now permitted to tell our friends that we were going to get married.

I kept my word about my letter writing. Every day I wrote Kevin a letter and once a week I received one in return. In my letters I asked him about his day at work and who he'd chatted to after the meetings. Once the work started on the house my letters were filled with ideas of how I'd like it. I'd tell him about my day and how I'd sit daydreaming about him instead of getting on with my work. I wrote about my dreams of when we were married and being able to kiss and cuddle him every day. I finished each letter with lots of hugs and kisses and always sprayed some perfume on the page before putting it in the envelope. Kevin's letters were short and always about his work and the house. He sent me little swatches of wallpaper and pictures of kitchens to help us choose together in the best way we could. Each Saturday evening we were allowed to talk on the phone for an hour.

In March 1987, in Bristol, Kevin and I met again in person five months after our first brief conversation. I wanted him to take me in his arms and kiss me but that was forbidden.

We stood together in awkward silence for a few minutes. It was like meeting for the first time. Those five months had been so long. I moved closer to him, wanting to smell him and feel the warmth of his body close to me. I looked him up and down, taking in every bit of him. He still looked cute to me with his stocky frame and wide smile.

Standing there in the car park of the Bristol meeting hall surrounded by hundreds of Brethren, I could feel many eyes on us. This was my husband-to-be, and I felt proud and happy to be standing next to him. No other man would love me like Kevin would, I told myself, as I watched him make his way to his place among the men while I took my place among the women.

Once the meeting was finished, Kevin and I rushed out to our arranged meeting place and, standing in the shadow of some trees, we stood close, whispering sweet nothings in each other's ears. It all felt so romantic, but it was over all too soon when half an hour later one of my friends told me to hurry, as the coach would be leaving in five minutes. Kevin and I ran to where all the coaches were parked and, finding the one bound for home, I ran to the back of the coach where I stood by the rear window waving vigorously to Kevin until he was out of sight. Everyone laughed at me for being so soppy, but I didn't care.

Around this time Mr Symington decreed that young couples who were almost ready to get married but didn't live in the same city could meet once a month at the Bristol fellowship meeting. So, every month I made that same journey from the far north of England to Bristol. My family couldn't afford to pay for a train, so I had to make the gruelling journey by coach, but it was worth every mile. Every time Kevin and I met it took us a few minutes to get reacquainted because it had been weeks between each meeting, but each time we met I felt that excitement in my body and was sure that I was in love.

Apart from one weekend in summer 1987, when my family and I visited Kevin's family and to see the new house, these monthly meetings with an hour and a half's conversation together were the full extent of our permitted courtship. Added to that we had our letters and our permitted one-hour phone call once a week. I realise now that there is no way these rushed meet-ups, scribbled letters and limited phone calls could ever be enough time to get to know a future husband. By the time we got married that autumn, we had only met in person six times.

# NINE

Mr Symington died on 23 April 1987 while I was preparing for my marriage to Kevin. He had been ill for many years. No one talked about his illness at the time, but I now know that he, just like his predecessor, JT Junior, had died from an alcohol-related disorder.

His passing brought shock to the worldwide Brethren community because he hadn't made it clear before his death who the next Man of God should be. Now many Brethren elders were competing for that place. We were without direction. Rudderless. Every meeting and every social gathering was now dominated by discussions about who would be the next Man of God. With no Man of God, I couldn't help worrying, would our Brethren way of life fall apart? The whole situation began to make me feel ill. My doubts about my own readiness for the Rapture and for marriage began to surface again.

Two months after Mr Symington's death, amid all this uncertainty, my parents, my unmarried siblings and I visited Kevin's town to see my new married home. It was the first time I'd been back since my relationship with him had begun. Despite my initial excitement, doubts started to creep in, but most days I was able to push them to the back of my mind by keeping busy with planning my wedding and thinking about a new home and a new life in the South with the man I loved.

I was nervous to visit the town where I would soon be living. What if Kevin's family didn't like me? What if the local brethren weren't friendly towards me? Would I like the house that was going to be my new home?

I wasn't allowed to stay with Kevin and his family in their home as the elders believed that staying in the same house before marriage could lead to the temptation of physical intimacy, so, apart from my brother Brian, who stayed at Kevin's parents' home, the rest of us were sent to stay with a family who lived close by. As was often the way when you stayed with Brethren hosts in a new city, we had never met this family before. They were a family of five: the parents, two girls and a boy.

At this stage in our courtship, Kevin and I were supposed to spend as much time together as possible, but we had to have another adult present at all times and under no circumstances were we allowed to have any physical contact. Both our parents were keeping a constant close eye on us.

On the Saturday, my family and I went to look around what was to become my new home. Kevin had described in detail how every Saturday since he'd got the keys to the house he'd gathered a team of young Brethren lads to help him get the place ready. They'd been knocking down walls and redecorating. They were about to start fitting a kitchen. At the end of the day they'd go back to Kevin's parents for a meal and plenty of alcohol. This is common practice among the younger Brethren men. With no competitive sports, no television, no paid working at the weekend, no cinema, no holidays, the young Brethren men often queue up to spend time in each other's company hammering and knocking down walls.

As we walked the short distance from the meeting room to the new house, it suddenly struck me that my life was about to change dramatically. This narrow street was a far cry from our affluent street back home with its double-fronted detached houses and the seaside right on our doorstep. A continuous row of narrow terraced houses stretched down one side of the street, a mixture of semi-detached, detached and more terraced houses on the other. In the middle of the street was the huge Brethren meeting room. Kevin's house – *our* house, *my* house – was right next door. It was semi-detached and joined to another Brethren family house. We would be surrounded by Brethren! This should have made me feel secure and safe, but instead I had a gloomy sense of being hemmed in and overlooked.

But once Kevin had led the way up the very short garden path and opened the front door, my spirits lifted. The kitchen/diner was a long L-shaped room and, although it had no kitchen yet, it was an ideal size for entertaining. As I looked around, I tried to imagine myself in those rooms, entertaining twenty or more Brethren.

My parents and I filed upstairs. Upstairs was much smaller – a tiny bathroom with just a bath, two double bedrooms and a box room. Kevin took my hand and winked at me as he led me into what would be our bedroom. He'd papered the walls in pastel pink and blue patterned wallpaper, installed a vanity unit and, all along one wall, he'd installed built-in wardrobes. I was impressed. I looked around and imagined this being my home. I imagined bringing up children here, and although it was a far cry from the life I was used to living by the sea, I felt it was as good as I could get so far from home. As Kevin took my hand, I gave it a squeeze and thanked him for everything he had done.

Our next stop was H.Samuel the jewellers to buy the ring. A wedding ring is the only jewellery a Brethren woman is permitted to wear, so this was a highlight of the trip for me. Claire was sent with us as chaperone but she was happy to head off to other shops, so we found ourselves alone for the first time with no one watching us, looking in the window of H.Samuel. Kevin wasted no time. He put his arm around my waist. A thrill went through my body. If I felt this with his touch through my clothes, what would it be like when he touched my bare flesh? I whispered a silent, 'Holy Spirit help me. Keep my mind pure.'

That evening we went to Kevin's parents for a meal. It gave me a chance to get to know his family better. His mum seemed kind but she was almost completely silent, and although Kevin had warned me that his dad was very strict, that evening he was lively and funny. I was relieved to feel at ease in their home. On our final night we were invited out for a meal to another Brethren family.

It's dark as we head out from our host's residence and prepare to drive the few miles across the city back to Kevin's home. Kevin opens the back doors of the Coopers' minibus and leads me in behind him. The back row of seats is rear-facing. I can see from the glint in Kevin's eyes that he knows they won't be able to see us. Mr Cooper notices what Kevin is doing and asks Emily, the youngest Cooper girl, to climb in with us. As I guess is the case for Kevin, I long to snuggle up and feel the touch of my betrothed – but I don't want to break Brethren rules and get into trouble.

We haven't got far down the road when Kevin's hand starts to wander. First, he puts his arm around my shoulder while he glances over the back of the seat to make sure no one can see him. Emily is busy fumbling in her handbag and doesn't notice. Gradually his hand moves down towards my right breast. He feels for my nipple under my blouse and bra. He rubs his fingers gently over my nipple. Although my nipple responds, my body freezes. What is he doing?

'Please don't do that yet,' I whisper urgently in his ear. 'Just wait a few more weeks and my body will be yours.'

He doesn't seem to hear me. He keeps his hand on my breast and continues to stroke my nipple. He doesn't seem to even see me. I look up at him with an urgency but his eyes are closed and his other hand is on his crotch. I'm paralysed, terrified we'll be seen. Emily has heard me whispering and looks in our direction. Nudging Kevin, I quickly move myself away from him. He seems to wake from his trance and quickly removes his hand. He whispers an apology. He tries to take my hand, but I don't want him to touch me now. He's done something I haven't agreed to and it's going to get us both in trouble. I move as far away from him as I can. Who is this man I am about to marry?

The next morning, as we left to take the long journey back up north, I felt a sort of relief that we were leaving. I needed time to think. As the doubts had begun to creep in, I had become tense and anxious and now, as we drove further away from Kevin, I felt myself relax.

'Maria,' Claire whispered in the car, 'all weekend you've hardly said a word. Are you all right? You seemed almost scared of Kevin sometimes.'

I shrugged. I wasn't scared of him, but I wasn't sure who he was.

Emily reported what she'd seen in the back of the minibus to her dad. Kevin was in trouble. He had to go before the local leaders and confess his sins and ask for forgiveness. Trouble was waiting for us back home too: Kevin's local leader had told our local leader. I was called to speak to the elders. I explained that I hadn't done anything.

'But,' one of them asked me, 'if that was the case, why didn't you tell him to stop?'

No matter what I said, in our local leader's eyes I'd encouraged it and enjoyed it. According to him I'd let him down badly and he was ashamed that one of his Brethren had sinned in such a way. The only way to get out of this situation was to say I was sorry and promise never to do it again. It wasn't worth an argument. The leader was always right.

Later, Kevin told me he'd thought I would drop him right there and then. Maybe I should have done but it took weeks for me to stop and consider if what I was doing was what I wanted. It was only four weeks from my wedding day when I finally broke down to my parents and told them that I didn't think I should marry Kevin. At first they were shocked, but then they assured me that it was quite normal to have those thoughts and doubts as we approached marriage. It was just nerves.

Mum suggested that I should speak with my older sister Deb and her husband Cecil, as Deb had had the same doubts when she was getting married. Deb and Cecil said all the same things: that it was quite normal to have doubts but everything would be fine and everyone was looking forward to the wedding day. Mum told me again that she was sure that me marrying Kevin was the Lord's will. I told myself that Kevin was a good person. Of course he was a good person: he was one of the Brethren. Brethren trusted each other. I told myself that once I was married I would be more relaxed in his company and would come back to myself.

# TEN

Since the age of fourteen I'd been fantasising about my wedding day; as teenage girls, we talked of little else. In the ten months since I'd met Kevin I'd spent hours leafing through forbidden glossy wedding magazines that I'd hidden under my bed, transported into a world of white wedding cars, endless flowers, tiered wedding cakes, professional photographers and church weddings. I tried to imagine what it would feel like to be driven to church in a beautiful wedding car. Or walking down the aisle on my dad's arm, dressed in an off-the-shoulder, low-cut ivory wedding dress with a long train flowing behind me like the forbidden pictures I'd seen of the dress Princess Diana had worn a few years earlier. What would it be like to have a wedding reception in a beautiful location surrounded by my family and lots of friends? Yet every time I closed those magazines I was taken back to reality: I was an *Exclusive Brethren* young woman and *not* a young woman of this world. Those things weren't for me.

Brethren weddings are simple, unfussy, un-worldly affairs. No fancy cars. No honeymoons. No dancing late into the night. No bands or flowers. They also had to take place on a Tuesday for some reason I never understood. I'd be allowed to buy and wear a white wedding dress, and Kevin would be permitted to wear a suit. There'd be a simple ceremony in our Brethren meeting hall. Most of the Brethren I knew would come. We'd both make our promises. Then I'd say goodbye to my parents and family and we'd stay in a relative's house overnight before travelling to the southeast of England, where my new life as a Brethren wife would begin.

On the morning of the autumn day set for my wedding, I woke from a fitful night with a strange sense of dread. I had a fear of being alone down south without my family; fear of when I would ever see them again; fear of meeting new people. The huge life-changing step that I was about to take was weighing heavy on my mind. In a few short hours my life would no longer be my own. As a young Brethren woman I would be giving my life over to my husband. The scripture in Ephesians 5 had been whirling around in my head all night:

> Wives, submit to your own husbands, as to the Lord. For the husband is the head of the wife as also Christ is the head of the church; and He is Saviour of the body. Therefore, just as the church is subject to Christ, so let the wives be to their own husbands in everything.

Brethren men were often quoting those lines at their wives, using them to shore up their power in their own homes. Of course, they never mentioned the following verse that says: 'Husbands, love your wives, as Christ loved the church and gave himself up for it.'

So, as I entered into marriage with a man I barely knew, I had to trust that he would be the kind, caring and loving husband that he was supposed to be. I had to trust that he would be a man I could learn to love. I couldn't say I loved him yet, because despite our many letters back and forth, I hardly knew him, but that was fine because the 'Man of God' had told us that love comes after marriage. How I longed to find true love inside my marriage. When I climbed out of my single bed for the last time that morning and pulled back my bedroom curtains, the clear blue sky and bright sunlight of an Indian summer lifted my spirits.

The day started as it was supposed to with breakfast as normal with my parents, siblings and grandma. Then, after breakfast, I changed into a dinner dress that my best friend Linda had made me. It was a smart navy-and-green checked dress with contrasting pleats on the bodice and sleeves. It sat neatly on my slim figure and, as I looked in the mirror that morning, I knew that Kevin would approve. This was the dress I would wear until I changed into my wedding dress later.

At 11 a.m. my future husband, my married siblings, my nieces and nephew, my grandma and my best friend Linda arrived. Contrary to the wedding custom of the 'worldlies', a Brethren bride sees her husband-to-be on their wedding day *before* they meet in church, when he comes to the bride's family home.

It didn't feel like a Tuesday. In some respects, it felt like a Saturday, when all the family would come round for one of Mum's roast dinners and my young nieces and nephew would run riot around the house. But today was different. Today a new member was joining us for this meal and that was Kevin. It felt strange having him in our home for the first time. It felt strange having him sat next to me for our midday wedding meal, his aftershave filling the air around me. I wanted to touch him, to reach out and run my hand up and down his muscled leg. I wanted to kiss him and hold him close to me, but it would be 5 p.m. before that happened.

The thought made me nervous. Would I disappoint him? What was I supposed to do? I knew very little of what would be expected of me in the bedroom. Brethren didn't talk about those things. Most of what I knew I'd picked up from the girls in school and from the little blue book called 'All About Sexual Intercourse' which Mum had given me to read a few days before. As we popped champagne and ate my favourite meal of roast lamb, I did my best to put my fears and nerves to the back of my mind and enjoy the day.

At 3 o'clock Mum and Linda helped me get into my wedding dress while Kevin dressed in his suit. After months of searching, I had found my dream dress in a shop in Carlisle, all puffy leg-of-mutton sleeves that were so fashionable in the '80s, trimmed with tiny pin-tucks, ribbons and pearls. But sadly the dress I'd found was ivory silk and I wasn't allowed to wear anything but pure white. White was a sign of purity and would show that I was a virgin on my wedding day.

Mum was a fine seamstress, so she offered to make a replica of the dress I'd seen in the shop. She made it in pure white and adapted the sailor collar so it wouldn't reveal any cleavage. The bodice sat tight against the curve of my breasts with a 'V' waistline sitting neatly on my slim waist. The skirt sat over a layered net petticoat, making it puff out like something from *Cinderella*. The back was fastened with tiny pearl buttons and was finished off with a huge bow. Mum added the required waist-length veil held on my head by a simple headdress. I chose silk pumps to complement the outfit. I may not have had the exact fairytale dress I'd dreamt of, but I felt amazing. I did a little twirl in front of the full-length mirror, giggling with excitement and hugging my mother with gratitude.

Although Brethren brides were not allowed bridesmaids, and the mother of the bride was not supposed to dress elaborately, I felt and shared my mother's desire to push the rules as far as we dared. She wore a pretty jade-green dress with a white collar trimmed by a navy bow and a beautiful silk headscarf in jade, navy and white. My sister Claire, who was my witness that day, wore a navy and cerise spotted Laura Ashley dress and a matching silk headscarf. My mother made blue dresses trimmed with white sailor collars to match my dress for my seven-year-old sister Chloe and my four young nieces. This was as close as we dared to go to worldly wedding traditions.

Only my immediate family and a small number of my friends were invited to the wedding lunch. None of Kevin's family was invited. That was the rule. If a young man married outside of his local city, then his family weren't permitted to attend the wedding. Once the wedding was over I'd leave my family to live in the South, to be part of his family.

As I reached the bottom of the stairs I took a deep breath before turning the wooden knob on the lounge door. Stepping into the room, blushing from pleasure and shyness, I saw my bridegroom stood waiting for me, looking handsome in a navy suit and turquoise-blue tie. He took my hands in his as cheers and clapping went up from the small gathering of people around us.

Once the cheers had died down, everyone made their way to the garden to enjoy the weather and join in the celebrations. Dad had laid out a red carpet for me to stand on to keep my dress clean. Everyone stood around drinking champagne or whiskey while Mum and my sisters passed around trays of finger food. As I stood on the red-carpet square, I lifted my eyes up to the blue sky and gave thanks for my family and friends around me. I gave thanks for the beautiful weather we'd been given for this special day.

At 4.15 p.m. Dad went to lay a white sheet across the back seat of his car to keep my dress clean on the journey to the meeting room. Now there was no turning back. Linda helped me tidy myself up, and I reached for the little white drawstring handbag Mum had made, which was just big enough to hold a new lace silk hanky and my new hymn book and Bible that I had been allowed to buy for the occasion from the Bible and Gospel Trust Depot. My initials M.J.W, boldly embossed in gold, shone bright and clear on the front corner of my Bible. Miss Maria Joan Compton was about to become Mrs Maria Joan White.

As I squeezed into the back seat of the car with my dress and petticoats almost up to my ears, I took one last look at the big old house that had been my childhood home for eighteen years. The next time I stepped over the threshold I would be a married woman. Dad climbed into the driver's seat with Mum beside him and Kevin squeezed in the back beside me. As we made our journey towards the hall, with Kevin holding my hand, I looked out of the car window to see for the last time all the familiar sites and landmarks I'd passed so many times on this journey. Still, I was asking myself the question I'd been asking all my life: was I ready?

Kevin and I were the first to arrive at the meeting room. The bride and groom should always be seated before the rest of the congregation arrives, so he and I took our seats on the front circle of the room, the other rows racked up behind us. The front row is usually for the leaders and elders but, on her wedding day, the bride, now the centre of attention, is permitted to sit there. As I sat myself down, arranging my full skirts around me, I took a good look around to take it all in one last time – this old windowless meeting room with its high fences, fluorescent lighting, ugly green carpet and black seats had been like a second home to me. I had sat in this meeting hall four or five times every week since I was a baby. This place held so many memories for me, both good and bad. There were times when the high fences, locked doors and locked gates had made me feel safe; then there were other times when I felt closed in by it all; times when I had wanted to run away from the shouting preacher or the boring monotonous voices of the old men.

Soon the room was full of Brethren from the various meetings around Northern England. These people were my friends. I watched them smiling fondly at me as they took their seats. These were *my* people, *my* friends, *my* family, and I loved them, and I knew they loved me too. Now I was going to have to make new friends in a new place as a good Brethren wife. This was everything it was supposed to be but, again, I felt a flicker of fear. Why was I so afraid?

At 5 p.m. our registrar brother Mr Turner took his place behind the table and, with microphone in hand, he asked us to rise. Kevin and I rose from our seats and faced him at the table to say our vows. I could feel my whole body shaking as I spoke. I could sense Kevin's nervousness too, but we still couldn't touch each other for reassurance. The meeting room was a sacred place, a place of worship, and as such it was not a place for physical touch between a man and a woman.

After we'd said our vows and everyone had said their amens in the right places, after the legal jargon was completed and we signed the papers, the meeting began. I have no memory of who ministered that evening. All I could think of was our wedding night. What would it feel like to passionately kiss my husband and be kissed in return? What would it feel like to be touched by this man? A shiver of anticipation ran through me. Would he want sex on that first night? Much as I was impatient to experience sex for the first time, I had always hoped that there would be a lead up to it. In my mind, to 'make love' would be so much better than just having sex, though I didn't really know what the differences were. The authors of 'All About Sexual Intercourse' hadn't said anything about that.

The meeting soon ended and, after much 'oohing' and 'ahhing' over my beautiful dress from my sisters and friends, we finally got in the car to head back to my parents' house for a buffet meal with family and more photos before we changed into our 'going away' outfits. For our first night together we'd be staying at my sister and her husband's home. I couldn't help thinking of those fancy marital suites I'd seen in the magazines – what it would be like to have a big four-poster bed, our own bathroom and lots of privacy. But I reminded myself firmly that wasn't the Brethren way. I had vowed to live a life as a good Brethren wife – a simple life of having children, keeping the house clean and pleasing my husband.

As soon as Kevin and I were in the back of my parents' car and my father was pulling out of the meeting room car park, Kevin pulled me close and kissed me full on the lips. We spent much of that journey kissing and cuddling. My parents were inches away in the front of the car, but they kept their eyes to the front and, apart from the occasional clearing of throats in embarrassment, they left us to it. By the time we drove into my parents' drive we were so wrapped up in each other among the skirts of my wedding dress that it would have been hard to tell that there were two people in the back seat of the car. As I disentangled myself and reached for the door handle, I gave Kevin a smile and a wink and whispered in his ear, 'Later, Husband.'

The evening was lively. As I sat next to Kevin, I watched my family milling around me, making sure to remember every last moment: my four nieces and my little nephew running amok through the house; Richard's once-white shirt stained with orange juice as he ran around with a beaker in hand; my youngest niece, eight months old, sitting in her highchair with baby food smeared on her cheeks, banging a toy on the tray; my little sister Chloe sitting in the corner, trying to read a book while her young nieces pulled at her dress, begging her to come and play; Dad and Edward cracking jokes; Mum milling about in the kitchen with my sisters.

Mum set endless amounts of food on the table that evening but I couldn't eat a thing. Soon Kevin and I would have to go upstairs to my bedroom to change out of our wedding attire. It would be our first-ever time alone. I was going to have to undress in front of him. He was my husband, but he was also a stranger. Why couldn't Mum help me out of my dress? Why couldn't Kevin and I wait until later when there weren't adults and children downstairs hearing our every move through those creaky floorboards?

It was 9 p.m. when Kevin and I made our way upstairs to my bedroom. The adults gathered in the hallway to watch us mount the stairs. There were wolf whistles, jokes and cheering. I'd done the whistles and jokes too when others had got married. You were supposed to. But now that I was on the receiving end, I felt embarrassed and alone. I wanted our first time alone to feel private and romantic, not all nudge-nudge-wink-wink. I closed the old wooden door behind us and stepped forward to draw the curtains.

Before I move away from the window, Kevin is already up behind me. He starts unbuttoning my dress. I had imagined him slowly unfastening each button of this fairytale dress one by one, glimpsing a little of my lacy bra and then gradually revealing all. But now he is wrenching and tearing at each button with frustration. I am rooted to the spot, still holding the edges of the curtains. I'm unable to move. Within seconds my dress falls to the floor. He pulls me around to face him. There's a look in his eyes that frightens me. He looks like some crazed animal as he gropes at my breasts under my silk lacy bra. He's hurting me. I want to stop him, slow him down. I want us both to enjoy the experience but he's not seeing me. I step out of my dress and move towards my outfit hanging on the wardrobe door, hoping that if I get my clothes back on, I can get out and downstairs quickly. Now he is pulling his own clothes off. I want to love this man, I want to be intimate, but I can't rush it. Then, as I reach for my blouse, he comes up behind me again. This time I can feel his nakedness pressing against my skin. I can feel his hardness against my bottom as he roughly undoes my bra and pulls down my pretty silk knickers. I'm standing in just my suspenders and white lace stockings as he spins me round to face him.

'Oh! Very nice,' he says. 'I love suspenders.'

I have no words. This is my husband, I tell myself. He is standing naked in front of me, and I need to make him happy. I need to submit to whatever he wants. I reach awkwardly to the floor to retrieve my fallen bra and knickers, but he pulls me back against him. I turn my face away, embarrassed at his nakedness. I want this, I tell myself, but not here, not now. Not in my old bedroom. Not in my parents' house with all my family downstairs. I want to plead with him to wait. But isn't it my duty to submit fully to my husband? Suddenly he picks me up and almost throws me onto my single bed. Again, I'm too shocked to speak and too scared to resist. I feel his weight on top of me as he pulls my legs apart and tries to push his penis inside me. I plead. My voice is a loud panicky whisper:

'Please, Kevin. Please wait. They'll be waiting for us downstairs. They'll be wondering what's keeping us.'

But he doesn't seem to hear me as he continues to try and enter me. Why is he doing this? Can't he see he's hurting me? But in that almost animal-like state, he seems to see and feel nothing but his own pent-up sexual desires. Who is this man? I ask myself. Who have I married?

Suddenly there are screams of a child somewhere downstairs, then the sound of feet running up the stairs. Kevin snaps out of his trance and jumps off the bed, grabbing his boxers. Mum is banging on the door, shouting.

'What on earth is taking you so long? Young Richard has fallen and split his head open. He needs to go to the hospital. For goodness' sake, hurry up!'

As I grab my clothes, I call out as calmly as possible: 'OK, Mum, we'll be down in a minute.' If she knew what she had just saved me from, would she have been shocked or would she have told me that this was what marriage was all about? Did all marriages start like this? Is this how it was supposed to be?

I did my best to dress quickly, but my hands were shaking so much I couldn't fasten the buttons on my blouse. Kevin came to help me while he apologised for what he had done. He kept saying that he should have waited for the right time. That crazed look had left him now. He was the handsome, gentle, smiling Kevin again, the man I'd married a few hours earlier, so I gave him a quick hug and kiss and told him it was OK, that I forgave him. But as I folded my wedding dress up, placed it in our suitcase and we made our way downstairs, I felt a shiver run over me. Who had I married? Who was this man? What had I done?

# PART TWO

# ELEVEN

I'd imagined a man making love to me. I had dreamt of sensual touches, gentle caresses and soft kisses. As a teenager, in the quiet of the night, lying in my single bed, those dreams and fantasies had led to a stirring of sensation within me: a pleasure I seemed to have no control over. I dreamt of a life like I'd read about in those forbidden novels that I'd hidden under my mattress as a teenager. I longed for the love that Mr Darcy showed to Elizabeth Bennet in *Pride and Prejudice*, or the lovemaking I'd read about in *A Kind of Loving*, which I'd read for my CSE English Literature coursework.

I had never heard the words 'orgasm' or 'masturbate' but I found ways of making those pleasurable feelings more intense until I felt the pleasure peak and take over my whole body. As a Brethren teenager with no sex education, I had no idea what was happening within my body, but I was certain that these pleasurable stirrings, whatever they were called, were meant to be kept for marriage.

Now that I'd married Kevin, all those pleasurable feelings seemed to have disappeared. What was wrong with me? For years I had longed to have those feelings of pleasure when my husband had sex with me, but as I lay on my back waiting until he came, I felt nothing. It was all over so quickly. Was this my duty to my husband? Was this marriage?

I longed to ask my mother if this was normal, but in those days the Brethren man was master in his own home. A woman's duty was to obey him in all things and not ask questions. No one was allowed to interfere. So I kept my questions and feelings to myself. It never occurred to me that there might have been something wrong with Kevin. I'd heard that worldly people were sex maniacs, that they were all doing it all the time both inside and outside of marriage. I had never imagined that sex maniacs existed in the Brethren too and that I would marry one.

Right from the start, the more sex Kevin had, the more he seemed to want. He could never seem to get enough: first thing in the morning, as soon as he came home from work, even at lunchtime, and then last thing at night. Yet nothing seemed to satisfy him. He often had a crazed look in his eyes. It frightened me.

I no longer felt like a person. I felt like an object to be used for my husband's satisfaction and pleasure. I was sore and bruised. I was getting thrush and urine infections. I was going to the doctor for pessaries and creams. But even though Kevin could see the pain and discomfort I was suffering, he didn't stop. He couldn't stop. I longed to be able to show my new husband affection and love. I longed for what I had imagined marriage meant, what my parents seemed to have: cuddles on the sofa, snatched kisses in the kitchen, or just companionship in comfortable silence, but instead I could feel myself retreating further and further away from Kevin, bruised and confused, terrified that if I showed him any signs of affection it would only multiply his sexual demands upon me.

One Saturday morning, only a few short weeks after our wedding, I awake to Kevin's hand between my legs again, but this time, exhausted, sore and certain I am pregnant, I feign sleep. Staying in a foetal position, facing the white veneer wardrobe in our bedroom, I lie as still as possible, hardly daring to breathe. Looking at the bedside clock, I read the big red numbers: it's 6 a.m. The fumbling stops and I feel his familiar hardness pressing between my legs as his breathing becomes more rapid. I must stop this. I've had enough. Turning over suddenly, I face him and plead:

'Please, Kevin. I'm just so tired. Can we do this another time?'

Moving away from me slightly, he props himself up on one elbow and, grabbing one of my breasts with his free hand, he gives it a painful squeeze.

'Why not now?' he asks angrily, with that wild look in his eyes again. 'Don't you love me?' Wrenching myself free from his grasp, I roll over and turn my back on him.

'It's not about love,' I mumble. 'It's about how tired I am right now.' Moving as close to the edge of the bed as I can, I pull the heavy winter quilt up around me and do my best to go back to sleep.

The next thing I know, the alarm clock is bleeping. The big red numbers say 8 a.m. now. Turning over, I see that Kevin is already up. His side of the bed is cold so he must have been up for a while. Relieved, I bath quickly and, wrapping my big white towel around me, I go to sit on the edge of our bed. Opening my underwear drawer, I reach in to take out my knickers and bra, but find the drawer is empty. I check all the other drawers, but my underwear is all missing, even my lovely lace-top stockings and tan nylon tights.

I search through my wardrobe, pulling jumpers and tops off the shelves, throwing everything around me, but still, I find no underwear. My towel has fallen to the ground in my agitation. Then I sense I'm being watched. Looking up, I see Kevin dressed in his smart clothes for the meeting, leaning against the door frame with a carrier bag in his hand. He's watching me running around naked, frantically looking for my clothes. He's enjoying it.

Then he throws the bag onto the bed contemptuously.

'Here's your underwear,' he jeers. 'That'll teach you.' Then he disappears downstairs.

I empty the contents of the bag onto the bed: my knickers, bras, stockings, suspenders and tights are all there. I take a deep breath to calm myself as I try to dress for the meeting, but my hands have started shaking. Tears are staining my white cotton blouse. As I struggle to tie the knot of my headscarf, I try to make sense of what has just happened. What had Kevin just said? 'Teach you.' Teach me what? Teach me to never say no to sex? Is that what he had meant? What kind of strange punishment is this? We are just weeks into our marriage and he is already acting so strangely. I want to go home. I want Mum. I want to see my family. I collapse onto the bed and sob into the pillow.

I didn't go to the meeting that day. I became ill. I had developed a heartsickness – perhaps you might call it homesickness. It was a longing that never fully left me in the eighteen years that I lived down south. Kevin apologised for his behaviour later that day, but I knew now that this wouldn't be the last time he'd punish me if he didn't get what he wanted. I was afraid.

The following week I found out that I was pregnant with my first child. There was no going back home now. I was going to have to find ways to bear this new life. But, as I came out of the doctors' surgery that day with a positive pregnancy test tucked into my pocket, I was asking myself not 'What is wrong with Kevin?' but 'What is wrong with me?'

The weeks turned into months. As my marriage to Kevin struggled on, I battled with constant homesickness, trying to fit in with the local Brethren and my perpetual doubts about the Brethren system while also trying my best to be a good Brethren sister and mother and to satisfy my husband's sexual desires.

A few months before I gave birth, Kevin went to confess his sins to our local leader, David Johnston, and his second-in-command, Alfred Robinson. He'd told them about his use of pornography, his masturbation and his overwhelming sexual desires. It must have been deeply shameful for him.

Instead of just accepting Kevin's remorse and granting him forgiveness, or encouraging him to get professional help, the two elders wheedled further intimate details out of him about these so-called sins, causing him further humiliation and embarrassment. Then they determined that Kevin and I were to 'act' as though we were 'shut up' for six weeks, to get us 'right with the Lord' again. This put us into a strange limbo: we were allowed to attend all the meetings, but were not permitted to talk to anyone afterwards and had to go straight home. This way, the elders reasoned, Kevin would get help from the daily meetings and become more repentant, but he – and I, because, according to them, being his wife made me a part of his sin – would not corrupt anyone else.

No one in the fellowship apart from the two local leaders knew the details of Kevin's confession, so when we left the meeting room abruptly every day they were left to gossip and surmise about what we had done. But during those six weeks, the leaders brought up the subject of 'the flesh' in almost every meeting, quoting sections of the Bible such as the verse in Romans 8, verse 5: 'For they that are according to flesh, mind the things of the flesh; and they that are according to Spirit, the things of the Spirit'.

No one could have been left in any doubt about the reasons for our quarantine. Finally, once David and Alfred had decided that Kevin was fully repentant of his sins, we had our full Brethren privileges restored.

Looking back, and knowing what I know now, I understand that what Kevin probably needed was some professional counselling for his likely sex addiction, not two Brethren men – or priests, as they were called – preaching fear and damnation to him several times a week. No one spoke to me about Kevin's confession. No one asked me if I was all right. The two men punished us, then severely restricted my access to my parents for years, perhaps for fear that I would tell them what Kevin was doing to me. Over the years I did tell my parents, drip by drip, about what was happening to me, but in those first years I teetered on from day to day, praying some days for deliverance, dreaming on other days of escape. I tried to quiet my mind, focusing on the next meal, the next meeting, the next weekend when I would have to host Brethren visitors, and the welfare of my children.

Years later, after I had left the Brethren, I talked to a friend about her experience of sex inside marriage. I told her about Kevin and about how he could never get enough; about the wild look that came into his eyes; how he would often want sex three or more times a day, and how I'd been told it was my duty to always give him what he wanted.

I was still puzzled. I still found it hard to talk about.

'The underwear,' she said, her eyes wide. 'Why did he want to hide it?'

I told her how he was always hiding things that I cared about, and how later, when the children came, he'd sometimes do the same to them. It was his way of controlling us. It was his way of punishing us.

'He did it because he could,' I said. 'Perhaps he thought he should. He did it because in his own home no one was supposed to contradict him. He was the Brethren man of the house and could do anything he wanted. He wanted to make sure we knew that.'

'Would you have called what Kevin did to you . . . rape?' she asked carefully. 'I mean, people out here might call it rape. After all, you didn't exactly consent, did you? He just did what he wanted, and you didn't dare resist. You were too frightened.'

I couldn't answer her question.

I still find it hard to answer it.

# TWELVE

Although only nineteen years old when I became a mother for the first time, some joy was brought into my life by having a beautiful little human who was dependent on me. My children gave me a purpose to keep going even though the strain and responsibility of young motherhood wore me down, diminishing what little self-worth I had left. I had two pregnancies in close succession, and we were blessed with two sons, Oliver and Bradley. But any support that I needed as a young mother was hard to come by; my parents were now living 300 miles away, a full day's travel, and we weren't allowed to visit each other without getting special permission.

The demands of conforming to the system to avoid disapproval were constant and exhausting. Often, it felt simpler just to stay low-key and fulfil the expectations of being a good Brethren wife in order to steer clear of any public humiliation. However, I often think back with incomprehension and shame at the things I did and said as a Brethren wife and mother. The Brethren system required all of us to run it, of course. It depended on mothers as well as fathers to indoctrinate our children, turning them into obedient and cowering drones who would in turn shape their children into the same. Whether we believed Brethren teachings or nursed secret doubts, we were too fearful to oppose the rules, and if you didn't oppose those rules you had no choice but to enforce them and report on others who broke them.

There's one Sunday that sticks out clearly in my memory as an instance of shame. It was a winter in the early 1990s and was one of the coldest on record. The snow had started to fall one Friday. It didn't stop until the Sunday of that weekend. I've never seen snow like it before or since. It was a strange heavy snow that seemed to cling to everything. It caused chaos: electricity wires snapped under the weight, plunging us all into darkness for days. Phone lines were down. Around our home, the snow settled in two-foot-high drifts, making it virtually impossible to get out of the house.

But nothing must stop the Brethren from reaching the Lord in their meeting room, especially for the first meeting on the Lord's Day, the Lord's Supper. It was a matter of faith and honour. One of the Men of God had once said: 'Crawl there if you have to.'

'The Lord,' our local leader proclaimed, 'has sent the severe weather to test our commitment to Him and His assembly.'

Four thirty in the morning: my alarm wakes me, red numbers pulsing in the dark. Kevin is snoring beside me. I want to stay in our bed, listening to the wind howl outside, staying warm, but I know that I must get up. We mustn't be late for the Supper. The Lord won't wait for us.

The cold hits me as soon as I lift the covers. I tiptoe downstairs in the dark. Our electricity is still off, so I fumble around in the dark, feeling for the candles and matches that I made sure to leave out the night before. With the candlelight casting flickering light around the kitchen, I open the boiler cupboard and light the gas with a match. Peeping through the net curtains I see that the snow is continuing to fall. Lighting a ring on the gas hob, I warm some milk for eighteen-month-old Oliver. Then I boil some water in a saucepan and sterilise a bottle for eight-month-old Bradley. All the while I'm checking the clock. I need to make sure everything is ready on time.

As I tiptoe back upstairs, I'm thankful that I remembered to lay our clothes out the night before. Kevin's ironed crisp white shirt and smart navy trousers are ready and hanging on the fitted wardrobe door.

Five a.m. Kevin crawls out of bed, yawning and sighing as he makes his way to the bathroom. I get dressed in my Sunday best: a tweed skirt and warm polo-neck jumper. Once my long hair is brushed, I finish my outfit with a matching silk headscarf and my long-length winter boots.

Five fifteen a.m. In the flickering candlelight I pull back little Oliver's bedclothes to dress him in his sleep. I ease on his white shirt and his navy corduroy trousers over his little legs, trying not to wake him as I sit his half-asleep body up and slip a warm jumper over his head. Once he's dressed, I lay him back down and pull his bedclothes back over him, leaving him to sleep in the warmth of his bed until it's almost time to leave. Looking at Bradley asleep in his cot, I decide not to dress him. If we take him to the Supper in his pyjamas, warm fleece sleep suit and bundle him up in blankets, no one will notice what he is wearing.

Five forty-five. I put on my warm winter coat and gloves before gently lifting Bradley from his cot. It's time for our little family to brave the winter elements and do what we do every Lord's Day: remember and celebrate Jesus' death. I wrap Bradley in blankets and put his woolly hat on his head, then lay his sleeping body over my shoulder. Kevin lifts Oliver from his bed. We both take a deep breath, open the front door into the darkness and set off on the short but snowy walk to the Supper.

A walk that normally takes us two minutes takes ten minutes because the drifts are so deep and the ice slippery underfoot. We're thankful when we reach the brightly lit meeting hall. As we open the oak swing doors and step into the large foyer, a welcome warmth greets us. The town meeting hall has a back-up generator when the power is off so we can all keep warm through the hour-long service. This hall holds hundreds when full but, for the Lord's Supper, we are only a small gathering of about fifty.

We make our way down the long slope to the centre circles and take our seats. Kevin sits in the front circle with Oliver next to him, while I sit behind in the outer circle with a sleepy but wriggling Bradley in my arms, his still-warm, still-untouched bottle of milk tucked in my bag; he mustn't have his bottle until after 'the Emblems' have been taken – 'It's an affront to The Lord,' we've been told.

Five fifty-five. It's important that we start the Supper before six o'clock. The Lord Jesus will join us 'in Spirit' at 6 a.m., so we have to be seated before then.

During the hymn I'm relieved to feel little Bradley nestle against me and fall back to sleep. After the hymn has ended, Alfred Robinson takes his place beside the table where the Emblems – the bread and wine – have been neatly set upon a pure white linen tablecloth. Speaking through the stand microphone, he gives elaborate and lengthy thanks as we sit with our heads bowed. He then breaks the loaf in two and places the bread neatly in its basket before passing it to the sister behind him. I watch the loaf pass from one sister to another, as it comes my way. Each of us pulls off a small morsel and puts it in our mouth before passing it to the brothers.

Eight-month-old Bradley stirs in my arms, excited to see the basket of bread approaching. As soon as a Brethren baby is weaned at around five months old, everyone watches them closely at the Lord's Supper. The first time any baby reaches for the bread, it is taken as a sign from the Lord that he is ready. Ready for what? I often wondered. How can a baby understand about the body and blood of the Lord? Isn't he just hungry? The trouble was that when a baby reached for the Holy Bread, his mother must make sure to give him a crumb of that bread. And once he had reached for and eaten the bread, then his mother must also make sure he drinks the wine. All of my babies have loved the bread and hated the wine.

Bradley is wide-awake now, and once his small crumb of bread is finished he starts to fret. He seems to know what's coming. But I have to make sure he drinks the wine before I'm allowed to give him his bottle of warm milk. Every week since he's started taking the Emblems, it's been a struggle to get his lips to even touch the side of that large shiny cup. I watch as the cup gets passed from one sister to another, getting ever closer to our turn. I get ready for battle. As I take it from the sister next to me, the struggle begins. After taking a quick glug myself, I bring it towards the wriggling

Bradley, but he is having none of it. All eyes are on us. Bradley shakes his head, his chin trembling. He pushes it away, almost spilling the contents. I put my arms around him in a brace to hold him tight as I make another attempt to bring the cup to his mouth. Spitting and blowing bubbles, he turns his little head away again, but still, I must persist. Everyone is watching. Kevin is looking at me sternly. After another minute of struggling, I give up. I feel like I've failed in my duty to my son, my husband and the Brethren. Next time I need to try harder.

From the outside, I can now look back and analyse this system that I found so cruel and see how it replicates itself from generation to generation. Not just by fear, but from what seems to me to be coercion. I not only lifted my children out of their warm beds every Sunday morning, but I forced my babies to drink wine, and later, I shamed my teenagers when they came to tell me they had transgressed. Why did I do all these things? Because if you didn't comply you could be punished. If you asked awkward questions in public or in private, you could be 'shut up'. And if you didn't capitulate after you'd been shut up, if you didn't confess and contort yourself back into complete simpering obedience, you'd be 'withdrawn from'. And if you were a mother and you were withdrawn from, you'd probably never see your children again.

# THIRTEEN

When Oliver and Bradley were still pre-school age, and I was still in my early twenties, I fell pregnant with my third child. I'd been married for less than five years, and soon we would be a family of five.

It wasn't an easy pregnancy. I'd been more than usually sick and very tired. Looking after two toddlers and the constant Brethren entertaining and going to all the meetings added to my exhaustion. I thought about my own mum and couldn't help but admire her for bringing six children into this world. I had rarely seen her flustered while she washed, cooked, entertained, cared for us children and kept the house clean and tidy while Dad was busy working to make his business a success. I missed my mother sorely. I was longing for the time when she would be allowed to be with me for a few weeks once the new baby was born.

But just as my pregnancy reached its end, the new Man of God, John Hales, received new light again. According to him, God had told him that it was no longer necessary for a mother to travel miles from her Brethren locality to help her daughter after childbirth unless it was her first child. Instead, Mr Hales ruled, a Brethren husband should take a week off work to help his wife after childbirth. I was devastated. I couldn't see how I was going to cope with a new baby while recovering from the birth and caring for two very young children without my mum. I longed to see her. And I knew that Kevin, like most Brethren husbands, didn't help much with the children at the best of times. He didn't consider it his role. He was supposed to be the breadwinner, according to the Brethren. But I dreaded him being at home for a week. He seemed to have a way of winding up the children, which made him angry and then he'd lash out at them.

Looking back, I wonder if this new rule, this new light, was put in place to prevent Brethren women from travelling alone, or to prevent mothers and daughters from talking to each other, sharing experiences, reporting back, raising alarms. Or perhaps it was a way to reduce the mother-in-law's influence within Brethren marriages so that the Man of the House could always remain the Man of the House. Whatever the reasoning from on high, my world as a Brethren wife seemed to be getting smaller and smaller, and more and more constrained.

Mum was also upset about this new rule. She had always loved the short periods in which she was allowed to come to our house to help me with my babies. She missed me too. But there was no arguing with this 'new light' or with the authority of the Man of God. I had many tearful phone calls with Mum during those last weeks of my pregnancy, discussing how I was going to cope without her help.

During one of these calls Dad came up with an idea. If he and Mum were going to support me without breaking any rules, then one way for them to do this was to have Oliver come and stay with them for a couple of weeks. Then I'd only have two children at home while I recovered. This sounded like a great idea to all of us, including Kevin. It would be simple. Mum would arrive as soon as the baby was born. Kevin would meet her at the railway station with Oliver and she'd take him with her on the next train home.

Our only stumbling block was getting permission from David Johnston. We were supposed to get permission from the local leader for everything. Travel was yet another aspect of Brethren life that was controlled – in later years, when we had access to mobile phones, even these would be monitored to keep us in line. We could never travel away for more than a day without permission. This was going to be difficult. Not only did David not like us, but he also didn't like my father. I never really understood the reason for this. Given that we were already only granted permission to see my parents once a year, we knew it would be difficult.

With so much stacked against us, and the constant censure from the local leaders, it was no wonder that Kevin quaked at the thought of asking permission for Oliver's visit to my parents. We put off the request for as long as we could, but two weeks before my due date, we knew time was running out.

After a prayer meeting on a Monday evening, I sat chatting to the other mums, watching Kevin approach David Johnston. I held my breath, trying my best to listen to the women's conversation without giving my eavesdropping away.

'Mr Johnston,' I heard Kevin begin, doing his best to sound confident. 'I want to ask you something.'

'Go ahead, young man, he said cheerily. 'What can I do for you?'

'As Maria's mum can't come after the birth of our next baby,' Kevin blurted out, 'we thought we'd send Oliver to her parents' home for a couple of weeks. Would you be happy with that?'

With dread, I saw the cheery expression leave David's face.

'Why are you asking me?' he roared, making us all jump. 'You know what I'll say. Why would you want to send your young son so far away from his mother's care? A child should be with its mother at all times.'

I couldn't believe what I was hearing. I knew Oliver wouldn't be in any danger staying with my parents. David Johnston was only saying this to keep control.

I watched Kevin take a step back with a look of fear and defeat. I could see the other mums looking at me nervously at the sound of David's raised voice. I kept my head down as he continued his tirade.

'Any man with any sense in our fellowship will tell you that you can't send a four-year-old child that far! You ask anyone.'

I watched Kevin gather his thoughts. Then, to my amazement, he said, 'All right, I'll go ask someone else's opinion and take their advice.'

'Well,' David said, somewhat taken aback. 'You just let me know when you get your answer.'

I felt proud of Kevin for keeping his nerve, but I couldn't help but wonder who he was going to ask who would give him a different answer. As we made our way home that evening, he put his arm around me reassuringly.

'Don't worry,' he said, with a glint in his eye. 'I've got a plan. I'll ask someone who I know will say yes.'

'But who?' I said. 'Surely no one is going to contradict David Johnston.'

'I'll ask Cyril from next door. He can't stand Johnston's bullying, but he's practical and will be honest with his answer. I'll call round this evening and ask him.'

Cyril and Jennifer Dunn, our Brethren neighbours, had not been blessed with children of their own, but they loved children and children loved them back. They were practical and down to earth, sympathetic, kindly, well respected. They did their best to avoid the politics of the local Brethren. Kevin had made a good choice.

'I see no reason why he shouldn't go,' Cyril told Kevin. 'It'll help Maria if she has one less child for a couple of weeks. It makes sense. And it won't break any rules.'

Thanking Cyril for his answer, Kevin hurried back to our house and called Dad so that plans could be put into place. When he told him the story of what David Johnston had said and how he'd instead had to go Cyril Dunn for his approval, Dad was furious at first then he saw the funny side.

'Stupid man,' he said. 'He hasn't got a clue.'

We spent the next twenty-four hours putting plans in place: as soon as I went into labour, my mother would catch the train. Although I still longed to see her and have her at my side during the first days after labour, I was thankful that we were doing the next best thing. Knowing that David Johnston would probably be furious about us going behind his back to get Cyril's advice, I was thankful that Kevin decided not to tell him about his conversation with Cyril until the very last moment. Kevin did his best to reassure me: he'd done what David had asked by getting someone else's opinion and approval.

But there was still one more hurdle to cross before we could send Oliver to my parents. Kevin would have to announce the news publicly after a meeting. That was another Brethren rule: the Brethren of a particular fellowship must always know where a member of a meeting is if they miss a meeting, even if that person was a small child.

Kevin decided to leave this announcement until the day before Oliver was due to leave so that no one had time to make a fuss or attempt to change our plans. The plan was in place, but we were all braced for its repercussions.

I went into labour on a September day in 1992. Kyle was born in the afternoon. He was perfect, with his shock of dark hair against his wrinkled new-born skin. As we had planned, as soon as Mum got the news of the birth from Kevin, she booked her train for the following day. With the quick turnaround at the station, Oliver would be in the north of England that same night.

Kevin brought Oliver and Bradley with him to the hospital the next morning to see their new baby brother, a rushed visit before the evening meeting. I gave Oliver an extra-tight hug as I kissed him goodbye. David Johnston's suggestion of him not being safe had made me nervous. Was sending him to Mum and Dad a mistake? I looked down at the little bundle of Kyle in my arms, and at Bradley jumping excitedly around the hospital bed, and reminded myself why we were doing this: there was no way I could cope with all three children on my own. This was the best way forward for all of us. Oliver was beside himself with excitement at the adventure of going to Granny and Grandpa's on his own.

I walked with Kevin and the boys along the corridor. When we reached the big swing doors Kevin gave me goodbye peck on my cheek. He'd announce Oliver's 'going away' after the meeting that evening. I gave the boys a last kiss and Oliver an extra-tight hug with a gnawing sense of apprehension. Then, leaning against the doorpost for support, I watched all three of them disappear down the corridor. Oliver turned and blew me a kiss and a wave. I blew one back and waved until they disappeared.

At the next visiting hours, Kevin told me what had happened when he'd announced Oliver's trip at the meeting. No one had publicly objected to the plans, he said. He had hurried home after the meeting, relieved to get the children to bed and finish Oliver's packing ready for the journey the next day. He'd just tucked the boys up in bed when the phone rang. David Johnston had bellowed down the line, ranting and raving.

'How dare you disobey my advice! What sort of a father are you, sending your own son away? Why did you go and ask a "yes man" like Cyril Dunn? Cyril wouldn't say boo to a goose. You asked him because you knew he wouldn't say no. You knew he'd say exactly what you wanted to hear. How dare you!'

'With all due respect, Mr Johnston,' Kevin interrupted carefully, 'I've done exactly as you suggested. I asked for someone else's advice and opinion. I've no fear for my son going to stay with his grandparents. My wife needs help after the birth of another child, and if her mother can't come here to help, then why can't my son go there? I am breaking no rules.'

'Cancel that train now or you'll regret your decision,' David roared back. 'If you don't, we might just have to take further action against you and your wife.'

I started to cry hot angry tears that we were being threatened with 'further action' like this. But Kevin put his arm around me and told me not to worry. He had stood his ground. He had told David that he was sorry, but as parents we felt we were making the right decision. He'd been quaking in his shoes as he'd said those words, he said, but he couldn't say if the shaking was from anger or fear. He had, he said, slammed the phone down on David Johnston.

As I drew the curtain around my hospital bed that evening and brought my baby to my breast, I braced myself. I sent a silent prayer up to Heaven asking that David Johnston's threats of 'further action' wouldn't materialise, though I had witnessed people being thrown out of the Brethren for far less than our little act of rebellion. I determined to put it all to the back of my mind and trust for the best, but David

Johnston and his second-in-command, Alfred Robinson, were already planning their revenge.

Six days later we had Kyle baptised. According to Brethren rules, before a baby can attend the daily meetings, they must be baptised within a week, as both mother and baby are supposed to attend the meetings as soon as possible after the birth and no one is allowed to attend a meeting unless they have been baptised. Brethren baptisms always take place in the family bathtub, and until now only the chosen baptising brother and the immediate family, including grandparents, were permitted to be present. The most recent 'new light' dictated that now only the parents and siblings and a couple of chosen members of the immediate fellowship could attend.

For Brethren mothers, baptisms can be scary because the newborn baby's whole head must be submerged in the bath water. Things can go wrong. When Oliver was baptised, he had started wailing just as the nervous baptising brother dunked him into the water. The brother had failed to cover his mouth with his hand, so poor newborn Oliver had swallowed a lot of water. He came up coughing, spluttering and flushed in the face. Thankfully my mother had acted quickly, giving Oliver a sharp slap on his back to get his lungs going again. Bradley's baptism had been more straightforward, but I couldn't help but be nervous for Kyle.

So, that Monday evening, in autumn 1992, we stand huddled in our tiny bathroom – the brothers in their white shirts and navy trousers; the sisters standing with their head-scarfed heads bowed.

I give Kyle a brief kiss on his tiny head, unwrap his bare little body from the towel and hand him to the officiating brother. Taking him in his arms he clears his throat and solemnly says the mandatory words, 'We baptise thee, Kyle White, in the name of the Father, the Son and the Holy Spirit.' Just as he finishes the sentence, he quickly turns Kyle over in his big hand before whisking him swiftly through the water, making sure that all his body gets submerged.

As soon as the proceedings are over, I take Kyle to dress him while the baptism guests have a cup of tea downstairs.

Once dressed and wrapped in his white shawl we make our way to the Prayer Meeting in the main hall next door. With Kyle fast asleep in my arms, I walk down the long slope to the centre rows where I take my seat with the sisters.

Kyle whimpers a little at first, but as soon as we start to sing the opening hymn, he settles. One by one the brothers stand on their feet and submit a prayer to God. There are many 'ums', 'ahs' and 'amens' from the brothers as each prays. I keep my eyes closed as is expected of us sisters, enjoying the warmth and gentle breathing of my newborn baby against my body.

For me, Prayer Meetings are a time when I can let my mind wander – a time of quiet, a time to relax once I have shut out the drone of the men's voices. But now I'm conscious that Alfred Robinson is on his feet, submitting his prayer to God. I freeze, remembering he still has unfinished business with us.

'Our Father,' Alfred prays, 'we ask you to protect and keep your hand over our young brother Oliver White while he is away from us. Protect him and bring him back safely to us.' David Johnston utters a loud 'amen' in agreement. My tears are of anger, embarrassment and fear for my child, as well as the exhaustion of a trapped animal. I want to get up and run from this place. Why would our leaders ask God such a thing in a public setting?

Keeping my head bowed for the rest of the meeting, I cry silent tears. I can't bring myself to sing the closing hymn and, although it is customary to stand around socialising after a baptism, both Kevin and I get up straight away and walk home. Carrying a sleeping Bradley in one arm, Kevin puts his free arm around my shoulders as we make the short walk back to our home.

In times like this there was a sort of unity between Kevin and I as even he could see the cruelty of the system. Once home, we settle Bradley in his cot and then sit on our old worn settee, holding our newborn baby and each other close. We don't need to say anything. We both know how the other is feeling and that talking won't change anything. All I want is to call my mum and to know that Oliver is safe. When I call her and tell her what has been said in the prayer meeting, about how we've been publicly shamed, she assures us that Oliver is 'as happy as Larry'.

Two weeks later Kevin caught the train up north to meet Mum and Oliver. He and Oliver returned that night and I hugged my eldest son. But the elders' words had put a new fear in me – a fear that God would punish me for sending my little boy away. All my life within the Brethren seemed to be filled with a constant fear of God's punishment upon me. Even after I'd left the Brethren, it took years for that fear to leave me.

# FOURTEEN

As the years rolled by, I was struck by how the Brethren way of life allowed Kevin to continue in his ways and denied me my voice. Now with three boys under five years old, through the nappies and the bottles and the sleepless nights and the shock of responsibility, I still lived through Kevin's constant and increasing demands for sex. It seemed never-ending. There were times while the babies and toddlers would be alone downstairs when Kevin, just home from work, would lure me to the bedroom, pretending he had something important to say. Then, once I was in the bedroom, he would lock the door and demand that I undress so he could have sex with me. I didn't refuse; refusing meant conflict, and I had no strength left for that. Also, I daren't risk leaving the children downstairs alone for long.

Kevin demanded sex through each of my pregnancies, right up until the day I gave birth. Abstaining from sex in the six weeks after labour, as the doctors insisted was necessary for my recovery, almost drove him crazy. With no contraception, oral sex or masturbation allowed, I lived from month to month in fear of getting pregnant. I learnt to read my body clock, but this meant that to be safe, to avoid a further pregnancy too soon on the last, Kevin and I had to abstain from sex at certain times of the month. Those times drove him demented. I watched him toss and turn in our bed, trying to satisfy his desires without breaking any Brethren rules. I became afraid of these periods of abstinence, afraid of that wild look in his eyes. It felt safer for me to let him do what he wanted with my bruised and abused body. It was no longer mine to govern.

Now that I have left the Brethren, people often ask me why I didn't confide in anyone about the abuse I suffered in my long marriage. 'Weren't there other women you could go to?' they ask. 'Special friends you could confide in?' But the Brethren were very strict about close friendships. They discouraged them, perhaps because they were afraid that strong loyalties between individuals would undermine their power. I was even afraid to confide in my parents, as parents were forbidden from interfering in their children's marriages.

When I got married, my best friend Linda and I drifted apart. I had a new life in a new part of the country. At first we made a few attempts to talk to each other on the phone, but Kevin soon put a stop to this. I did make a few friends among the other young married sisters and young mothers locally but the 'no special friends' rule was even stricter there. In the kitchens that we spent so much time in, we women would discuss our children and maybe gossip about the latest scandal. If you'd been a fly on the wall during one of those Sundays, you would have found a group of sisters in the kitchen talking in whispers about how so and so had been caught doing some naughty deed or other; about how short so and so's skirt was, or whether some sister had dared to dye her hair or not. Looking back, I'm ashamed of how critical I was about other Brethren, but it was just the Brethren's way.

Yet, in all these conversations I would never have dared to confide in any of these women. You could trust no one with your thoughts, doubts and fears. Like most Brethren, I had become highly skilled at concealing my true feelings. One of my therapists said to me once, 'You could win an Oscar for your acting skills.' Year on year, from child to teenager to young mother and wife, I learnt to put on a mask, to smile and nod and be compliant, and to keep my tears to those rare moments when I could lock myself behind a closed door out of earshot of anyone else.

Kevin's demands were putting a great deal of strain on my mental health. I was deeply unhappy, exhausted and very lonely. My spiritual doubts increased, tumbling around my mind as I washed nappies and cooked and cleaned; as I braced myself for the sound of my husband's key in the lock and the sexual demands that would follow. Was the Bible true? Were the Brethren right? Was I going to Hell? Was I saved? Was this really my life forever? Had God meant this for me?

When I look back now, it's not the fact that I had several mental breakdowns that surprises me, but the fact that I weathered Kevin's psychological and physical brutality for so long before the first breakdown came. To protect myself and my children for all those years I must have developed complex survival strategies that had to evolve with each new era, with each new child, with each new rule imposed by the Brethren. Those strategies are impossible to map or to describe now. There are many incidents in the long decades of my marriage that I remember only as fragments – sounds and images.

When I left the Brethren, I heard the word 'trauma' for the first time. I had to ask what it meant. Someone explained that trauma is like a mental wound. It leaves a scar on your heart or your brain. And that scar can keep opening up again if something triggers a memory. Sometimes the wound means that your heart or brain stops you from remembering certain things. Someone said that was called 'repression'. Perhaps that's what has happened to me. Perhaps I've had to repress the memories of those repeated assaults on my body to save a small part of myself. Perhaps I took my mind somewhere else when the bad things were happening. Maybe this was my way of coping with the twenty-five years of my marriage. Yet, though so many memories are shattered into broken shards, oddly, there are some incidents that remain crystal clear in my mind: some incidents that were so awful that my mind could not repress them.

It was a Saturday in the summer of 1994. Often on a Saturday, after we'd attended the morning meeting, I would pack up a picnic and Kevin and I would take the children for a day out. Brethren families were not allowed to go to circuses, fairs or swimming pools or to play or watch any organised sports at weekends, but they were allowed to go to zoos, some museums, farms and safari parks on Saturdays. On that day, like many other Saturdays in the summer, we took the three boys to the zoo.

It was a fine day – a blue sky, pink clouds. Kevin and I pushed the two buggies around so the boys could watch the elephants being fed. We laughed at the chimps and their silly antics, pointed at the hippos in their swampy lake and sat with the sun warming our faces, eating ice creams. By mid-afternoon, when we were all tired and hungry, Kevin and I pushed the buggies to the car, bundled the children in and set off to find a suitable place for a picnic. That day I was happy in a way that I had long ago forgotten how to be; happy in a way that I often pretended to be so that my children would see me happy in the way that mums are supposed to be happy. But I'd forgotten that sort of happiness never lasted very long.

Kevin said he'd come across a nice park while travelling for work the previous week. It was a bit 'off the beaten track', he said, but the long drive would give the boys a chance to take a short nap on the journey.

An hour later Kevin pulled up at what looked like a deserted playground on the edge of a wood: chipped, faded, with rusty play equipment and a single picnic table near the trees. I was baffled.

'Why here?' I asked, wondering if he'd got mixed up or lost his way. Why had we driven so far to come here, to this? There were so many beautiful picnic spots close to our home.

'We've had a day surrounded by worldly people,' Kevin said in his 'no-nonsense, don't argue with me' voice. 'Now we need to have some time as a family before the Lord's Supper in the morning. The boys can have the whole playground to themselves, and we can sit together on the picnic bench and have our picnic. It'll be nice.'

I knew I couldn't argue with him, so I unclipped my seatbelt and got out of the car. The boys were wide awake now and excited at the sight of the swings and slide. It didn't matter to them how worn and faded this place was. Taking the picnic basket and cool box over to the worn wooden table, I laid out the tablecloth and arranged the food prettily. I listened to the birds in the trees above and counted my blessings as Mum had taught me to do. I rested my head in my hands and took it all in, enjoying the moment of peace, the sun, the shadows from the trees, the sound of the birdsong, the sight of Kevin pushing Kyle on the baby swing, Kyle squealing with delight, Oliver pushing Bradley on the rusty old roundabout. I closed my eyes for a few minutes, enjoying the moment.

Minutes later I am awoken from my reverie by the touch of Kevin's hands on my shoulders. At his touch, I feel my body tense. Leaning my head back I look up at him, smiling, hoping that he doesn't sense my tension. I tell myself to relax. After all, we're in a public place. Nothing can happen here. Then I feel his hands move around my body. Taking a breast in each hand he gropes them tightly, pinching my nipples hard. I try to remove his hands as I look up at him again and plead, 'Not here. Not now. The children will see what you're doing.'

Keeping a firm hold on my breasts, Kevin leans in close to my ear, whispering in a desperate voice, 'If you just stand up and bend over this picnic table, I'll take you right now. It'll be over before the children even notice. I want you now, right here, right now.'

Dragging his hands off me and shoving him hard with my elbows, I stand and turn to face him. This time he has gone too far. I am furious, my heart is pounding, but I try to keep my voice low and calm so as not to alarm the children.

'Are you crazy? How dare you!' I whisper. 'How dare you even think of having sex here, in a public place with our children around us!'

Kevin grabs my arm roughly before I can step back. He brings his face right up close to mine. I can smell his hot breath. 'Bitch!' he hisses. Then he pushes me away and storms off into the woods. I'm shaking, rooted to the spot, staring towards the woods where he has disappeared.

Then I come to.

Kyle is crying. Kevin has left him sitting on the motionless swing; his little legs are dangling, his head leant back in a long wail. I run over and lift him from the swing to comfort him. He nuzzles his head against my shoulder. Holding back tears, I walk back to the picnic bench and call Oliver and Bradley to come and eat. Clambering up on the bench opposite me they ask in unison, 'Where's Daddy?'

'I think he's gone into the woods to go to the toilet,' I say, forcing a bright smile, relieved to see them chatter on, oblivious to what has just happened.

The boys have finished their sandwiches and crisps before Kevin returns, his face thunderous. He sits down at the table in silence and helps himself to the remaining food. We don't look at each other. I help Kyle with his food but can't face eating anything myself. As we drive away from that awful park, Kevin's driving is erratic and bordering on dangerous. Driving fast and crunching the gears is one of the many ways he punishes me, especially if the children are in the car. He likes to scare me. He likes to show me who is in control. Closing my eyes, I say a silent prayer for a safe journey home.

I wonder now how many Brethren wives had to tolerate husbands like Kevin. The constant pregnancies are difficult enough for Brethren mothers – the isolation, the subjugation – but now I can see how cruel the whole system was: the lack of sex education, the ban on masturbation, the teenage self-loathing, confusion and guilt followed by the absolute, apparently Biblically sanctioned control husbands had over their wives from the first day of marriage, and the culture of silence over what happened in the marital bedroom. All these things were cruel and mentally destructive for both men and women, and disastrous for the health of many marriages, but divorce was not permitted in the Brethren at that time. I think of my daughter Juliet again and feel a sense of dread and fear creep over me.

Years later, I meet a friend for coffee. She left the Brethren as a child in the 1960s. She has written a memoir about the impact of the Brethren system on her family. When the book won a prize, readers, not just ex-Brethren readers but journalists and lawyers and judges began to write to her about Brethren-related matters, their memories, their stories.

Knowing about Kevin's compulsive behaviour, she tells me about a psychotherapist she has just met, a worldly. He wrote to her after he read her book, then came to interview her. He had a Brethren client, he told her. He was treating her in an expensive clinic in London.

I recognise the name of the clinic. I remember people in the Brethren talking about that clinic in hushed voices. It's where Brethren sometimes disappeared to when they got ill in the head.

'Rick's an addiction counsellor,' my friend says pointedly, expecting me to see where she is headed. 'His specialism is addiction.'

I'm confused. I understand what addiction is – it is another of those new words that I've heard since I left – but why would a Brethren client be treated by an addiction counsellor? It made no sense.

'Many of Rick's male Brethren clients have addictions such as gambling and drinking,' she says, seeing I am struggling to follow, treading softly for my sake, spelling it out.

I'm not surprised to hear about gambling and drinking. I've heard of Brethren men getting into trouble for excessive drinking, even gambling, but I had not thought of it as addiction. It makes a kind of sense to call it that.

She goes on.

'Rick, the therapist, says some of his Brethren clients grow to hate themselves for their addictions. Their compulsions sometimes bring them close to suicide.'

I nod. I can understand that too. I can empathise.

'But the thing is,' she says, 'many of the Brethren men that Rick treats are sex or porn addicts.' She raises her eyebrows, watching me closely, checking I am following her drift.

I lean in.

'Sex addict?' I say, 'What do you mean by sex addict?'

Bringing her head close to mine so as not to be heard by those around us in that busy coffee shop, she says in a low voice, 'Think of the Brethren boys you and I knew. Some of them grew up lonely and sad, struggling with doubts and rules, breaking rules, feeling bad and terrified of shaming their parents. And then all the hormones hit them in their teens. They probably touched themselves for comfort under the sheets in the dark because they couldn't help it. But they were told that masturbation was a terrible sin, so they started to feel guilty and ashamed and afraid. But the more they tried, the more they couldn't stop thinking about sex. The shame grows. The fear grows. This kind of sin could mean they'd be left behind when the Rapture comes. If they were caught, they'd be withdrawn from. They'd have to confess in public. They'd shame their parents. They'd get thrown out. They'd never see their families again. Despite the stakes, despite all the shame, these boys were desperate. Soon they were buying porn magazines and hiding them. Then the shame grew even bigger.'

I think back now to all the Tuesday After Meetings I attended in my teens; how I listened to those words I hadn't understood at the time: fornication, sodomy, adultery, fondling, masturbation. I think of all the miserable shameful confessions that were extracted from so many men by my father and grandfather. Not just the men who'd been caught visiting prostitutes or touching another man's wife, but the men who had been made to confess to touching themselves as teenagers, perhaps only once or twice, or the ones who had glanced at forbidden magazines. And then I think of all those teenagers like me who sat through those After Meetings confused and terrified at what might happen to us if we gave in to similar desires. Then I think of the poor people who ended up at this special addiction clinic in London, or, worse still, those who confessed to a sexual misdemeanour in front of everyone they knew and then were withdrawn from, the Brethren door closing on them forever, made to live a half-life outside, forever shamed, forever abandoned by everyone they knew, always on edge.

I think of Kevin, and I wonder if an expensive clinic would have helped him. But I also think, with shame, of my sons who came to me full of self-loathing as teenagers, whispering in my ear in the safety of their bedroom about what they believed to be sinful thoughts but were in fact just a part of growing up, when a young person's hormones are raging.

And because I was a good Brethren mother and knew no different, I'd tell them to do what I always did when I was tormented by wicked thoughts: 'Repeat the words "Holy Spirit" in your head over and over again,' I had told them, 'until the wicked thoughts go away.'

I hope that my sons will be better husbands to their wives than their father was to me, and that when they take up their traditional roles as husbands, they will be able to show them tenderness and love. I hope that they will listen and that they will laugh together and be happy.

Since I have left the Brethren I have met people who have taught me to unlearn these Brethren ways, to talk about my feelings, to say what I like or don't like in bed, to ask for love and tenderness and to express my own sexual desires. I know I am one of the lucky ones.

# FIFTEEN

While family life remained very difficult, members of the Brethren community around us added to the struggles. After our manoeuvres around the rules for Kyle's birth, David Johnston had it in for us. At any opportunity he would pull us up on something. As the children got older David's bullying extended to our children, especially Bradley. If we weren't being told to take our noisy child out of the meeting, Bradley was getting pulled aside after the meeting for a talking-to, during which David would instruct Bradley on the importance of sitting still in the meeting and listening to what The Lord had to say. Bradley received the brunt of David's wrath well into his teens. By keeping my head down, and keeping out of David's way, I usually fared better. I was determined not to give him the satisfaction of shaming or bullying me in public, but even I was not bulletproof.

Vicky Morris, one of our local Brethren, was only twenty years old when she woke up one morning to find that she was paralysed from her waist down. She was rushed to the hospital. Everyone was in shock. We all prayed fervently that she would be healed. As the weeks went on it became apparent that Vicky would never walk again.

I wanted to do something to make her smile. I spent a long time searching in the shops for a gift that would put a smile on her face when I visited her for the first time. Eventually, I settled on a large Laurel and Hardy figurine that I found in a second-hand shop. When Vicky pulled off the wrappings, she laughed with delight. She put the figurine in pride of place on her bedside table among the bowls of grapes and cards. Seeing their funny, cheeky faces there every day, she said, would keep her spirits up more than anything else.

The following morning, our phone rang before Kevin had left for work.

'Yes, I'll speak to her,' I heard him say. 'Yes, I'll let her know how you feel and get back to you.'

Kevin came into the bedroom looking cowed.

'That was Mr Cooper,' he said. 'He's very concerned about the gift that you gave Vicky.'

'Very concerned?' I said. 'What about?'

Kevin explained that Mrs Cooper had gone into hospital to see Vicky after my visit. She had seen the figurine on the table and listened to Vicky saying how much she loved it and how it made her smile every time she looked at it.

'Good,' I said. 'That's what I bought it for.'

'The Coopers feel,' Kevin went on, and I could hear the incomprehension in his voice, 'that by giving such a gift, you have promoted the love of idols. The Coopers have spoken to the elders. They want you to go to the hospital and remove it.'

'Idols?' I said, still completely baffled.

'They say that Laurel and Hardy are worldly comedians. By giving Vicky a figurine of them you have turned them into idols. Look, I don't agree with them either, but we have to keep the priests off our backs, so just go to the hospital and get it back.'

And that was that. Although Kevin could see the whole thing as ridiculous, he wasn't prepared to risk the consequences of not conforming. That was frustrating for me, yet I understood. There were times over the years when Kevin did risk not conforming, but he was so unpredictable I gave up trying to work him out. In this case, though, it was clear I was going to have to toe the line too.

I couldn't bear the thought of going to the hospital alone to take my gift back from poor Vicky. But who could I trust to come with me? Although we weren't particularly close, I went to see my sister-in-law, Kevin's sister, and asked her to come with me. From snippets of conversations that we'd had over the years I knew that she didn't agree with all of the rules and regulations.

'What if Vicky won't let me take it back?' I said. 'What am I supposed to do then?'

'Let's cross that bridge when we come to it,' Nina said, equally shocked by the severity of the elders' response. None of us had ever faced a Brethren censure of the 'don't worship idols' kind like this before but Brethren censures could so easily snowball if you didn't respond to them quickly and show all the appropriate contrition, so I decided to act swiftly.

Vicky's mum was at her bedside when we entered the ward. They were surprised but happy to see us. 'Great to see you again!' Vicky exclaimed, reaching for her lifting bar. 'Is everything OK? You look like you've been crying.' I burst into tears and was immediately ashamed of my distress. My worry was nothing compared to Vicky's suffering.

'Maria has been asked to come and see you today,' Nina said, putting her arm protectively around me. 'The elders have—'

'Vicky,' I said, jumping in, picking up the figurine and blurting everything out at once, 'some of the Brethren – Mr Johnston and the Coopers – think I've encouraged you to worship idols by buying you this. They want me to remove it.'

Vicky pulled herself up with her lifting bar and turned to me angrily.

'You go back and tell David Johnston and the Coopers that they have no right to say what gifts I can and can't receive from my friends. If they don't want to see that figurine, then they're not welcome to visit my bedside!'

We all laughed then at her courage. I hugged her.

I thanked Nina and went home happy. Kevin made the call to Mr Cooper that evening and Mr Cooper said he would pass the message on to David Johnston. I hoped that would be the end of it. We all did.

The next day, a Friday, I was too busy with washing and cleaning and housework to dwell on what had just happened. I had done what Mr Johnston had asked of me. Vicky had refused to give up her gift. That was that. No one was going to censure Vicky in her condition.

Friday evening was the same as any other Brethren Friday: I supervised the boys' homework after school, prepared and served the family meal and then, when most worldly households were settling down to watch television together, we spent forty-five minutes together preparing for the evening meeting, making sure we were all looking spick and span, hair brushed, clothes ironed, Bibles in hands.

Friday Reading Meetings were conversational meetings – less formal, but the local leader would usually lead the meeting if he were present. After the usual hymn had been sung and the prayer submitted, one of the elders placed the microphone in front of David Johnston, and he proceeded.

'Let's read from Exodus twenty, verses three to six,' he began, tight-lipped. Still, I did not see what was coming over the hill. There was a rustling of pages as we all found the scripture in our Bibles. In a stern and serious tone, he read the words in his usual declamatory fashion: 'Thou shalt have no other gods before me. Thou shalt not make thyself any graven image nor any form of what is in the heavens above or what is in the earth beneath, or what is in the waters under the earth. Thou shalt not bow down thyself to them nor serve them; for I, Jehovah thy God, am a jealous God, visiting the iniquity of the fathers upon the sons to the third and fourth generation of them that hate me, and shewing love and mercy unto thousands of them that love me and keep my commandments.'

I froze. Was he pointing the finger at me? Had everyone been judging me as an idolater?

'Let's read a second scripture,' David Johnston sneered, turning to the next marked-up page in his Bible: 'One John Five, verse twenty-one: "Children," John says, "keep yourselves from idols."'

Now I knew that David Johnston's fat finger was definitely pointed at me I was scared. Would I be 'shut up'? Would my children be taken to live with other families until he decided I had got myself 'right with the Lord' about the figurine? I felt myself shrink into that hard wooden chair. I wanted to crawl under it, but I had to sit tight and pretend nothing was wrong.

'We've had an issue this week,' Johnston began as he opened his address, pausing for dramatic effect, still avoiding looking directly at me. 'We have had an issue this week with people promoting idols. Idolatry, brothers and sisters, is a sin!'

Now I could feel his eyes on me for the first time.

'Sinner,' he declaimed, 'get free from sin! Sinner, get free from idols! Sinner, repent and be saved!'

I was relieved to see Kevin glance over at me and roll his eyes. At least he was on my side on this one, though I knew he'd have no choice but to toe the line if David Johnston decided to shut me up.

I was used to feeling trapped, hounded, cornered. But now, I felt something that I can only describe as like being buried alive. David Johnston's wrath was like a storm surge. You couldn't stand in its path or you'd be swept away. All you could do was grab onto something solid and hold your breath. And if you were a woman being censured it was much worse: women must be seen and not heard. Any attempt to defend myself would be used by him as further evidence of my not being 'right with the Lord'. I put on my impassive face, set it in stone, and tried to switch my mind to happy thoughts as I always tried to do when the mood in Brethren meetings darkened. I fantasised at first, thought about what life outside of the Brethren might be like. Then I prayed. 'Lord,' I prayed, weakly, 'show me your love, not your judgement.' But there was nothing but silence.

I weathered Johnston's wrath, his storm surge. I was not shut up. But on top of everything else – the exhaustion, the domestic expectations, the isolation, the impossibility of talking to anyone about my doubts and fears – this new assault made sure I continued to diminish. Now that I walked on knives daily, I no longer cared about my appearance or my clothes. I only wanted to get through the day. To survive one more. To hold onto something. To make sure my children ate a meal, finished their homework – to find small moments of quiet somewhere, somehow.

# SIXTEEN

By the year 2000 we were parents to five children. Lincoln was born in 1998 and Juliet, my first and only girl, two years later. Just six weeks after her birth I suffered a bout of depression. I struggled to get out of bed, I struggled to look after the boys, and I seemed to spend hours crying. I was confused by this, as I knew I should be over the moon with finally having a little girl. Eventually I visited the doctor but, as always, I was careful not to mention my unhappy marriage or anything about my Brethren life. I was diagnosed as suffering with post-natal depression and was prescribed my first dose of antidepressants. Just as I was beginning to feel like I could cope I discovered I was pregnant again. The medication had to stop, and life went back into a state of merely existing as I struggled to hold everything together. Just fifteen months after Juliet's birth, I gave birth to our sixth child, Aaron.

A new Man of God was appointed in 2001 when Australian Bruce Hales succeeded his father, John Hales. This change brought its own challenges as new rules seemed to come thick and fast – as they usually did when a new leader was appointed. New leaders are keen to make their mark. Bruce Hales seemed to be getting new light from the Lord every week, often about the most minute details of family life. Now, for instance, he decreed that every child was supposed to have their own bedroom. The only way to comply with this new rule was to extend our house. So I spent the nine months of my sixth pregnancy struggling with morning sickness, looking after the four boys and baby Juliet, while Kevin, with the help of lots of young local brothers, built a large extension on our house.

Other new rules concerned 'fleshly activity'. Now, Bruce Hales decreed, we must abstain from any sexual activity on Saturdays and until after 6 p.m. on a Sunday. The Sabbath is the day of rest, he told us. It is a time to think about the Lord's Supper. I had no idea why the Lord might have chosen 6 p.m. as a cut-off point but I was deeply grateful for a temporary respite from Kevin's sexual demands. For Kevin, however, almost two whole days of abstinence was more than he could cope with.

It was also around this time that, under the guidance and agreement of my parents, I started to take the contraceptive pill. I had given birth to six children. I had served my purpose as a Brethren mother. Even the Brethren elders knew that some Brethren mothers began to struggle with their mental health when they had very large numbers of children. I was already struggling. I often thought of the mother I saw at the three-day meeting all those years earlier, who'd had thirteen children. How had she coped? That same mother went on to have fifteen children in total.

Brethren women were only permitted to use contraception in rare circumstances and with the support and intervention of their parents. When my parents agreed that between my ongoing back problems and post-natal depression, my request was granted. No one talked about the impact of years of sexual abuse, or the mental and physical strain it was putting me under. No one talked about it because at this point, fourteen years into my marriage, I had not told anyone but my parents, in part because I knew no words to describe it and because I would not have known that I had any right to question my husband's absolute control over my body. It was a Sunday night in summer 2003 that everything broke inside me for the first time.

We'd had a Brethren family of ten staying with us for the weekend from another town so, between meetings, caring for my own six kids, cleaning and tidying, I'd also cooked several meals for seventeen people. By 10 p.m., when everyone had finally settled for the night and I'd finished the last of the dishes, I was exhausted and desperate to sleep. But it was Sunday night – several hours after the sex curfew had been lifted: sleep was far from Kevin's mind after two days of abstinence. I curled myself up into the foetal position and let him take me from behind, praying it would be over quickly, and then fell into a fretful sleep.

The following day was the first week of the school holidays. My eldest child was fifteen years old and my youngest was two. I woke at 6 a.m. feeling sick to the stomach at the prospect of all the extra work the school holidays would bring: the children under my feet every day, the noise and the mess and the need to keep them entertained. Then I heard Kevin whispering in my ear, 'Come on, let's have a quickie before the children wake up.'

Again, I didn't resist. I was too tired physically and emotionally to face the consequence of saying no. So I rolled onto my back wordlessly. Lying with my eyes closed, I let him do what he wanted to me. But as he humped up and down, groaning again, I could hear an inner voice screaming, *Get off me! Please just leave me alone!*

As soon as he'd finished, I curled myself back into a foetal position and sobbed silently until I heard the front door close as he left for work. Listening to the summer rain beating against the bedroom window I tried to make a plan for occupying six children on a wet summer's day, but everything was going round and round. Pulling the quilt up over my head, I prayed that I might curl up and die. I was used to crying, but this time I couldn't seem to stop, no matter how hard I tried.

It wasn't long before Juliet and Aaron toddled into our bedroom. Pulling the covers back, they climbed in beside me for a cuddle. Lying in the middle of the bed with one on either side of me I put my arms around them, hugging them close while I kissed them gently on their foreheads, but still, I kept on crying. What was wrong with me? My children needed me to be happy and strong. I had to pull myself together again.

'Don't cry, Mummy,' Aaron said, propping himself up on his little elbows, a frown clouding his face. Doing my best to smile, I dried my tears with the back of my hand, gave him another kiss and forced myself to get out of bed and pull on my fluffy pink dressing gown.

Taking a deep breath, I lifted Aaron onto my hip and took Juliet's hand. We headed downstairs for breakfast. Oliver, Bradley, Kyle and Lincoln joined us at the breakfast bar. While they tucked into bowls of cereal, I emptied the dishwasher and put on a load of washing. But still the tears would not stop. I kept angrily brushing them away. Don't let the children see you crying, I told myself sternly. They need you to be happy. After all, it's their school holidays – a time to enjoy, a time to make memories.

Leaving the older boys in charge, I slipped away to have a shower, hoping I'd be able to pull myself together. But as I stood there with the warm water flowing over me, the tears still would not stop. All I could see was my life stretching out before me: a life of trying to please everyone; a life of keeping Kevin satisfied; a life of keeping the peace in our family; a life of looking after children; a life of constant entertaining; a life of endless meetings; a life of living with constant homesickness. A life of walking on knives.

Wrapped in a big towel, I sit on the edge of the bed listening to the distant noise and chatter of the children downstairs as they empty the Lego onto the floor. I can hear the *bumm bumm* of Bradley practising his bass guitar in the next bedroom. I should be thankful. I should be happy. But all I can do is sit here, stare out the window and cry. I pull on my clothes slowly, feeling the weight of every limb, then I stand by the big front window and look to the ground below, to the wet tarmac of the drive. I open the window. I lean out. What would happen if I jumped? Would I die down there? Is it high enough? Do I want to die?

The rain brings me back to my senses with a jolt. What am I doing? What am I thinking? I panic. I need to talk to someone. I dial Mum's number. She answers on the second ring.

'It's me. It's Maria,' I say, gulping back tears. 'Mum, I can't do this anymore. I can't live like this anymore. I've had enough.'

'Maria, what on earth is wrong? What has got you so wound up?'

Mum and Dad know what life with Kevin is like, but they are not allowed to interfere. It's not their place.

'It's just everything,' I sob as I throw myself onto the bed. 'I need to get away from here, Mum. You have to get me away from here.' Mum is scared. I can tell. She goes to speak to Dad. I can hear them talking to each other in the background. She comes back on the phone.

'Dad and I are going to drive down and get you and the children. We're going to bring you back home for the summer so we can get you better. Dad's ringing Kevin now to tell him what's happening. Don't worry, he's not going to give Kevin a choice about it. Now go and get Oliver. Put him on the line.'

Mum explains the plan to Oliver. She tells him to help me with the packing as best as he can and then she will finish it when she gets to our house.

As we left the house the following day, suitcases piled in the back of Dad's car, me bundled into the back wrapped up like a patient from an asylum, I saw that Kevin was fighting back tears.

'I'm so sorry, Maria,' he said. 'This is all my fault. I'm so sorry for how I've treated you.'

I had heard so many of Kevin's apologies by now that I knew they meant nothing. And I also knew that if he did feel some small tweak of genuine remorse, he was powerless to change his behaviour within a system that gave him absolute power in his own home.

We arrived in Wellfleet after midnight. The next morning, the four oldest boys were sent to stay with my sisters locally while Juliet and Aaron stayed with me. Mum took me to the local doctor that afternoon and I was prescribed a cocktail of antidepressants and sleeping tablets. Not once did the doctor ask me what was making me so unhappy. Mum did all the talking while I sat next to her, weeping inconsolably.

Those six weeks in Wellfleet are a blur of heat, drugs, sleep and drug-induced nightmares. When I wasn't sleeping in the sun or on the settee in my parents' lounge, I dragged my drugged body from one room to another. When I attended an occasional local Brethren meeting no one asked why the children and I were there. Sick mothers were often whisked off to stay with their parents. Sometimes they disappeared altogether, and you'd assume they'd been sent into one of the Brethren-approved clinics. No questions would be asked.

In all those long weeks, no one asked me about my marriage even though my parents and siblings knew what was going on. My parents gave me precious respite, for which I will be forever grateful. It couldn't have been easy for them to care for Juliet, Aaron and me while they were in their sixties. They nursed me back to health, carefully, lovingly, tenderly, and then, because no one is allowed to come between a man and his wife in the Brethren, they had no choice but to send me right back to my abuser.

On my return down south I was put under the care of psychiatrists. Unable to speak about the unhappy life I was living, the relentlessness of Kevin's physical and mental demands, the misery of my daily life, I used the bringing up of six children as my excuse for my sickness. The psychiatrists asked probing questions – they pressed, and they did their best to understand, but my guard was up. I had been told that I could not betray the secrets of Brethren ways to these worldly people. And even if I had been prepared to speak out, I had no concepts or words to describe what I had been suffering, let alone any sense that my rights as a human being were being violated: my right to be listened to, to say no, to choose how I lived, to be happy.

Then, to my astonishment, new light came in about Brethren relocating to less-populated meeting areas, and, perhaps to absolve him of any guilt about my mistreatment, Kevin decided we should request a move up north. The southern meeting was huge in comparison to Wellfleet, so he knew our request would meet the Brethren new relocation criteria. I had so often dreamt of moving back up north, but I would never have dared suggest it. So, when the new relocation rule came in and Kevin proposed we volunteer, I was overjoyed. I thought it would be the answer to all my problems, the answer to my prayers.

First, however, we had to get the formal approval of the Brethren 'relocation committee', which had been set up in each locality to examine each new relocation request. Moving to where your family lived was always looked on as a bit suspicious. We were meant to move to strengthen the Lord's position, not to be near our family. So we had our work cut out to convince them.

We went through endless meetings with the 'relocation committee'. Two assigned brothers came to our house again and again late in the evening when the children were in bed to discuss our move. Kevin would show them into our big lounge, where we'd all sit around on the comfy burgundy velour settees. The two brothers sat on one side of the room while Kevin and I sat on the other. I was expected to show my 'subject wife' attitude in these meetings. There were many times that I had to bite my tongue so hard I was afraid it might bleed.

The evening meetings went on for a couple of months. There were meetings about where Kevin would work; meetings about whether we were committed to the Lord's work; meetings about my mental health; meetings about our financial circumstances. Then there were meetings with the children to make sure that they were happy; meetings with Kevin's family to make sure they were in agreement. So they went on and on until eventually we were granted permission to move to Wellfleet. We sold our house quickly and arrived in the North with our removal vans to start a new life among the Brethren there.

# PART THREE

PART THREE

# SEVENTEEN

Moving to Wellfleet did make my life happier and easier for a time. Now I could visit my large family as often as I wanted without having to ask for permission. The Brethren community up north was also more relaxed. We were initially better off financially: Kevin was working for my family's business and was still being paid out from his family's mechanic business. From the sale of our house, we were able to buy a beautiful six-bedroom detached home in Wellfleet. David Johnston and his cronies no longer had any control over us. But more importantly for me, now that Kevin was travelling all over the North as a salesman for my family's business, I saw far less of him. Sometimes he would leave as early as 3 a.m. to travel to Scotland. But however far his journeys took him he'd always have to be back for the local evening meeting, as Brethren were not allowed to stay in hotels or to miss a meeting.

Although I often felt like a single parent during those years, I much preferred this new way of life because in Kevin's absence during the day, I was able to follow my own more lenient rules with the children rather than his strict but arbitrary rules. As soon as he walked through the door in the evening, though, the children knew the regime had changed and a darker mood settled over us all.

Although I was happier living in Wellfleet, Kevin struggled to fit in. He didn't understand northern humour and found his new job role difficult and exhausting. He spent those early years swinging from one mood to another. I'd never know which Kevin would walk through the front door at the end of the day. Would it be the angry Kevin who would lash out at the children and shout at me about the most stupid things? Would it be the crying Kevin who shut himself in the bedroom and wailed loud enough for us all to hear? Would it be the exhausted Kevin who spent any free time asleep and snoring on the settee while I took the children out of his way so as not to provoke his anger? Or would it be the depressed Kevin who used as much sex as he could get to ease his depression?

I understand better now why he struggled. The roles had been reversed and he missed his family and friends just as I had missed mine. Whereas I started to have breakfast over at my parents' house every day, he barely saw his family. The Wellfleet Brethren also teased him relentlessly – about being a 'soft southerner', about his finicky food tastes, about his aftershave. Looking back now, I would call it bullying. But teasing was the Brethren way, and even more so up north. It was also around this time that new light came in about credit cards – until around 2000 they had been prohibited but now they were encouraged. Since Bruce Hales had come into power around the year 2000, 'keeping up with the Joneses' had become paramount. Now everything was about status and money. The more money you had, the more popular you became within the 'rank and file' of the Brethren. Neither Kevin nor I had any money sense and, like many other Brethren we knew, we soon started living well beyond our means, spending up to the limit on our new credit cards. Our mounting debts became a new cause of Kevin's rage and frustration and a new source of anxiety for me.

As the years went on Kevin's mood swings started to affect our children and me more and more. We walked on eggshells, bracing ourselves for the sound of Kevin's key in the lock, steeling ourselves against his next tirade, his next violent tantrum. When he roared at me for making some simple decision with the children that he disagreed with, I'd watch the younger children wince or cower as the storm broke around us, and watch the older boys clench their fists behind their backs.

One sunny summer evening, I took the children to a park for a few hours. When Kevin came home from work and we had gathered around our big pine farmhouse table for dinner, he asked if the children had finished all their homework. I told him I had thought, with the day being so fine, that just for once the homework could wait. So I'd taken them to the park. Kevin brought his fist down on the table hard, making us all jump.

'You know what the rules are!' he yelled. 'All homework must be done before I come home!' I made the mistake of trying to defend myself.

'But it's been such a hot day. We had a lovely time.'

Kevin slammed his fist down hard again on the wooden table.

'I don't care how hot a day it is. If I say homework should be done before I get home, how dare you disobey me!'

By now we all knew how it went. We all knew that once Kevin started on at me like this he'd not be able to stop, so the children watched me leave the room again and lock myself in our bedroom until he had calmed down. Sooner or later Bradley would come and find me to check I was all right, and, trying hard not to show how upset I was, I'd pretend nothing was wrong, that I was just getting ready for the evening meeting. That was my job as a Brethren mother: keep up the cheerful façade, play happy families, even if you are dying inside. And the children had their roles too: look away, drop your gaze, go to your room and lock the door, don't ask any questions.

Often in those days – around five o'clock, about an hour before Kevin was due home – I'd open the dresser cupboard where we kept the alcohol and whiskey glasses and I'd pour myself a tumbler of neat whiskey. I've no idea how many measures that glass took. Brethren didn't measure their drinks. It was probably at least four measures, and it was enough to help me through any abuse that might be hurled at me as soon as my husband walked through the door. Enough to help me keep up the smiling, cheerful façade.

Every evening, once the children were tucked up in bed, I would do the remaining household chores: empty the dishwasher, put on the daily pile of washing, pick up toys and give the kitchen floor a quick mop. I enjoyed this time of day when I was alone and had peace and time to think.

Kevin would take himself off to the lounge with a tumbler of whiskey in hand to read some of the Man of God's ministry, as he was supposed to do, but, more often than not, by the time I'd finished my chores I would find his glass empty and he'd be fast asleep in the leather reclining chair with the ministry book open on his knee or fallen to the floor. In those moments, seeing him asleep like that, I often felt a rare jolt of joy and relief knowing that if I could just get into bed and be asleep before he joined me a couple of hours later, I might escape his sexual demands.

One evening in December 2006, I found Kevin in his usual pose in the armchair, asleep and snoring loudly. I picked up the ministry book from the floor and gave him a gentle shake. I told him I was going to bed. He replied with a sleepy 'OK' before closing his eyes again and falling back to sleep.

I surface from sleep several hours later. I am struggling to breathe. I am lying on my back and someone is holding me down. Something is being held over my nose and mouth. Turning my head from side to side I try to release myself, but the grip is so tight that I can't get free. My heart is racing in panic.

In the darkness of the room I can't see what's happening, but my other senses are wide-awake now. A strong smell and taste of aftershave fills my mouth and nose. Reaching my one free hand up to my face, I try to prise the hand away, but it's too strong. Suddenly I feel my legs being pulled apart and I can feel the hardness of a penis being pushed into me. Everything is happening so fast that my brain can't process what's happening. Is this a nightmare?

As my eyes adjust to the darkness I see Kevin's face looming above me, his expression wild and hateful. He has one hand held tightly over my nose and mouth. He is using the other to thrust his penis into me. Using all my strength, I lift my legs up and try to push his body off me. But Kevin is incredibly strong. As he struggles to keep hold of me, he finally moves his hand away from my face.

As I feel air fill my lungs again, I try to scream at him to stop but no sound comes out of my mouth. Kevin in his animal-like state doesn't even seem to see me. He continues thrusting in and out, in and out. Closing my eyes tight I wait for it all to stop.

A groan. Then panting. Then it's all over. Kevin collapses on the bed next to me.

Suddenly released, I jump up and rush into the en-suite, locking the door behind me. Still I haven't made a sound. Not a sound. Now I sit down and begin to sob quietly. What has just happened?

I sat on that cold toilet until Kevin's snores had reached the volume where I knew it was safe to move. Then, creeping out of the bedroom, I went downstairs into the lounge and quietly closed the door. I curled up on the sofa, pulling the throw around me, and continued to cry. I was still trying to catch my breath.

The word 'rape' swirled around in my head. Was it rape? I wasn't even sure what rape was, though I'd sometimes glimpsed the word in forbidden newspaper and magazine headlines and deduced the rest. What Kevin had done to me sounded like rape. But could a husband rape a wife?

I couldn't sleep. Every time I closed my eyes I was back in the bed in the darkness, suffocating, struggling to get the hand off my face, my body drenched in a panicky sweat, the smell of aftershave thick in the air, the taste in my mouth, Kevin's face full of hate looming above me.

I must have dozed off for a bit as I woke with a start, a gentle shake on my shoulder and the sound of my name being whispered in my ear. Sitting upright in panic, I saw Kevin leaning over me. Where was I? What had happened? Had I had a nightmare? As soon as I saw Kevin's tear-stained, crestfallen, guilty face, I knew that it had all been real.

Kevin tried to put his arm around me, but I shook him off.

'I'm so sorry about what happened earlier,' he said, as though it had been just another time that he had overstepped a mark, been a bit rough. 'I didn't mean to hurt you.'

'What on earth were you thinking?' I heard myself hiss. 'What were you trying to do? Were you trying to kill me?'

Kevin knelt at my feet, his head buried in his hands. I could see fear in his eyes; fear that I would tell an elder, report him.

'When I climbed into bed,' he said, as if this were sufficient excuse, 'I asked you at least three times for sex and you just turned away from me and refused. I was angry. I don't know what came over me. I'm so sorry. I didn't mean to hurt you.'

I rose to my feet. I glared down at him, my eyes full of the hatred and contempt and disgust that I felt for him. Then, taking a deep breath, I told him that I thought what he had just done was rape. Kevin stood up, staring at me in disbelief, the corners of his mouth curling contemptuously.

'No, Maria,' he said, in his Brethren 'we will hear no more nonsense from you' tone. 'I didn't rape you. There's no such thing as a husband raping a wife.' Then he left the room as though he meant there'd be no more talk about it.

My mind was awhirl, veering between guilt and anger. Had I brought this on myself? Was this my fault? How could a husband do that to his wife? How could I get into bed with my husband ever again? What was happening to me? What was happening to *us*? I sat staring into space, unable to move, my face wet with tears.

An hour later I heard the front door slam. Kevin had left for work. I waited until I heard the sound of his car on the gravel before daring to leave the room. I could hear the sounds of the children upstairs starting their day. I knew that I had to do my best to pretend that everything was normal. I knew I'd have to pretend again. But nothing could ever be normal again.

By the time I had dropped the children at school, my head felt like it was going to burst. I had to tell someone what had happened. And I knew at the same time that I wasn't well. Was I having another breakdown? I've no memory of taking the journey from school to my parents' house but that's where I found myself. I stumbled through their backdoor and into the kitchen, where I collapsed on the armchair in the corner.

Screams are echoing around the empty room. Who is screaming? Then Mum and Dad are running into the kitchen. Mum is at my feet, taking my hands in hers. I can see her mouthing, 'What on earth is wrong?' but I can't hear her for the screams. I can't hear anything for the screams. Dad is yelling, 'Maria, stop!' But what does he want me to stop?

Now I realise that the screaming is coming from me. Then the screams stop and the tears come – wrenching sobs from deep within me.

'What on earth is wrong?' Mum keeps saying. But still I can't say anything. I can't breathe. I can't catch my breath. I'm suffocating.

'Should we call a doctor?' Dad asks Mum.

I don't want to go to a doctor. Doctors don't help. Doctors can't help. Perhaps no one can help anymore. Not even my parents. I shake my head.

Bit by bit, fragment by fragment, I told my parents what had happened in the early hours of that morning. As Mum leant over me, holding me tight, I knew that she at least believed every word that I was saying. As she leant in close, comforting me, I whispered in her ear in desperation:

'Mum, what is happening to me? I can't do this anymore.' Before letting go of me, and facing Dad, she gave me a reassuring hug.

'Don't worry,' she said. 'Dad is going to sort this out.'

How on earth was Dad going to sort this out? I thought. Brethren parents aren't allowed to interfere in their children's marriages. You can get punished for that. You can get shut up for that.

Later that evening my father summoned Kevin to my parents' home. It was brave of him, but he had authority in the Wellfleet meeting and he'd chosen to use it. I have no idea what Dad said to Kevin that evening but, soon afterwards, a 'priestly meeting' was set up. Two elders who acted as priests in Wellfleet met with Kevin. For the next six weeks, he had a meeting with those priests twice a week. I knew how this worked. I had seen it happen so often. They would have interrogated him. They would have asked him endless questions about porn, masturbation and sex. When they had finished with him, when they had heard enough detail, seen enough tears, and been satisfied that Kevin was sorry and full of shame, they would have told him that he had received the Lord's forgiveness. That he was free to go back to his wife and family and his marital bed.

The priests did not speak to me. They did not ask me any questions. They did not ask me how I felt or what had happened or if anything like it had happened before. This, they would have said, was a matter for the men. Only for the men. *They* would decide what was right for me and for Kevin. *They* would decide our future. I know now that I should never have been expected to go back and live with my husband again, let alone sleep in the same bed as him. I should have received counselling to help me heal from what I now know was marital rape, but, instead, I had to battle on and accept that if the Lord had forgiven my husband, then I had to forgive him too.

# EIGHTEEN

So, despite the intervention, life continued as before. Kevin had been lectured and forgiven, and so our marriage limped on with little to no change, until external forces intervened. By 2008 our financial situation had changed. The recession had hit. Kevin's family back in the South were struggling to keep their car repair company afloat. They told Kevin that they'd have to stop paying him his share. We were mortgaged to the hilt. Our credit card debts were out of control. We took out a further mortgage against our home to help the situation.

The cost of living for a Brethren family is high. You're expected to entertain at least once a fortnight and, by the time you've bought enough food and alcohol to feed a group of twenty, there isn't a lot left over to feed yourselves. I did my best to feed the family during the week as economically as possible so that we could afford to entertain at weekends. There was one payment that we could never cut back on, though. Every Sunday at the Lord's Supper we were expected to put money into the collection box to help pay for the expenses in running the local meeting hall. And on the first Sunday of every month, we had to give a larger amount to be distributed among the important leaders of the Brethren. The Man of God received a percentage of these monthly collections. We had to look after the Lord's interests first, they told us. If we looked after the Lord's interests then He would look after us financially. But that didn't seem to be working for us.

Many Brethren businesses were suffering as a result of the recession. Now Bruce Hales received new light: in very dire circumstances, he told us, married Brethren women could go to work for their husbands or within a family business. If the family needed them to, married women could undertake filing or answer emails alongside the unmarried women, just so long as they remained entirely subservient to all the men in the company.

When I left school back in the mid-1980s and began working for my dad, I had longed to do so much more than secretarial work. I knew, because I had watched the men, that I could have run a business, managed accounts, developed business or marketing strategy and headed up meetings. I was bored doing menial tasks. My skills were wasted. Stuck in these dull roles with no promotion prospects, I can see why so many women longed to escape into marriage.

When the elders announced that for the time being married women could work, I decided to use it to my advantage. I didn't want to go back to work for my dad or for my brother, I wanted to run my own small business. I had an idea for selling homemade hair accessories such as colourful, knotted Alice bands and scrunchies to gift shops. I'd always had to spend so much time on my own hair that I'd become adept at finding different ways to tie it back, make it look pretty. But there were no Brethren role models to look to. I knew of no other married women running their own business without the influence of a man. I'd have to find my own way.

Kevin and I discussed my business concept with Dad and my brother Edward. It would be small, I told them. I could run it from home. I thought my main stumbling block would be the need for me to go out into the world to sell face-to-face. But, to my surprise, Dad and Edward didn't bat an eyelid and thought it a good idea. Maybe they thought it would help my mental health and give me something different to focus on. Whatever the reason, my business idea passed their scrutiny.

I wasted no time. I knew that the new rule was almost certainly time-limited, so I wanted to make the most of the opportunity. When the recession eased, I knew I'd have to go back to being a full-time mother and housewife again.

———

In October 2008 I launched my tiny start-up company, Promos Unlimited. Soon I was off travelling the country, visiting customers and potential clients. For the first time since I'd got married, I was meeting people, worldly people, talking to customers over the phone and interacting with the outside world. With my briefcase of samples in hand, I walked through the doors of 'worldly run' organisations. Despite my sheltered life and lack of business experience, my sales skills appeared to be good. People liked what I was offering.

Now I leapt out of bed in the morning, eager to start my day. For the first time in my life I had power, autonomy and self-esteem. I secured accounts with some big tourist boards and gift shops up and down the country. Although Brethren rules dictated that I couldn't even share a cup of coffee with my customers, I went out of my way to be as friendly as possible.

My brother, husband and father kept a close eye on me to start with, conferring with each other and checking to see that I was sticking to the rules. On one occasion my brother Edward insisted on coming with me to meet a new client. On the way home in the car, Edward turned to me and said, 'You're too friendly with those people.'

'What do you mean, too friendly?' I asked, feigning surprise. I wasn't stupid. I knew I wasn't behaving in Brethrenly ways.

'Maria, you need to keep your distance from the world,' he warned, and I nodded, thanking him for his advice and guidance, knowing that I'd have to be more careful if I wanted to keep going. But I didn't want to keep my distance from worldly people. I *liked* them. They fascinated me. I wanted to learn more about them and the way they lived, dressed and behaved.

What did my customers make of the woman who turned up to meetings in frumpy dark clothes, with no jewellery or makeup, her own hair long and loose down her back, and her head covered with either a headscarf or headband while I was selling such pretty feminine things? I looked so different from the other saleswomen I'd seen: the smart trouser suits, designer handbags, perfect makeup and earrings. I longed to dress like those women but I could never have dared to break the Brethren rules about clothing. If I did, however far I drove from Wellfleet for a business meeting, someone from another Brethren fellowship might spot me and report me.

But whatever my customers thought of me or my strange appearance, they continued to buy from me. Maybe I had an unforgettable look. Maybe my strange clothes made me stand out from my competitors. Maybe I was just good at selling.

My work was time-consuming and labour-intensive. I spent hours at the sewing machine and the family dining table designing and printing the packaging and then many more hours labelling and wrapping the products. After school and work, the children helped me wrap up the orders. I set up a little production line on our big dining room table and we often worked long into the night to fulfil each order.

In 2010 I secured a major contract with a distributor. Because our dining table would no longer be big enough for the new orders, my uncle offered me space in his business premises. Now, for the first time, I was able to separate home from work. I no longer had to tidy up the dining room every time we needed to entertain. But now I was working even longer hours while still running the home, taking the children to school, keeping everyone happy and entertaining at the weekends.

I had no regrets, despite my exhaustion. I was happy. During this time, Kevin and I were on a more level field with each other. We discussed business. Kevin seemed proud of me. He would often compliment my work ethic and sales and marketing skills. He made fewer sexual demands on me. We were both exhausted. I began to think that maybe God had listened to my prayers and that maybe we could salvage our marriage.

In April 2011 we decided to ease our financial situation by selling our large detached house and moving into a smaller detached cottage. This move and the income from my business enabled us to pay off our mortgage and our credit card debts. I fell in love with the cottage, and although it was much smaller than what we had been used to, we managed to make it work. We were even able to give the children a bedroom each, which was still required by Brethren rules.

After the move I was exhausted. I had made some profit in my business, but the workload, which had once been so stimulating and a source of joy and freedom, was having an adverse effect on my mental health, my physical health and the family. Looking back, I'm not surprised that I burnt out. Everything was stacked against me; trying to be a good Brethren wife and mother while single-handedly running my own business was an impossible task. Maybe Dad and Edward knew this too; maybe they knew that, eventually, I would have to give up and go back to my old life. So, when I finally told them I wanted to sell the company, they already had a plan in place. A Brethren company that sold promotional gifts would buy it from me.

I completed the sale the following month and returned to my normal life. But although I did not know it then, now that I had tasted a little of life outside the Brethren, seen for myself how kind and interesting these worldly people were, my doubts about our rules and beliefs began to multiply. Was the world really as evil as we were being taught?

# NINETEEN

Now that I was back at home and at Kevin's beck and call, his sexual demands quickly became obsessive again. He was increasingly depressed and frustrated with his work. When he came home, he would ease his anger by lashing out at the children with his hands and fists. Sometimes I'd have to physically pull him off the boys. He would often ease his depression and frustration by performing rushed, aggressive sex on me. I had no strength or energy to stop him. I would either lie on my back staring at the ceiling, studying each crack and stain and wishing they would swallow me up, or I'd lie curled up in a ball on my side staring at the cream-painted wall next to me. I knew every bump and cranny of that wall.

One day in May 2012, a month after I had given up my business, things between Kevin and me came to a head. I came out of the en-suite in our bedroom to find him roaring with rage, the latest novel I was reading, *Pride and Prejudice*, in his hand. I had discovered books again while I'd been free to travel for the business. I bought them from second-hand shops – classics, romance novels – anything that might take me away from my humdrum life. I read them greedily and dropped them into bins in the street when I'd finished with them for fear I'd be caught. I had taken to hiding them either under the mattress or under the bed.

Now Kevin waved my pretty hardback copy of Jane Austen's novel so close to my face that I had to take a step back so he wouldn't hit me with it.

'What is this?' he bellowed. With no energy or means to defend myself, I just shrugged.

'It's a harmless novel. It's just a book.'

'No novel is harmless!' he went on, throwing the book onto the top of the wardrobe and out of my reach. I heard it hit the wall before falling down the back. I would have no way of reaching it now without moving the heavy wardrobe, and I wanted so much to know what happened to Elizabeth after she'd bumped into Darcy at Pemberley.

'The next one I find goes in the bin and I'll tell the priests,' he snarled before storming off into the en-suite.

I climb into our king-size bed, curl my body up on the very edge and face that well-known cream wall. I want to cry but I daren't make a sound. I don't want him to know that he's upsetting me.

Minutes later Kevin is climbing into bed beside me. He wrenches at my shoulder, forcing me to roll over onto my back. He starts up again, berating me about reading, telling me that novels will defile my mind, reminding me of Bruce Hales's recent ministry: 'No Christian should put themselves into the defiled mind of an author.' Defiled. *Defiled.* I think of my book down there in the dust behind the wardrobe. I think of Elizabeth and Darcy. I think of Pemberley. I don't feel defiled.

I lie very still on my back, praying that if I wait long enough Kevin's anger will blow itself out and I'll be able to get some sleep. But he rants on and on, reminding me of my every fault, and my disobedience to him and the Brethren. He tells me that if I don't change my ways by submitting fully to him and the Brethren I won't make it to the end and I know he means that I won't make it to Heaven. I'll be left behind. I will shame us all.

I try to pull myself upright in the bed. I want to tell him to stop shouting, to be quiet, that the children will hear, that I don't deserve this, that it is just a book, but what happens next scares him more than any of my words ever could.

I can't speak. The words I want to say are formed in my mind, my mouth is open to say them, but no sound comes out. Collapsing back onto my pillow, I stare at the ceiling. I begin to shake. I can hear Kevin asking me what's wrong, but he sounds very far away. I try again to speak but still no sound comes. I fix my eyes on a stain up there on the ceiling, trying to anchor myself so that I won't float away forever. I hear Kevin asking me if he should ring my parents. I try to nod.

Then, as I slip in and out of consciousness, Mum and Dad are in our bedroom. Mum sits on the edge of the bed next to me. She takes my hands in hers. She talks softly and simply, trying to get my attention. I hear her and Dad's voices as they discuss what to do next. I hear panic rising in their voices. Dad says that he thinks I'm having a stroke. I watch wide-eyed as he phones for an ambulance. An ambulance? Why do I need an ambulance? *Am* I having a stroke?

There is so much I want to say. I want to tell them about Kevin's tirades, his constant demands on me, his incessant yelling at the children and me. I want to tell them that I'm just so exhausted from everything that I can't go on anymore, but all I can do is stare at the ceiling and that stain. I am scared and I am speechless.

Then there are men in medical uniform standing in our bedroom. A blue light is flashing on the ceiling. The men are putting blood pressure monitors on my arm. They are speaking softly to me, to my parents, to Kevin. They are measuring my heart rate, one of them says. I am not to worry, he says. They ask me questions – endless questions – but my voice has gone. All I can do is nod or shake my head.

At the hospital the doctors and nurses try to understand what is going on. None of their observations so far are pointing to a stroke. I hear them ask Kevin what happened. They want more details. I hear Kevin tell them that I was in bed and that he had asked me a question and when I didn't reply, he got worried.

I need to tell them what really happened. I won't have them listen to his lies, his evasions. When Kevin has gone to fetch tea, I pull myself up. I signal to the young nurse who's standing by my bedside. I use my hands to show her that I need a paper and pencil.

I write. I write about how I feel useless, about how I feel like I can't go on, about how I'm not happy in my marriage, about the financial worries we've had, about my exhaustion, about the strains of bringing up six children. I don't write about the rape or the sexual abuse, or about the strange life I live within the Brethren. I can't write about any of those things; those things must be kept secret; those things aren't for worldly people to know. As soon as I've written those words on the paper, I feel some sense of relief. I can feel some of the burden lift. I test my voice but it's still silent.

The nurse squeezes my hand. She takes my scribbled notes away. A few minutes later a female doctor sits on the edge of the bed next to me. She explains that my brain needs a rest, and this is its way of saying, 'enough'. She tells me that I've done a good thing; that writing down my thoughts will help my speech to return. She tells me to rest, that she will be back in the morning.

Then Kevin is sitting on the chair next to me and taking hold of my hand. He tells me again that he is so sorry for everything he has done. I know he wants me to keep quiet, to reassure him that I will keep his secrets. But I'm too tired to listen to his apologies now, too tired to reassure him. I close my eyes and drift into a light sleep.

When I awoke four hours later, Kevin was asleep on the chair next to me. I gave him a tap on his shoulder to wake him. I asked what the time was and if I could go home. He looked at me like a frightened child.

'Oh, thank goodness,' he said, 'you're talking again.'

Bending over, he kissed my forehead and whispered 'sorry' in my ear again. It was always the same: sorry, sorry, sorry. I lay back and I thought about what had transpired over the last twelve hours and how frightened I had been. At that moment I realised that I couldn't let things get that bad again. Something had to change – or I would go mad again and stay mad.

The doctor came to see me before discharging me and recommended that I be referred to a psychiatrist. I was happy to comply. An appointment was set up for the following day. She also increased the dosage of my antidepressant medication again to as high as it was safe to go. I'd been taking it now for ten years.

The following day I went to my psychiatrist appointment. I still couldn't talk about what had happened to me or was

155

happening to me. Looking back, I suppose I wasn't fully aware at that point that my life wasn't normal. It was all I had ever known.

The kind female psychiatrist I spoke to that day helped to change my life forever. She suggested that, as well as my one-to-one sessions with her, it would be good if I was enrolled in some self-esteem group classes the clinic was running. Self-esteem. I'd managed to snatch only very brief moments of this feeling when I'd first started my business, but I didn't know you could take classes in it. I did know that the Brethren elders would never allow me to attend such events, so this time I didn't ask. I'd go secretly.

Those nine self-esteem classes I attended over the following weeks helped to dislodge my mind a little from its lifetime of dogma. It was only a little, but it was enough, a start. I listened to other people talk about their battles with depression or with addiction or with abusive partners. Week by week, as our counsellor taught us how to value ourselves, respect ourselves and have the strength to walk away from unhealthy situations, I came to see that it was not only my marriage that was crushing me but also the Brethren's way of life. I came to understand that if I was to go on living and breathing, if I was to stop myself from going mad and staying mad, something had to change, and I was the only one who had the power to change it.

# PART FOUR

# TWENTY

After those classes I knew that something had to change yet I still didn't know how. The little crack of light had become bigger, and I was starting to see that my life wasn't normal. Over the next six months my mindset continued to shift. I spent time at the library researching how people had managed to leave strict religious sects. I battled constantly with myself about how to escape that life. I found it difficult to imagine ever being able to step into the outside world. That day, suicide felt like my only way out.

## Friday 18 January 2013. Wellfleet

The breakfast dishes are washed and put away, the sofa cushions plumped up and the rubbish has been taken out. Kevin and the three older boys have all gone to work. I have dropped my three youngest children at school just as I have always done. Since dawn I have worked hard to keep everything normal. I've smiled over the breakfast table, I've asked about homework and bills and suggested plans for the weekend. I've been careful not to let anyone suspect anything is different. I know that I can't live like this anymore. Something has to stop. Once the house is tidy, I take a deep breath and reach for my coat.

There is a frost outside. Putting the hood of my coat up, I keep my head down as I walk along the seafront towards the pier. I usually say hello to anyone I pass, but not today.

Today I'm just concentrating on putting one foot in front of the other. I'm conscious of people passing me, but I don't see them.

I find myself at the end of the long slab of the concrete pier, the steel grey of the sea stretching all the way to the horizon.

I like the pier. I often come here to clear my head. I like to drink in the smell of the salty water and listen to the waves as they lap or crash against the concrete wall underneath me. The icy wind sweeps through my hair as I lean against the safety railing. Resting my elbows on the cold black steel, I lean my body over slightly and stare into the dark bottomless water below. I am afraid of the water. I still can't swim. But maybe, I think now, maybe the sea is my answer.

I glance back along the pier. There's a woman in the far distance with a dog, but, apart from that, I am alone. How long would it take for a non-swimmer like me to drown? Would it be quicker in winter temperatures? I look down again into the deep black water and then back down the pier.

No one can see me. I could slip over the railings, sit down on the edge and quietly slip in. Disappear. Better to finish it once and for all. Death is surely better than the life I'm living.

Suddenly, I hear a voice inside my head: 'Stop! Choose a new life,' it says.

The urgency of the voice makes me jump. I step back from the railing. Do I *have* a choice? Is it time for me to choose a new life, a different life? The thought makes my heart thump in terror. Could there be a life for me outside of the Brethren? Would God punish me for turning my back on the light as the Brethren have always said He would? Or, worse still, would He strike my children down? What will happen to me or to those I love if I step into freedom?

Pulling my coat around me against the sea wind, I turn around, towards the woman with her dog, towards the shore, towards home. If I am to choose life, then it will have to be a life outside of the Brethren. I can see now that I must find a way to make the break even if it means

I can never see my children or family again. If I stay in this life, I will drown.

Taking the route home through town, past the coffee shops and restaurants, I feel an unfamiliar lightness. Some of that awful weight has lifted. Peering through the steamed-up windows of a coffee shop, I watch people inside enjoying hot drinks with friends. I try to imagine going into a café to share a coffee with a worldly friend. What would it be like to eat or drink with those in the outside world? What would it be like to not practise the Brethren rule of separation? I glimpse my reflection in the steamed-up windows. In my headscarf and frumpy clothes, my hair down my back, I look more like sixty than a woman in her forties. Who is this lost woman? What has happened to her?

For over forty years I've been told that evil is outside our small fellowship and that it is everywhere: in coffee shops, cinemas, radios, television sets, pop music, pubs, computers and restaurants. But today I don't see evil when I look into that steamy coffee shop, watching people sitting in close conversation, smiling at each other. I see freedom and light.

I spend the next week in a state of panic and fear. I know what I need to do but I don't know how to do it. I try to think of ways to get away, lying awake, tossing and turning. Could I get someone in the outside world to kidnap me? But who? I don't know anyone in the outside world.

Could I provoke the Brethren elders to withdraw from me? I think of things I could do that would get me excommunicated from the Brethren. If I ate with a worldly person, that would be enough for them to withdraw from me. Even walking into a pub would do it.

I think of the snippets of conversations I've heard about how other Brethren have managed to get away. Some have climbed out of bedroom windows and disappeared into the night. Some have made friendships in the outside world and got help. Some have gone to the police and been put into safe houses called refuges. But none of the ex-members I've heard about have been married women. It's almost impossible for married women to leave. The costs are too high.

And what about my children? I can't leave them behind and go on living with myself, yet I know that my older sons almost certainly won't come with me, not now they are working, earning good wages, counting the days until they get their detached house and their choice of a young Brethren wife. They'd have to leave all their friends behind too if they came with me – and for what? To follow their mother into a world that they believe is ruled by Satan? The odds are completely stacked against me.

Would my three youngest come with me? The courts might grant me custody for them until they are sixteen and deemed able to decide for themselves. But, even if the courts did grant me custody, how would I get us out and keep them safe and hidden? I have no money of my own. I have no job. I go round and round inside a kind of maze. I can't see a way out, or at least, I tell myself, I can't see one yet.

For six long days I play the good Brethren wife to my husband and the good mother to my children, making meals, supervising homework, hoovering, polishing and doing laundry. Each day I wonder if this is going to be my last day in this life, in this house.

Every night I go to the Brethren meeting. No one must suspect what's going on in my mind. Then I begin to worry that God is going to punish me for what I am about to do. Will He suddenly strike one of my children down? Or one of my parents? How will God punish me for my wicked thoughts and plans?

## Thursday 24 January 2013

Kevin leaves home at five o'clock in the morning to travel to South Wales, some 200 miles away. He needs to be there at eight o'clock to get his sales calls done before travelling back home in time for the daily Brethren meeting at seven-thirty.

He always calls me around one o'clock in the afternoon – regular as clockwork. But five o'clock comes round and I've heard nothing from him. I've rung him on his Brethren-monitored mobile several times, but his phone is going straight to voicemail. Normally I wouldn't be worried, but now my heart is racing and my palms are sweating. Is *this* God's punishment? Although my husband isn't a nice person, he is the father of my children. I wish him no harm. Has God struck my husband down to warn me to put an end to my wicked thoughts about leaving?

At a quarter past five, my brother Edward, who is now the manager of our family business, rings me and asks if I've heard anything from Kevin.

'No, nothing,' I tell him, trying to keep the panic out of my voice.

'Neither have we,' he says. 'We've been trying to get hold of him since two o'clock this afternoon and his phone keeps going straight to voicemail.'

'Do you think something bad has happened?' I ask carefully.

'I'm sure there's a good reason,' Edward says. 'Maybe his phone isn't working. Let's give it another couple of hours before we start to worry. Let me know when he arrives home.'

I get the children's dinner ready, pretending that nothing is wrong. I tell myself I'm over-reacting. I mustn't let a little scare like this blow my cover. As I finish loading the dishwasher and busy myself with tidying the kitchen, I look at the clock: it's almost seven. It's been almost two hours since Edward phoned me. In my panic I've been calling Kevin every five minutes but his phone is still going straight to voicemail.

I go into Oliver's bedroom, sit on his bed and burst into tears. Between sobs I tell him how worried I am that his dad isn't home yet. The other children slope into the bedroom. They look confused – I'm usually the one keeping everyone calm in situations like this. They have no idea how I am reading Kevin's silence – that I think he's had an accident and that it's all my fault.

I do my best to pull myself together. I need to get to the meeting tonight or it'll raise suspicion among the Brethren. I tell the children that everything will be fine and that I'm just worrying about nothing. I tell them to hurry and get ready for the meeting. I'm bracing myself for news.

Then I hear a car in the drive. I run from the bedroom into the hallway and get to the front door in time to see Kevin stepping out of his car. He looks completely unperturbed.

'Sorry I couldn't call you,' he says as he rushes past me and into the house to get washed and changed ready for the meeting. 'My phone died, and my charger broke.'

Scolding myself for being so paranoid, I make a decision right there and then that this weekend I'm going to somehow find the courage to tell my husband, my children and my parents that not only am I finished with my marriage, I'm finished with the Brethren.

Over the last few days I have started thinking a little more carefully. I have nowhere to run to for refuge because everyone I know – my parents, my friends, my siblings – are all part of the Brethren. I don't know anyone outside the Brethren. I can't run and hide somewhere with no money and no job. With no income I'll be forced to go back sooner or later. So I need to find a way to stay in the family home. Without the house I won't have anywhere to live or to keep the children safe and clothed and fed. I don't want to leave my children behind in Kevin's care. I never want them to say that I walked away from them. I refuse to slip away into the night, and I'm going to fight to keep them. At this point I've still no clear idea how I'm going to do any of this. I've no idea what's going to happen. But I do know it will be done.

## Sunday 27 January 2013: 4.30 a.m.

My alarm sounds. I've slept very little, but I have to get ready for the Lord's Supper. We need to be in our seats by 5.45 a.m. Although my children now range in age from their twenties down to early teens, they still rely on me to wake them up.

I go through the motions just as I do every Lord's Day: I have my shower, get dressed in my Sunday best, bring my husband a cup of tea, wake the children and get them a drink if they want it. I'm grateful to be busy getting everyone organised. It takes my mind off my worry. Taking care of the family is what a good Brethren wife and mother does. That's what I have always done. The routine is comforting.

Then it strikes me that this will probably be the last time that I need to get up so long before dawn for the Lord's Supper. Rather than feeling sad at the thought, I feel excited at how much my life – and the life of my children – is going to change. But I am also terrified. All my life I have been making deals with God, trading one thing for another, asking for signs of approval or disapproval of plans and decisions. Today is no different. Then I remember – in my fitful sleep in the middle of the night I had cried out in silent prayer to God, pleading to Him, bargaining with Him.

'God,' I had said, 'if what I'm doing is wrong, then the Supper is the time to show me. God, if you get me through this next meeting without one of my family, my children or myself being struck down dead, then I'll know you want me to take this path towards freedom.'

It is the most shocking bargain I have ever made. I have massively upped the stakes.

It's a cold morning. Kevin and I and our six children take the short walk as always to the windowless meeting room with its high fence and tall fir trees hiding it from the prying eyes of the world. It's still dark. I'm shivering outwardly and shaking inwardly. I've made a bargain with God. What if He strikes someone down as we sit in the meeting this morning? How am I going to live with that?

Juliet and I take our seats alongside the other sisters in the outer circle. Kevin and our five boys – Oliver, Bradley and Kyle in their early twenties, and Lincoln and young Aaron still at school – take their seats within the front circles, their shirts identically white and pressed. At the Lord's Supper the brothers always stand up individually through the service to offer a prayer of thanks to God or Jesus. Even boys as young as three years old are encouraged to do this. I've seen my sons tremble at the prospect of doing it for the first time. I feel for them. Once I get us all outside, once we leave, surely things will be better for them.

I usually sit next to Mum at the Supper, but this morning I can't. Mum can read me like a book. I know she will sense something is wrong with me if she sees me up close. Sitting

165

next to her would make me more nervous, and I might break my resolve. I can't do that. Not now.

Everyone is gathered under the bright strip lights, the sky still dark outside. The brothers are all dressed in their white shirts and smart trousers. We sisters are seated behind them in subjection with our eyes down on our hymn books, keeping quiet and still and doing nothing except choosing a hymn when we feel the Spirit moves us to do so.

We've all been taught that it's important to greet each other at the Supper by making eye contact. So while I do my best to meet the eyes of each member as usual, I can't help but think that this could be the last time I greet these people, my friends, my family. I am close to tears but I cannot cry. It will give me away.

Once everyone is assembled, I watch Mum carry the Emblems to the table, which is set in the centre. I watch her place the bread and cup carefully in their assigned places. I watch her every move, my heart thumping, waiting for God to trip her up or strike her down dead, but nothing happens. I watch as silently, with her head bent in subjection, she walks back to her seat. I breathe a sigh of relief.

It's not long before a hymn is announced. A brother starts singing the words before we all join in:

*O Lord what burdens thou didst bear*
*Our load was laid on Thee*
*Thou stoodest for the sinner there*
*To bear all ill for me*
*A victim led, Thy blood was shed*
*Now there's no load on me.*

*Death and the curse were in our cup*
*O Lord was full for Thee*
*But Thou has drained the last dark drop,*
*'Tis empty now for me.*
*That bitter cup . . . love drank it up*
*Left but the love for me.*

*That bitter cup is mine.* I do my best to sing the words without breaking down, but the lyrics are almost my undoing. This is one of my favourite hymns. I've chosen it myself many times at the start of the Lord's Supper. It reminds me of my own suffering at the hands of my husband. My voice is thickening in my throat now. I keep my head bent, hoping no one will notice. As the hymn finishes, I take my neatly folded white hanky from the front of my hymn book and discreetly blow my nose and dry my tears.

I feel like a traitor to be here at all, but I still need to pretend that nothing is wrong. As I take a piece of bread from the broken loaf that is passed to me, I remind myself that if I see the end of this meeting without anything happening, then this will be the last time that I attend the Supper; this will be the last time I take a morsel of the bread; the last time I taste the wine; the last time I will 'break bread' with these people, my people, the only people I have ever known.

Time passes. I sense movement. Everyone is getting off their seats and making their way out of the hall. The meeting is over. I follow everyone out, sighing with relief. I speak to no one, and, to my relief, no one speaks to me. We've been instructed that there should be no conversation after the Lord's Supper, and today I'm glad of that rule. I have survived. My family has survived. God hasn't struck any of us down. The way is clear.

Now I must see the rest of this last Lord's Day through. At the end of the day I'm going to stand in front of my husband and tell him that our marriage is over, but, not only that, I'm going to tell him that I am never going to a Brethren meeting ever again. I imagine the look on his face, his mouth open, gawping, frozen in disbelief.

Then, once I've told Kevin, I'll take each of my children aside and tell them of my decision. They will listen. They will understand. After that, I have no idea what will happen. One thing I do know is that though many hearts will be broken by my decision, I must do this for myself. I've spent all my life pleasing others, looking after others, biting my lip, and doing my best to be a good wife and mother. I've lain on my back staring at the ceiling while my husband takes his conjugal rights brutally over and over, but now it's time to go. I just have to get through this very last day.

———

This morning we're going to a neighbouring Brethren meeting for the scripture reading and preachings. After a quick breakfast, we all pile into our people carrier. As I climb into the front next to Kevin, I can sense that the atmosphere is tense. He is in one of his darkest moods. Taking the road out of Wellfleet, we head up the hill towards the motorway.

Kevin is driving extremely fast and at every corner we're all thrown around. The children and I are silent. We've learnt over the years that it only makes him drive faster if we try to plead with him to slow down, so we grip the handlebars of the car and pray silently as we've always done, raising our eyebrows surreptitiously at each other. I glance over at the speedometer. He is way over the speed limit.

Then I catch sight of flashing blue lights in the rear-view mirror. A police car overtakes us and pulls us over. Kevin slams on the brakes and curses under his breath. The policeman slowly gets out of his car and approaches our vehicle. He knocks on Kevin's window but Kevin's head is down. To my astonishment, he is refusing to open the window. Taking a breath to calm my nerves and smiling as best I can, I signal to the policeman to come round to my side. I open my window. The policeman is puzzled, and I am scarlet with embarrassment, but there's nothing I can say. In the rear-view mirror I can see the children cowering in the back.

Leaning into my open window, the policeman speaks to Kevin.

'Sir,' he says, 'you were driving well over the speed limit.' Kevin nods but still refuses to make eye contact or answer. I can hear the children catching their breath in the back.

'Can I take some details and your driving licence please, sir?' the policeman asks politely.

Kevin reaches into his back pocket, pulls out his wallet, takes out his licence and silently, still without making eye contact, he hands it to the policeman. I scramble to sort out all the details so the policeman can issue a speeding ticket. I am polite and cheerful. The policeman smiles, thanks me and, as he takes a last look at us all in the vehicle, he looks straight at Kevin and says, 'Looks like you've got a lovely family here, sir. Make sure you look after them and take more care with your driving.'

As we pull away from the kerb, Oliver erupts.

'Dad, you're so weird! Why can't you just be normal?'

It is so unlike Oliver to speak to his father like this. He knows the risk he is taking. We are all on edge, less afraid that Kevin has broken the law, more that he will erupt again. But, emboldened by Oliver's outburst, suddenly all the children are joining in and berating their father. Kevin is purple. There is no stopping him now.

'How dare you speak to your father like that!' he says, shoving his foot down hard on the accelerator, crunching the gears. 'If I don't want to speak to a policeman, that's nothing to do with you.'

'As for you,' he says, turning to me, as I smell the rubber burning under the tyres, 'why did you have to speak to the police? Can't you keep your big mouth shut? Now I've got more points on my licence because of you.

'Stupid bitch,' I hear him mutter under his breath.

I open my mouth to defend myself but I know there's no point. I don't have the emotional energy for an argument, and I know it will only make things worse. I'm already exhausted with all that's going on inside my head. But Kevin's not finished with me yet.

'You're constantly defying me and being in-subject to me,' he says, veering towards the central reservation. 'What sort of an example do you set for our children? If their mother doesn't obey me, how can I expect my children to obey me?'

We make the rest of the journey in silence. We are all deep in our own thoughts, gripping the door handles. I mutter a prayer in my head, pleading, 'Please get me through this day. Please give me the courage and strength to do what I need to do.' I've no idea who I'm praying to, but I hope that whoever hears it will answer me.

After the delay of getting pulled over by the police, we arrive at the meeting room very late. The gate is shut. I am praying that the main doors aren't shut as well. When you arrive at a Brethren meeting more than ten minutes late, the doors get locked by the 'gatekeeper', so you then need to ring a little bell that notifies him that someone is waiting outside. It's a shameful thing to have happen to you.

Oliver opens the gate and we drive into the full car park. We all jump out and run to the meeting room doors, hoping they won't be locked. Kevin tries the door, but it's locked. He glares at me again, as if it's all my fault. We press the bell and wait. We hug our coats around us in silence, doing our best to keep out the freezing January air. Eventually the door is opened, and we're allowed in.

Walking into the full hall I can feel the eyes of approximately three hundred Brethren on us, the full shameful force of it. I take a deep breath, lower my head and, clutching Juliet's hand in mine, I head for the seats that my sister Chloe has kept for us. Sitting down, taking a deep breath so I can look calm and in control, I open my handbag and take out my hymn book and Bible.

Chloe leans forward and whispers, 'Everything OK?'

'Fine,' I whisper with a weak smile.

I try to listen to what's being said in the meeting, but I feel nothing. The words that are being said mean nothing to me anymore. I long for the meeting to end. At last, I sing my final hymn and listen to that last prayer.

After the meeting I exchange a few words with Mum and my oldest sister, Deb. I keep my head down, avoiding any questions. I know that this will probably be the last time I am free to speak to my mother and my sisters face to face, but though I long to hug them, tell them I love them, that I will always be there for them, I know they mustn't suspect anything.

Leaving the noisy bustling foyer, I go and sit in our people carrier. I need to be alone. But the peace doesn't last long. After a few minutes, Kevin opens the door and climbs in the seat beside me. He seems to have forgotten this morning's drama.

'What on earth is the matter with you?' he says. 'You've hardly spoken two words to me since yesterday.'

I turn towards him. I look him straight in the eyes.

'Kevin,' I say, 'after today things will never be the same. I can't go into details right now but later today you will know the truth.'

I'm shaking but I'm thankful that I've given him some warning, relieved that my plan has begun, that now I can't go back. To my surprise, Kevin doesn't look shocked, just terribly sad. Maybe he knows me better than I realised. With tears in his eyes, he puts his hand on my leg and starts to plead.

'Please, Maria, don't leave me. I promise I'll change.'

I no longer believe that this man can change. My mind is made up. I push his hand away from me and stare blankly out of the window into the car park where the Brethren are milling about. I close my ears to his pleading. I take in the scene before me: the groups of young men laughing and joking; the young women in little clusters gossiping; the old men in deep conversations; the mothers and grandmothers with children in their arms and at their heels; the little boys and girls running around playing. Part of me is sad that I won't witness this scene ever again but another part of me is full of new hope.

Soon our children are clambering into their car seats. It's time for us to go for a meal at a young Brethren couple's home.

I like this couple, especially the young brother. Over the last few years he's become close friends with us. As I help pass food around, I'm nervous; doubts are still running through my head even now that I am right on the verge of leaving. Am I having a midlife crisis? Do I need psychiatric help? And what if when I get out into the world all I've been taught about the evil and wickedness out there turns out to be true? What if I can't fit in? What if I can't make friends? What if no one wants me? What if I *am* mad?

*No!* I tell myself. *Nothing can be worse than the life you're living now. Stay true. Focus.*

Lunch is tense and awkward. The children are still annoyed with their dad after the police incident. Kevin is ignoring all of us and especially me since our earlier conversation. As I've been doing for years, I work hard to smooth things over with light conversation. I smile and smile. I help in the kitchen. I chat away with the other Brethren sisters as we load the dishwasher. I pray that our hosts don't notice the tense, fractured family that we really are. When it's time to leave I thank our hosts and say goodbye, but I can't bring myself to look into their eyes.

Thinking about the confrontations to come, I feel a shiver of fear run through me as I get into our vehicle and we drive off. I am nearly there. The time has nearly come. It's a quiet hour-long journey home. The children settle to sleep as usual. With the early start and all the meetings to attend on a Sunday, they are always exhausted by this point in the day. I press my head against the back of the seat and pretend to sleep too, but so many thoughts and emotions are running through my mind that I fear I will never sleep again.

When we arrive home the children go for their usual freshen-up before we all have to head off for the last meeting of the day. I follow Kevin into our bedroom and shut the door. I watch him change into a clean white shirt as I sit myself down on our king-size bed.

'I'm not going,' I say, my voice cracking.

'You have to,' he says, understanding the import of my words, reaching for the usual Brethren platitudes. 'Whatever is happening in your heart and soul needs healing. You need to listen to the gospel. You need to accept Jesus as your saviour. He will sort all your problems and all our problems.'

'No,' I say, more calmly now. 'It's too late. I've been praying and hoping for years that things will change, with us, with you, with the Brethren and with myself, but all my prayers go unanswered. I can't go to this meeting. I won't.'

He quickly changes tack – devout Brethren brother to authoritarian husband. 'I'm insisting you go,' he says in his 'don't you dare argue with me' voice.

'No,' I say again. 'I'm not going. I won't have you decide anymore what I can and can't do in my life.'

Have I really said those words out loud? I wait for Kevin to roar in anger, throw something, bring his fist down on something, but instead, he just turns away with a look of defeat. For the first time, he seems to realise that I mean every word that I've said.

A few minutes later I hear the front door close. Kevin and the children have gone to the meeting. I am alone. I lie down on the bed and close my eyes. My mind is a whir of doubts.

I remember the waves crashing against the end of the pier. I remind myself that I've chosen life *not* death and that means standing up against everything I've ever known. I am about to step into the unknown – I may lose everything and everyone I care about. But even though I know I'm going to break the hearts of everyone I love, I feel a strength and a power beyond myself take over me.

*You can do this. You will do this.*

I get off the bed and stand tall, holding my head high. I walk to the kitchen and make myself a strong cup of tea.

I sit and wait.

I hear a key turn in the front door lock. This is it. Now it is time. As Kevin enters the kitchen, alone, ahead of the children, I can see he's exhausted too. His eyes are red; he looks like he's been crying. He lurches towards me, trying to put his arms around me to effect some kind of reconciliation, but I turn away and walk back towards the bedroom. He closes the door behind us as he comes towards me again, clumsily fumbling for me, but I push him away.

'Don't touch me,' I say, my voice firm and clear. 'Our marriage is over. I don't want you near me ever again.'

Kevin begins to plead again: 'Please, Maria, don't leave me. You can't leave me. The Brethren won't allow it. I can't live without you. I'll change, I promise. I love you. I'll do anything to make you happy.'

It all feels very simple now. I shake my head.

'No, Kevin,' I say. 'I've heard all this before. This time I'm done for good. Not only am I finished with this marriage, I'm also finished with the Brethren. I'm never going to another meeting and I'm going to live my life outside. You will no longer dictate what I can and can't do. The Brethren will no longer dictate what I can and can't do.'

This time he steps back in shock. His complexion turns pure white.

'Done with the Brethren?' He can hardly breathe. 'You can't . . .' Silence stretches between us. 'Where will you go?' he asks.

'I'm going nowhere,' I say. 'I'm staying right here in this house. I won't walk away from our children. I will never do that. I've no idea how this is all going to work out, but our children are staying with me.'

Now I have my voice. Now I have my power. I fear no one's opinion or judgement. It's a heady feeling. I'm finished with the Brethren. They can say what they want but from this moment on I'm not one of them.

Kevin leaves the bedroom. I can hear him talking to the children. I can hear him telling them that their mum isn't feeling well and needs to rest for a bit. He comes back into the bedroom.

'Not well?' I say. 'I'm saner than I've ever been. Don't you dare tell the children I'm sick! Very soon I'm going to tell each of them exactly how I feel and what I'm doing and why.'

But I can already feel the doubt creeping in again. *Am* I ill? *Am* I going crazy? But I hear another voice too: *it's time to be honest with your children. You owe them your honesty. You'll be no use as a mother if you give up and choose to continue a living death rather than life and freedom. At least if you find a way to live a different life it gives us all some hope. Some hope of a relationship. Some hope of understanding and reconciliation.*

Kevin locks himself in the bathroom. The wails begin. Over the years I've learnt to cope with his collapses by just leaving him to it. Tonight, his wailing echoes through our small chalet cottage. I know the children can hear it, that they are listening. Soon they'll want to know what's going on.

Time is running out.

Things are coming to a head.

I step out into the hallway. Oliver appears at his bedroom door, his face ashen.

'Is everything OK?'

'No, Ollie, it's not OK,' I say. 'Can we talk?'

He looks at me in a puzzled way but nods. I follow him into his room and close the door. We both sit down together on his double bed. He props himself up against the pillows while I sit on the edge of his bed, facing him. Then, for the second time that evening, I say those shattering words.

'Ollie, I know how much this is going to hurt you, but I'm finished with your dad and with the Brethren.'

I watch the colour drain from his face. He looks ill. He leaps from the bed. He paces his room. He shakes his head in disbelief. My eyes follow his every move. My heart goes out to him, yet in saying these words for a second time, I can feel more of the weight lift. Eventually, he finds his voice.

'No, Mum, there must be another way. You can't do this. I know you and Dad aren't happy, but leaving the Brethren? No, you can't do that. You can't.' Tears are streaming down his face. He is shaking. His voice rises to an almost hysterical pitch.

'No! Please, Mum! Think about what you are doing! If you turn your back on the Brethren, you turn your back on God! You're turning your back on not just the Brethren but *all* of us! We are the Brethren! How can you do this to us?'

He throws himself down on his bed, sobbing. I'm crying now too, but I know I must be strong. I kneel on the floor next to his bed and put my arm around him.

'Ollie, I *must* do this. I can't carry on living a lie. There's so much within the Brethren and with your dad that just isn't right. I can't go on with it any longer. Please try to understand. I will never turn my back on you or your brothers and sister. I am not going to walk out our front door and leave any of you, but I am never going to a Brethren meeting again. I can't live with your dad again. Please try to understand.'

Oliver lifts his head to look at me with a sad, tear-stained face.

'Mum, promise me just one thing. Promise me you will talk to a responsible brother before you do this. Promise.'

'Son,' I say, 'my mind is made up, but I promise that I will talk to someone tomorrow, if that will make you feel any better.'

Oliver eases himself out of my arms and leaves the room. Have I lost my eldest son already, so easily? If telling Ollie has been so difficult, then how am I going to tell the rest of my children? I begin to panic; I need to get out of the house, but where can I go? I know no one outside the Brethren and, if I leave, will the front door already be locked against me when I get back?

When I go back into our bedroom, Kevin is lying still and silent on the bed.

'I'm going to take a drive,' I tell him. 'I need to get out of the house for a bit.' He sits up. His eyes are hollow.

'Where are you going?' he says. 'I should come with you.'

'No,' I say. 'You don't need to come with me. I'll be fine. I promise I'm not going to come to any harm, but I just need space away from here for a bit.'

For a bit? I can see hope in his eyes at my words. It frightens me.

I start up the engine of our people carrier and ease down the gravel drive. I've no idea where I'm going but I know that I must get away. All I can see is the heartbreak and judgement in Oliver's eyes. I'm not ready to face my other children. I can hardly see where I'm going for the tears.

It's a cold and dark January night. Soon I am driving past our old house. Why am I here? I see the lights on in our worldly ex-neighbour's house, the glow from their sitting room. I park on their drive. I cut the engine.

Barry and Ashlyn Fitzpatrick and their four children were the best 'worldly' neighbours that any Brethren could wish to have. They must have thought us so strange when we lived next door to them, but in those six years they always did their best to befriend us and to ignore our odd behaviour. Sometimes, when Ashlyn and I were hanging the washing out, we'd chat over the fence, so long as I knew no one could see us. Sometimes, when Kevin was away, our children would climb the fence and go and play in each other's gardens. Since we had moved away two years ago, I'd had no contact with them, yet here I was standing on their doorstep, my whole world falling apart.

I ring the doorbell. Ashlyn answers, apron on, TV remote in hand. I don't even give her a chance to speak before I blurt out in a hysterical voice:

'Ashlyn, I've left Kevin and the Brethren. I've no idea what I'm doing.'

She puts her arm around my shoulders and leads me gently into her home. She sits me down on the soft cream leather settee in her sitting room. She turns the television off, sends the children to their snug, where they can finish watching their programme. Their house smells of Sunday roast and wood smoke. I'm shaking. I'm struggling to breathe. Am I going mad again?

'Right,' Ashlyn says. 'I'm going to make you a hot, sweet cup of tea and when you're feeling a bit better you can tell me everything.'

While Ashlyn disappears to the kitchen to make tea, I look around me. What am I doing in this 'worldly' person's house? I shouldn't be here. There are TV sets and radios everywhere. Ashlyn sets a steaming cup on a side table next to me.

'Barry is away on business tonight. The children won't bother us. Take your time. Tell me.'

It all comes tumbling out. I tell Ashlyn about this evening. I tell her I've told both Kevin and Oliver that I'm leaving. 'I'm done with Kevin,' I say again. 'I'm done with the Brethren.'

It feels good to say those words. *Done with. Done with.* And then I wonder what I mean when I say I am done. What life could there ever be for me outside the Brethren? How will I ever be *done*?

'Maria,' she says, 'I don't think you were ever meant for a Brethren life. You're too much of a free spirit. You need a *real* life; a life where your husband doesn't control you; a life away from that cruel religion. I've watched you over the years. I've listened to how Kevin talks to you. No woman should have to put up with that. You've put up with it all for far too long.' Squeezing my hand, she goes on: 'Don't feel guilty. Your children love you, that's clear to everyone. They won't abandon you now. Trust them. See it through.'

I thank her, but her words make me feel lonelier than ever. She can't understand. She doesn't know how it is inside the Brethren. She doesn't understand that no matter how much my children love me, I felt that in time they would be turned against me. Unless you've lived a Brethren life, you can't understand how it all works. Finishing my tea, I wipe the last of my tears away and give Ashlyn a weak smile.

'Thank you,' I say, feigning relief. 'I don't know what led me to your door tonight, but you have given me fresh hope and fresh strength to go on. Thank you so much. I must go back home now and face what I must face and leave you in peace.'

We hug. She holds onto me. It's the first time anyone outside the Brethren has embraced me in such a loving way, and it feels good. On the threshold, I turn and thank Ashlyn again. She leans towards me and kisses me on my cheek before whispering in my ear, 'Anytime. I'm here if you need me. I'll be thinking of you.'

Once I'm back in the car, I look at my phone. There are ten missed calls from Kevin. He's in panic mode. I'm worried for the children. I take the five-minute drive back home.

Inside the house I meet a wall of noise: doors are slamming, children are crying. What have I done? Kevin, hearing the car, meets me at the door, tries to put his arms around me, but I push him aside to face the chaos.

'I've told them,' he says. 'They are all going crazy. Please, Maria, just think of your children. You can't do this to them. You know you can't.'

In the sitting room Kyle is on the settee, his head in his hands, sobbing. Juliet is there next to him, looking pale and confused. Aaron comes running down the spiral staircase. He almost knocks me over in his relief and panic. He puts his arms around my waist and I hold him tight. Even at eleven years old, he's still my baby. I drink in the smell of his hair. I have no words. What can I say? This is not how it was supposed to go.

Oliver comes out of his bedroom into the hallway. His complexion is grey, and his eyes are red from crying. I can hardly bear to look at him. Then Bradley comes out of the bedroom next door with Lincoln at his side and roars at me.

'What do you think you are doing, Mum? Who do you think you are to question God? God put you with the Brethren. It's not your choice to decide differently! Shame on you.'

I'm taken aback. Bradley is my son, but he is also my friend, the one who has always tried to push the most boundaries. Of all my children I thought he would be the one to understand, yet here he is bellowing at me. When I try to step towards him, try to talk to him, he retreats to his bedroom and slams the door. Now, following their brother's lead, Lincoln and Aaron step away from me and go back upstairs. Kyle and Juliet both get up from the settee and walk straight past me into their bedrooms. Oliver and Kevin follow them upstairs.

Doors slam.

Doors close.

I am alone.

# TWENTY-ONE

The next day, arguably one of the most significant – the first day of my new life – is actually rather blurred in my mind. There's much of that first day, and the days that followed, that I can't remember at all. The trauma of that time has caused blanks in my memory. Did I even eat in those first few days? Did I take the children to school? Did I do the daily housework? What remains in my memory however, like little islands in a fog, are the first conversations I had with my brother Edward and my mother.

Sometime during the first day, with the mood in the kitchen before everyone left for work or school inevitably dark, the children tight-lipped and pale, I remembered the promise I had made to Oliver to speak to a 'responsible' leader. I had made a promise. I was going to keep it. The first person that came to mind was Edward. Although he was only five years older than me, he was now one of our local leaders. As a leader he was known to be fair and kind, and I was hopeful that he would listen to me without judgement or anger. In a way it would have been easier if I could have talked to someone outside of my family, but as is common among the Brethren, many of us are related to each other. I knew it would be one of the most difficult conversations he and I had ever had, but it had to be done.

Once the house is empty, the breakfast ordeal over, I sigh with relief and sink down into the brown leather corner settee in our lounge. Above me on the wall hang the mandatory photographs of the seven Men of God, from

James Darby, the founder of the Exclusive Brethren movement in the 1830s through to Bruce Hales, the current leader of the Plymouth Brethren Christian Church based in Australia.

Under the close scrutiny of all these men, I take my Brethren-approved mobile out of my denim skirt pocket and dial Edward's number. The eyes of the leaders, stern and judgemental, seem to follow me around the room. I turn my back on them and climb the stairs to take refuge in Juliet's bedroom just as Edward answers my call.

'Hello? Is everything OK?'

'Edward,' I say, my breath shallow, 'I need to talk to you urgently.'

'Are you sick?' he asks in a worried tone.

'No, I'm not sick but . . .'

'Go on . . .'

'I need to end my marriage to Kevin,' I blurt out, knowing how impossible it sounds. Brethren don't divorce; Brethren wives rarely leave their husbands because they are not allowed to. I take another breath now for the next part: 'And, Edward,' I say, 'I am going to leave the Brethren.'

*There*, I think, *it's done with.* I've said it. I can't go back now. I've taken another major step. There's no way back – I just have to weather the storm. I brace myself.

'Wow, wow!' Edward says, his voice high-pitched with shock. 'Now, hang on a minute. I'm sure that's not really what you want to do. I know things aren't great between you and Kevin but I'm sure we can find a solution without being so drastic.'

Drastic? Is he accusing me of over-reacting? Does he really think this is another of my 'turns'?

I go on, keeping my nerve, remembering to take one step at a time. 'No,' I say. 'My mind is made up. I've had enough. I'm done.'

*I'm done.*

*I'm done.*

*I'm done.*

I have heard myself say those words so many times in the last twenty-four hours that I'm beginning to sound like a recording. But each time I say them I feel stronger. How many more times am I going to have to say those final words?

*I'm done.*

Edward hesitates, clears his throat.

'OK,' he says, slowing his words right down, reasoning with me as though I'm an overtired child having a tantrum. 'Calm down and listen. I'm going to get in my car right away and come to see you. You can tell me everything and then you'll feel a lot better.'

At first I'm surprised that he would leave work and travel an hour to talk with me, that he is taking my words seriously. But then I remember that he has to try and save me from the outside world. It's his job. That's what leading brothers are supposed to do. I need to talk to him in his pastoral role – I promised Ollie – but I also long to talk to my brother Edward. When he arrives, will he be Edward the Brethren leader and preach to me? Or will he be my brother Edward and listen and understand? I need him to understand and to let me go.

While I wait for him to arrive, I go into the children's bedrooms, looking for somewhere to wait that feels safe. The boys' bedrooms smell musty with boys' smells; Juliet's bedroom smells of perfumes and candles. I can't bear it. The smells of my individual children – three grown into young men, three still children, all of them finding their way – remind me of how I'm breaking each of their hearts and how much I will lose if everything goes wrong.

When I go back into the lounge, the Men of God in those photographs are still staring down at me. I can't stay there either. I retreat to my bedroom but there's Kevin's aftershave on the dressing table, and Kevin's discarded clothes from yesterday on the floor. I try the bathroom. I lock the door. My heart is racing, and my body is in a sweat.

At last, the doorbell rings. When I answer it, to my surprise, Edward, all six feet of him, puts his great arms out and hugs me. I smell his freshly pressed and laundered shirt as he holds me tight. Edward has never hugged me before. Why would he do that now? I feel myself hug him back. We stand on the doorstep like that for what seems like forever.

'It's such a beautiful day today,' Edward says at last, drawing away. 'Why don't I drive you to Holmbrook Beach? We can take a nice walk by the sea and have a chat?'

A walk on the beach? Edward wants to walk on the beach? We've never walked together before. He should be admonishing me. He should be telling me I'm a sinner. Is he going to help me instead? I grab my coat, a warm hat and gloves. I follow him to his car, hope rising.

We drive the ten miles to Holmbrook in silence. I watch the green fields race past as we drive along the familiar country roads towards the coast. It *is* a beautiful day. Edward's calmness has relaxed me. It gives me confidence that I might be able to tell him everything, explain everything. As we pull up to the kerb, I glance at my brother out of the corner of my eye and wonder what is going through his mind. I feel for him. I know that this decision of mine will be causing him the biggest stress he has ever had – or will ever have – to deal with as a Brethren leader, and for that I'm sorry. I am not just a wayward Brethren woman, I am his sister. Edward knows he is in a very difficult position. There is a great deal at stake for him. He can't get this wrong.

Edward and I get out of the car and walk side by side down onto the golden sand. Apart from a couple of dog walkers, we are alone. The sun is low in the clear blue January sky. A biting wind is blowing off the sea. We tug our hats down and pull on our gloves.

'OK,' Edward says, 'now just talk, walk and tell me exactly what's going on.'

Where do I start? As I begin to talk, it feels like a dam has opened. Everything comes pouring out. I tell him how for years Kevin has physically hurt the children, thumping them, kicking them, lashing out at them for no reason. I tell him about how I've watched him put Kyle through a partition wall. Then I tell him about how Kevin has raped me. How he's twisted my arm until I'm bruised, how every day he treats me as if I'm dirt, how for the decades of our marriage he has demanded sex – aggressive, bruising, loveless sex – sometimes up to three times a day, as soon as he sees me when he gets home from work, in the bedroom or kitchen, and how there has never been any love in his sexual attentions, only lust. I tell my brother that I don't love this man and don't know if I ever loved him. '*This man*,' I hear myself say as I go on, trying to catch my breath. *This man* – because I can no longer bring myself now to give him a name – '*This man* disgusts me, and I want no more to do with him. I've had enough of his bullying, and I've had enough of this loveless marriage.' I tell my brother how I long to feel the arms of a loving man around me. How I long for love.

My words are raw. I'm not softening anything. I can see Edward wince at some of my words, but he needs to know. He *has* to know.

For the second time today, I feel Edward's arm around me as we walk. Turning, he looks at me and, with tears in his eyes, he says, 'I had no idea things were so bad. I'm so sorry you've had to go through all that.' Then he says, 'Now tell me why you think leaving the Brethren is the answer to your problems.'

As we walk with the cold biting wind blowing in our faces, I feel my pace quicken at his question. I am ready for this. I have fire in my belly. I feel all my pent-up anger and frustration come flowing out. I tell Edward how I think the rule of 'separation from evil' is wrong. How I've witnessed so much hypocrisy within the Brethren; so much cruelty and bullying. I throw questions at him: why haven't I got a choice? Why can't we eat and drink with people outside our fellowship? Why must I be subject and submissive to my husband? How, I ask, can any of this be *right*? I talk about the inconsistencies within the Brethren, the crazy rules we are told to live under, the idea that the Brethren are God's chosen people and they will have a special place in Heaven. I don't go so far as to tell him that I even question the very existence of God. I'm not ready yet to admit *that* thought. If I admit that out loud, I fear that God Himself will instantly bring some punishment down on me.

Finally, I stop talking, stop walking, and turn to look at my brother. He must be angry with me now. But to my surprise I don't see anger in his eyes – only understanding and empathy. Does this important brother of mine have doubts too? Does he see the wrong that I see too?

'Let's walk back to the car,' he says.

As he turns and walks away in silence across the sand towards the car park, I run to keep up with him. When he finally speaks, his voice is calm, but I can sense him starting to prepare the speech that is expected of him as a leading brother, not as *my* brother.

'Maria,' he says, and my heart breaks as I hear the familiar Brethren phrases gather in his words, 'thank you for opening your heart to me. It's always good to get things out in the open and off our chests. I hear what you have to say and wish that I could give you the answers that you want, but I'm not here to answer your questions. I'm here to help your eternal soul. I want to help you dispel the doubts about the Brethren. What you are proposing to do will be disastrous not only for yourself but for your children and all of us. Please reconsider. You must reconsider.'

I hesitate before I answer him. My heart is breaking, seeing him in contortions like this, torn between his loyalty to the Brethren and his role as a sympathetic brother. But I know I must leave my emotions behind and stay strong. I take a deep breath. I choose my words carefully. Looking straight into those dark brown eyes of his, I say:

'Edward, thank you for listening to me and showing some understanding of what I have suffered, but my mind is made up. I can't go back to the life I've been living. I can't live a lie, pretending that I'm a good Brethren sister when underneath it all I've lost all trust in my marriage and in the Brethren system. I'm so sorry but it's over. It's time for me to move forward and not back.'

The light seems to go out of his eyes. I see tears. This time when he speaks his expression is one of defeat, disappointment and sadness.

'Is it OK,' he says, his voice breaking up as he struggles to keep talking as he is supposed to, 'is it OK if I come and see you again with our uncle, Cuthbert?'

'Sure,' I reply, 'but please don't put pressure on me to change my mind. I won't change my mind. I'm done.'

He manages to muster up a smile.

I know that this is just the start of the many conversations I will need to have with the Brethren over the coming weeks and months. If I'd fled during the night as others have, I wouldn't have had to go through these agonies, but I've chosen to stay put in our house so that I can keep my children with me. I will have to defend my ground – for me and for them. I hope I will have the strength to keep firm. But this first interview with Edward has given me the confidence to go on.

Edward and I drive back to Wellfleet in silence. I'm bracing myself now for the conversation I will need to have with my parents at some point later that day. That conversation is going to be the hardest of all. I don't feel ready to tell them face to face. I'm scared that I will crumble when I see their pain and tears and shame. As Edward drives along those winding country roads towards home, I decide that I will tell my parents of my decision with a phone call. It will be a start.

When Edward drops me at my front door, he tells me he will phone later with a time for him to come back with my uncle. I thank him again for his understanding. It is so much more than I could have hoped for. I have seen my brother in a new light, glimpsed tiny cracks in his certainties. Maybe a part of him is on my side after all. As I put my key in the front door, I hear Edward call my name. I turn around and see him leaning out of his car window as he says, 'Please don't do anything you will regret.'

Later that day, before collecting Lincoln, Juliet and Aaron from school, I make the dreaded phone call to Mum. With shaking hands, I punch her number into my mobile. She answers on the first ring.

'You didn't come for breakfast today,' she says, concern in her voice. Almost every morning since we moved to Wellfleet from the South, I have had breakfast at Mum and Dad's. But today I hadn't been able to go.

'Mum,' I say. 'I need to tell you something. It feels unfair to tell you over the phone, but I can't face you right now.'

'Are you ill?' she asks, her voice tight. Am I ill? How many times have I asked myself that question over the last week?

'No, I'm not ill, Mum,' I say, 'but I've made a huge decision that is going to change all our lives. I can't carry on living this life. If I do, I fear I will do myself some harm and never recover.' I'm back at the end of the pier, looking down into that cold dark water. I hear a slight gasp at the end of the phone as I go on. 'I told Kevin and the children last night that the marriage is over.'

'You did?'

'But not only that,' I say, my voice trembling. 'I'm leaving the Brethren.'

It feels like forever before she responds. I can hear her irregular breathing down the phone, and then she says something unexpected: 'Maria, if my husband had treated me like Kevin has treated you, I would be doing the same thing.'

Is Mum giving her blessing to my decision? It takes me a few seconds to gather my thoughts and reply.

'So, you're not angry with me?' I ask in surprise. 'You don't think I've gone crazy?' There's a long pause before she answers me.

'Maria, I'm not mad at you but I *am* concerned that maybe you're not well in your mind. You know you can't leave the Brethren. You know that's not a choice. God put you here. Come and live with us for a while and we'll get you well again and work through your marriage problems.'

I can understand Mum thinking I'm not well in my mind. After all, over the last year I have been prescribed the highest dose of antidepressants a person is allowed. Everyone will assume that I've gone crazy, but I feel in complete control of my thoughts and decisions. I need her to know that.

'No, Mum,' I say, 'I'm honestly not ill. I need to do this, and I mean what I say. I've spoken to Edward, and I've told him that my mind is made up.'

'Oh, I'm so glad to hear that,' she says. 'Edward will know what to do and how to help you. Then you can come and have a chat with Dad and me. We'll work this all out and everything will be fine.'

I remind myself that Mum is in turmoil too. She doesn't want me to leave, and yet part of her understands why I *need* to do so. The loving mother in her is at war with the good Brethren sister. She is as torn as I am. As I say goodbye, I promise to call and see both Dad and her later that day. But I know I will hold Mum's first reaction in my heart forever.

I can still hear her words: 'Maria, if my husband had treated me like Kevin has treated you, I would be doing the same thing.'

# TWENTY-TWO

As I awake on the second day of my new life, I feel a fresh sense of optimism. For two nights Kevin has been sleeping on a mattress on Aaron's bedroom floor, so I wake alone. I lie listening to the first of the morning birdsong, smiling at the thought of being free as a bird. As I roll over in our king-size bed it feels strange but good to be alone.

Now that I have told Edward and my parents of my decision, more of that weight has lifted from my shoulders. My burden is getting lighter every day with each new challenge and with each new dreaded conversation.

Today I am going to take my first steps into the outside world. Today I'm going to get rid of my Brethren clothes. I open my wardrobe door and look at the sea of long skirts and high-neck tops. I've always gone as close to the world as possible by wearing bright colours, smart shoes and matching handbags, despite the disapproving looks from the older Brethren sisters, but I've never worn a low top, or jewellery, or makeup, or a skirt above my knees. That would have got me into terrible trouble with both my husband and the elders. Before I married, Dad had to approve all my clothes. After I married, Kevin had always been the judge. Whenever I bought a new coat or a new skirt or top, I always had to be sure I could get a refund in case it didn't pass Kevin's approval.

This morning, as I run my hands along the clothes hanging in my wardrobe, feeling the ugly, frumpy material against my fingers, I want to pull out every last item and burn it. I can't wait to be rid of it all and wear exactly what

189

I want. Pulling out a long denim skirt and top, I tell myself that this is the last time I will wear these horrible clothes.

As soon as I've dropped Juliet, Lincoln and Aaron off at the Brethren school, I make my way to the shopping centre. I'm excited. I'm going to buy a pair of jeans. I've never been allowed to wear trousers. Perhaps I'll buy four pairs. Who's going to stop me?!

I remember a day when it had snowed a few years earlier. Kevin was away at work, so I had taken the children sledging. Somehow, in all the excitement and sense of holiday, I had managed to pull on a pair of Bradley's jeans, telling the children I couldn't go sledging in a skirt. None of my children had told me to take them off, perhaps because they didn't think we'd be seen or because they were too young to understand the punishments that would follow. I remember the feeling of denim against my skin, the freedom to stride and run.

As I make my way into the shopping mall, I think of the pictures of worldly women I've seen in magazines, the women in the supermarket who I've stared at, wearing ordinary but stylish, worldly clothes, well-cut clothes that they've chosen themselves, clothes that express who they are.

I run my hands along the endless rails of jeans in every shade of blue, feeling the texture of the denim against my fingers. I pick out a pair of boot-cut jeans and a navy scoop-neck top and make my way towards the changing rooms. A royal-blue leather jacket catches my eye. I grab that off the rail too. I find myself looking behind me to check there are no Brethren watching me, then smile when I remember that I don't need to do that anymore.

I slip off my dowdy denim skirt, tights and high-neck jumper. I tug on the jeans, pulling up the unfamiliar zip, relishing the feel of the material against my thighs and hips. I slip the top over my head and glance in the mirror. I notice my cleavage showing just above the neckline, the fine contours of my chest. I pull on the blue jacket, admiring the contrasting colours. Out in the communal changing room area, I can't help the gasp that escapes me in front of the mirror. I look good; I feel good. This is me; this is who I am.

But my face is still pale and tired, my hair frumpy and long. Once I have some makeup on my face, my hair cut and styled, then I won't stand out – I will look like a normal woman. I'll no longer be stared at or sniggered at. No one will shout 'hanky head' at me ever again. I'm surprised at how easy it is to transform myself from the dowdy old woman I see in the mirror every day to a woman of the world.

I spend the next five minutes admiring myself in the full-length mirror, looking at my image from every direction. For the first time I notice my long legs and I feel proud of them. I notice my full breasts with my attractive cleavage and feel proud of that too.

The sales assistant appears behind the curtain and asks if I need any help. I ask her what shoes she thinks would go with what I'm wearing. She comes back with boxes of boots and shoes, but one pair stands out for me: a pair of suede cowboy-style ankle boots. They seem to fit with the boot-cut jeans. I strut up and down the changing room area like a peacock. I'm sure that the sales assistant must think I'm crazy, but I don't care.

'Can I keep these clothes on?' I say. 'I mean, once I've bought them?'

She gives me an odd look and then smiles.

'Sure, that's no problem. Let me get some scissors and I'll cut the labels off.'

She brings me a carrier bag for my old clothes. If there had been a bonfire nearby, I would have thrown the bag and all the clothes straight onto it and watched them burn. Instead, I'm going to drop them into the nearest bin.

I'm having a reckless spending spree, but I don't care. Kevin is the wage earner, but for now, I don't care that the money is from our joint bank account. After all, it was my business that brought us back from the brink of bankruptcy and I never got to spend a penny of it. Now that I'm out in the world I'm like a child with her hand in the sweet jar, grabbing everything with both hands before it's taken away from me.

I'm not done yet. I notice the jewellery stand. The only jewellery I've ever been allowed to wear is my wedding ring. I gaze at the different styles of necklaces, bracelets, rings and earrings, then pick out a chunky silver and blue necklace with a matching bracelet. The blue is the same colour as my new jacket.

As I go to pay for everything, I ask the sales assistant if she'd mind taking the necklace out of its packaging so that I can put it on. She beckons me to a mirror and lifts the heavy necklace around my neck. I look at my reflection for the umpteenth time that morning and gasp.

'Thank you,' I say, breathlessly, with that huge grin still plastered across my face.

'My pleasure. You look amazing,' she replies. 'Special occasion?'

I smile shyly, unsure what to say. It *is* a special occasion but there's nothing I can say that will even begin to explain. As I complete my purchase, I thank her for her help.

My next stop is Debenhams to buy some makeup. Over the years I've found a way of occasionally wearing a very light foundation without anyone noticing, but I would never have dared buy my foundation in a public store for fear of being seen by a Brethren member. I'd always bought it in a little 'out of the way' chemists, yet here I am now dressed in jeans, wearing jewellery and boldly walking towards the Elizabeth Arden makeup counter for all to see.

But when I stand in front of the counters, I don't know what to buy. I don't even know what to ask for. Shyly, I approach a beautifully made-up sales assistant of a similar age to me.

'Excuse me,' I say, 'I wonder if you can help me to choose some makeup?'

'Of course,' she says. 'Have you worn the Elizabeth Arden range before?'

'I've, well,' I stumble, 'I've hardly ever worn makeup.'

She looks taken aback. I blush. This is awkward. 'Well, you see,' I blurt out, 'the thing is, I have just left a very strict religion. We weren't allowed to wear makeup. I really want to try some, but I don't know what to buy or what will suit me.'

There, I'd said it. Again I watch a look of shock pass over the assistant's face. She glances around. I can't tell whether I've impressed her or if she thinks I'm mad.

'Wow,' she says. Just wow. And then she beckons me towards a high chair right in plain view of everyone.

'My name's Liz,' she says, rubbing her hands with enthusiasm. 'How much time do you have? There's so much to show you. You've got such a lovely complexion, it just needs a little . . .' And then she's talking away about primers and foundations and cheekbone structures, opening drawers to pull out shiny packets of lipsticks.

I'm glancing over my shoulder again. What would the Brethren say if they saw me now? I think of Mrs Arnold who always tutted if she saw any of us even wearing a brooch, or David Johnston who had called trousers on women an abomination of Satan, and old man Robinson who would shake his head in disgust if he saw a woman showing too much leg.

*You're not one of them anymore*, I tell myself sternly as Liz busies herself finding the right products for my skin and starts to explain the different brushes and what they are all for. I drink in the warm scent of her perfume as she busies herself around me, her fingers on my face, plucking, smoothing, patting.

At last, she hands me a mirror. I look at my smooth skin, the accentuation of my eyes, the soft blush on my cheeks, the curve of my lips. I gasp again. I look so much younger.

Liz laughs at my expression. 'Well, do you like it?'

'Like it? I love it!' I exclaim.

I buy every product Liz has used, including all the correct brushes. She packs all the boxes into a carrier bag, tucks in some free samples and tells me I can come back anytime for more tips and techniques. I thank her again, tears in my eyes.

Now I need a mobile phone. My Brethren mobile isn't safe for me to use anymore. I've only ever been allowed to purchase a mobile phone from the Brethren business hub, the Universal Business Team (UBT).

I now want an Apple iPhone. Someone told me that Bruce Hales had said that Steve Jobs was 'of the Devil'. Many people are supposed to be 'of the Devil' – Charles Darwin, Elvis, Elton John and even the Beatles. But Steve Jobs, they always said, was *particularly* 'of the Devil'. The mark of the apple,

I had heard elders say, was the proof. I guessed they meant that Satan had persuaded Eve to eat the forbidden apple, so that apple on the phones and computers and laptops must have been a sure sign of Satan's work out in Satan's world.

Over the years, under the direction of so many different Men of God, we've been taught many strange beliefs about computers, the internet, phones, radio and television. Using the scripture from the Bible, where it says, 'Satan is the Prince of the Power of the Air', the Men of God have insisted this means that Satan is in charge of the internet, the radio and television, even though whoever wrote those lines all those centuries ago couldn't have conceived of soundwaves or the telephone, let alone the internet or smart TV.

In 2008, Bruce Hales had received new light about computers and mobile phones. The world recession was putting a great deal of pressure on Brethren businesses to compete. They couldn't afford any longer not to have computers and email. Bruce Hales received new light that even though Satan was still Prince of the Power of the Air, Brethren were now allowed to use special mobile phones and special computers just so long as they bought them from UBT. UBT made sure that all these new Brethren computers were adapted so that there was limited internet access. Now if a business or an individual wanted to access a website that wasn't on the approved list, they had to apply to UBT for permission.

We were lucky. Bradley knew how to unlock the restrictions on our home computer, so we were able to access anything we wanted. This had to be kept a strict secret within our house. Kevin allowed this to go on despite the risk of being punished. I wonder if that was because it meant he'd then been able to secretly watch porn.

Having access to the internet unsupervised had been a great blessing for me. When the house was empty I had watched documentaries and read other people's stories about cutting loose from strict religious sects. If you'd been able to peek through our tightly closed curtains on a Sunday evening you would have seen me and my children – and sometimes even Kevin – huddled around the computer screen watching YouTube videos, the curtains pulled tightly. Over the last couple of years we'd watched all of *Fawlty Towers*, *Mr Bean* and *Britain's Got Talent*. I had often wondered if most other Brethren families were doing exactly the same, swearing each other to secrecy and living in fear of being found out or denounced behind their closely drawn curtains.

Today I am Eve from the Bible, reaching up for that apple. She knew the punishment would come, but until it did, she was going to carry on reaching. I am testing God to see what punishment I will receive for being rebellious and disobedient. Will I be punished for tasting all this forbidden worldly fruit? I had asked God to show me a sign if He wanted me to stay in the Brethren. He hadn't stopped me from leaving but might He have been testing me? How far will I need to go before He strikes?

An hour later I emerge from Carphone Warehouse with the latest iPhone tucked in the back pocket of my new jeans.

Later that afternoon, I pick Juliet, Lincoln and Aaron up from school in the car. When they spot my new clothes, I see the three of them gape and then wince, but they say nothing. I leave my new phone on the passenger seat for them to see. Juliet picks it up and places it in the glove compartment out of sight.

When the older boys come home from work later, they each look me up and down, taking in my dramatic new clothes and makeup. Oliver looks at me sadly then takes himself off into his bedroom. Bradley sneers, 'Mum, do you realise how pathetic you look?' then also takes himself into his bedroom, slamming the door behind him. Lincoln has maintained the countenance of a surly teenager all week and has declined to comment. Kyle looks me up and down with an expression of pity then follows his brothers.

Is this how it's going to be? Are they all going to lock themselves in their rooms rather than face me? I know I'm hurting them with my actions, but I can't hide the feeling of freedom, liberation and confidence that my new clothes are giving me. I have been controlled for too long. Now it is time to be me. This way, so long as I am wearing these clothes, there is no going back. I take a deep breath.

———

That evening, I receive a visit from Edward and Uncle Cuthbert. They have been assigned as my priests. It will be their job to get me to change my mind and, if they fail, they will have to decide how to deal with me. They could choose to 'shut me up' but, because I have *chosen* to leave, I'm not looking for God's forgiveness so shutting me up would be pointless. They could choose to 'withdraw' from me, but I know they are unlikely to do this yet because they want me to return. The stakes are high. If they either shut me up or withdraw from me too early, they could get 'shut up' themselves. They will be keen to stick to the long-established Brethren rules about how to handle troublemakers. I know how this goes.

First, they have a conversation with Kevin and then they call me into the lounge. They both look up in shock as I walk into the room wearing jeans, makeup and jewellery. And in that moment, I enjoy seeing their reaction. I relish it. I am filled with a rebellious pride and in a way I *want* them to shut me up or even withdraw from me. Then I'll be *really* free, and they'll stop trying to get me back. But within seconds, reality hits – if they do that, they'll take my children away and I can't let that happen. I need to walk a tightrope, call their bluff, bide my time. Once Kevin has gone, and I hope they'll move him out sooner or later, then I'll have a chance to persuade the children to leave with me too.

Cuthbert looks embarrassed as he clears his throat and says, 'We feel it might be a good idea if Kevin moves out for now to give you some space. How do you feel about that?'

I can hardly believe my ears. This is exactly what I have hoped for. Once I have Kevin out of the house I will be free. The children can go on living with me and I'll be free to live my life exactly how I want.

'That will definitely help,' I say, doing my best to hide my delight.

'Good,' Edward says. 'Maybe time alone with the children will help you to think about what you are doing. We are praying that you will reconsider.'

I say nothing. Instead I smile politely. The less I say, the better. As I say goodbye to them at the door, I can hear Kevin in our bedroom emptying his wardrobe and gathering his belongings together. I ask him if he'd like some help, but he just turns his back on me. He hasn't said a word to me for two days.

Two hours later he is gone, and I am alone with our six children.

# TWENTY-THREE

It's 7 a.m. I can hear my older children getting up for work. Showers are running, doors are opening and closing, and there's a clattering of breakfast dishes. I lie staring at the ceiling of my bedroom listening to the familiar sounds around me. Sounds of family and life. Sounds that belong to this house.

Sitting bolt upright, I remember the events of the previous evening and realise that today I can leave my bedroom whenever I like. It's day three of my new life and I am finally free from my husband after more than twenty-five years. Kevin has gone. He has left this house. I didn't expect that to happen at all, let alone so quickly. I jump out of bed to face day three of my freedom. My children can't keep their doors shut against me forever. Now Kevin has gone I'll be able to explain, tell them about the new life I have planned for us all. They'll understand soon enough – I just need to give them a little time.

Today, as soon as I see the children off to work and school, I go to my hairdresser's appointment. For most of my life I have been forbidden to put scissors anywhere near my hair. Some Brethren women found inventive ways of coping with the split ends and the knots that inevitably plagued us. When I was young, and before I married, once a month Mum would pull down the roller blind in the kitchen to make sure no passing Brethren could see in, and she'd get my sisters and I lined up so she could singe our hair. She would light a match over the gas ring of the cooker and then, very carefully and quickly, she would run the match along the bottom of our hair, burning off the split ends niftily and cleverly, blowing out the flame as she went. I would stand very still for fear of all my hair catching fire as the smell of burning hair filled the kitchen. We were lucky. Most of the Brethren women didn't know the 'singeing trick', so their hair was left in a straggly mess of split ends. Mum hated seeing our hair in a poor state, and that was her way of getting around the rule.

'Well, I'm not cutting it, am I?' she'd say. To this day, when I light a match, I'm sure that I can smell burning hair.

Sadly, once I got married and moved south, singeing was no longer possible. My husband would never have allowed it, so, for the next twenty years, I never had my hair trimmed or even singed. It became a long straggly mess that I was forever ashamed of.

But in 2004 those rules changed. Brethren women were now permitted to have their hair trimmed – but *only trimmed* – and so we could go to the hairdresser's occasionally. I remember the excitement of the first time I set foot in a hairdresser's and asked for an inch to be trimmed off my messy locks.

Today though is going to be different. Today I am not going to get my hair trimmed; I am going to get it cut short, and I am going to have it coloured to get rid of my greys. I will have my hair styled and I will get rid of the very last of that Brethren look. Today I am going to leave the salon looking like a worldly woman.

As I enter the salon of the hairdresser who has trimmed my hair on many occasions, she does a double-take.

'Maria, what have you done? You look so different. You're wearing trousers!'

I laugh at the shock in her voice, but can't hide my pride.

'I've left them,' I say breathlessly. 'I've left the Brethren.'

'I wish you could see yourself,' Helen says. 'It's not just that you're wearing different clothes and makeup, but your whole countenance has changed. Your face and your eyes are alight, and you're smiling. I can't believe the trans-formation. It's like one of those TV make-over shows.'

Looking at myself in the mirror, I can see that she's right: I do look different. My bright blue eyes look brighter than I've ever seen them. My shoulders look squarer, and I'm smiling. Over the last three days I've felt a slow, inward transformation, but until this moment I haven't realised that I've started to show it outwardly.

'Now then,' Helen asks, 'what are we doing with your hair today?'

'Do whatever you think will suit me. Anything you like.'

Over the next three hours, Helen works her magic. She dyes my hair a beautiful chestnut brown to cover all my greys and runs blonde highlights through it. She washes, conditions and tones it. She cuts inches off my long hair until it sits just on my shoulders. She cuts layers into it and gives me a fringe. Since I was five years old, I have longed to have a fringe. I love it.

While Helen is busily transforming me, mixing the hair dye and foiling up the highlights, she is constantly asking me questions. How did you get involved with the Brethren? Why couldn't you cut your hair? Why don't the Brethren eat or drink with anyone from the outside world? Although Helen knows of the Plymouth Brethren Christian Church because many of the men visit her husband's barbershop next door, it's apparent that she knows very little detail about them, about us.

I tell her that Brethren's houses, businesses and schools must be detached and not joined to this 'evil world'. I tell her about how we must keep conversation with 'worldlies' to a minimum because we've been told the world will contaminate us. Even as I'm recounting the Brethren ways, it's hard to find the right words to fully explain what it was like.

Now that I'm speaking out and spilling the beans, describing life inside, I can't help feeling I will go to hell. As I answer Helen's questions and tell her the truth, even now that I'm certain I'm leaving for good, I can't help feeling that I'm being a traitor. I want to answer all the questions she is asking me, but fear still has a firm grip on me. The truth of my life is so jumbled in my head that I don't even know how to express it. I'm sure my answers made very little sense to Helen that day but I still couldn't comprehend – how could I? – that I had been living under an oppressive system. I still didn't know that the words 'abuse' or 'coercive control' even exist.

I do a few twirls in front of the mirror. Helen laughs at me, but I can't help admiring myself. As I pay, I thank her for everything and as she puts her arms around me, giving me a tight hug, I am again surprised by the kindness being shown to me by people I barely know. Taking a deep breath, I step outside, taking a last look at this new me, groomed, styled and elegant, in the shop window. Crossing the street, I decide to take a walk by the shore before driving home.

Although it's a cold winter's day, the skies are a clear blue and the sun shines bright in my eyes. Walking along the promenade I enjoy the feeling of a gentle breeze blowing through my hair. As I make my way along the wide pavement, the sea is glistening as the waves lap gently against the sea wall below. With every step, I lift my head a little higher and my pace gets a little quicker until, suddenly, I realise that I'm running. My newly styled shoulder-length hair is flowing behind me. People on the pavement are staring at me but I don't care. I am free, and I need to run. The feeling is like nothing I've ever felt before or since. A weight has suddenly lifted from my shoulders, and my whole body seems so light that I'm surprised my feet don't lift right off the ground as I run.

I keep running until I reach the end of the pier. I lean against the railing trying to get my breath back. Looking down into the deep blue water crested with white, I realise I am standing at exactly the same spot where I'd stood only a few days ago: the pier where I'd contemplated suicide. Oh, how glad I am now to have chosen life! As I lean on that railing again, I lift my head to the heavens and utter a hesitant prayer of thanks.

'Whoever or whatever might be up there listening to me right now, thank you for showing me to choose life, thank you for giving me the strength to choose freedom at whatever the cost, and thank you that this life is now mine to live as I should.'

Now, I feel like I am really free; now, I am ready to show the world that I am one of its citizens; now, I am no longer a weirdo with long hair, dowdy clothes and a headscarf. No, now I am Maria, and I am ready to take on the world. I know there are going to be challenges ahead but I am ready to face them.

My last challenge, on this third day of my freedom, was to visit the teachers at the Brethren school that Juliet, Lincoln and Aaron attended. I had to speak to them as soon as possible, to let them know what was happening before the Brethren elders intervened and told them I was ill or unstable or mad.

So, that Wednesday afternoon, just before school finished for the day, I parked my car next to the other Brethren mothers' cars and walked towards the school entrance. I held my head high, keeping my gaze straight ahead. With each step, I felt their eyes on me. I guessed from their looks what each of them was thinking:

Look at her! Who does she think she is?

She's wearing trousers!

Has she gone mad?

But I didn't care. No one could take this feeling of freedom away from me. No one could dampen my spirits. As I walked up the steps and reached for the swing doors, the Brethren children and teenagers started filing out. Some turned and stared at me. Some dropped their heads as though they didn't dare look at me – as though even looking at me dressed like a worldly was going to infect them. Some even jeered and called 'weirdo' after me. I understood that I was a weirdo in their eyes but I didn't allow anything to faze me. I kept my head held high as I looked each one of them in the eye and smiled.

Although it was a Brethren-run school, the teachers were all non-Brethren teachers. As Brethren were not allowed to go to university, they couldn't train to become teachers, so non-Brethren teachers were employed and kept under close surveillance by the elders. They were only allowed to teach Brethren-sanctioned lessons. Except for parent–teacher meetings, we had very little to do with the teachers. We were supposed to keep our distance and they were supposed to keep their distance from us. It was part of the deal of working in a well-funded Brethren school. I often wonder now why any of them chose to work in such a place, but I assume it must have been because they were paid well, and that Brethren children worked hard and were polite and the schools were very well resourced.

I knocked on the staffroom door where the teachers were gathering up their belongings for the end of the day. As I entered the room, I heard a collective gasp. At first no one spoke; they just stared. One teacher, Miss Marshall, looked me up and down, from my boots to my hair.

'What on earth, Maria?' she said. 'What have you done? You look like a different person! How come you're wearing trousers?'

I laughed. She was right. It *was* surreal and crazy to be standing in that Brethren school dressed in my worldly attire. The teachers had got used to obeying the local Brethren leaders, even down to how they dressed. The female teachers were forbidden to wear trousers to school, so for a Brethren mother to be standing in their staffroom dressed in those forbidden clothes must have seemed crazy – and perhaps even dangerous.

One of the teachers asked me to sit down. They asked questions. I answered and explained as best I could about my decision to leave the Brethren. I warned them of the effect my defection had already had on Lincoln, Juliet and Aaron; I warned them of the kind of things I suspected the Brethren would be saying about me to my children; about how they would do their best to persuade my children to leave me.

The teachers were kind. One by one, despite the risk to their jobs, they hugged me, patted me on the back, told me how proud they were of me. One of them told me I was a brave woman. They knew that if any one of them reported back to the Brethren elders, describing the encouraging words they were saying to me, they would all be in trouble. They assured me they would do all they could to help my children. As I left that meeting I had a sense yet again of how kind worldly people were. In only three days I had met nothing but kindness and encouragement. I was beginning to see that this world we'd been taught was so evil might be far from it.

―――――

As I lie in bed that night, alone in the silence of my bed, I think about all those questions Helen had asked me that morning. I know now that those questions are going to follow me all through my new life. I'll be forever explaining my past. I'll never get away from it. It's always going to come up in conversation: how did you get out? What was it like? Why didn't you confide in anyone? Why didn't you run away?

How will I answer them? How will I ever be able to explain to people what has happened to me?

# TWENTY-FOUR

When I left the Brethren in early 2013, I hoped that through me my children might see there could be a good and decent life to lead outside. I hoped we would face the outside world and all its adventures and challenges together. But only two weeks after I parted ways with the Brethren, the first of my six children left me. It broke my heart.

I had come home one afternoon still full of the excitement of my newfound freedom. Every day seemed like a new experience. With Kevin gone, I spent my days learning how to navigate this alien world. I was having coffee in cafés, going out and about shopping, and listening to worldly music. And amid all of this change I had the joy of all six of my children still living with me.

Kyle comes home from work as normal but, without even a hello to me or sitting down to eat the meal I have prepared, he goes straight upstairs to his bedroom. Hearing the banging of cupboard doors and drawers, I go upstairs to see what he's doing. There he is, busy pulling his belongings out of the cupboards and drawers and shoving them into a suitcase.

'What on earth are you doing?' I ask, taking a seat on his bed.

'Mum, I can't live here anymore,' Kyle says, his face red. 'I can't bear to watch my mum give herself to the world and the Devil. I'm sorry, Mum, but it just hurts too much. I'm going to live with Grandpa and Granny.'

My heart sinks when I hear those words, but I also realise how much must have been going on outside my house during these last two weeks: conversations with his grandparents and his uncles and the other elders, and insinuations and judgements about me. Kyle was being shamed because of me. He is in an impossible situation as a young man in the Brethren. Sooner or later, they were going to try to persuade him to make a choice. Of course they were. That's what they do.

I try to put my arms around my son, but he shrugs me off. He closes the suitcase and almost runs down the stairs. I follow him to the door, pleading with him not to go, but I know there is nothing I can do to make him change his mind. He has no choice. I watch him throw the suitcase into the boot of his car.

'Please come back and see me soon,' I shout feebly as he drives off.

I think at the time I didn't believe he was leaving me. I think I was hoping that he might stay with friends or family for a few days to get things straight in his mind and then return. He wouldn't *really* leave his mum for good. Or would he? As I stood at the front door watching his car disappear into the distance a cold sweat came over me. Was this it? Was this how it was going to be?

As I sit here now writing these words, I'm overcome by the fact that of all my children, my memories of Kyle are the ones that have faded the most.

My therapist is working hard to help me remember each of my lost children. She asks me whether I want to let them go, or whether, even though I may never see them again, I might want to keep them in my life, keep them dear to me, *carry them with me*. She is a bereavement therapist, but she has never had to work with this kind of bereavement before, where a grieving mother has lost six people forever but knows they are still alive, so she is working with the techniques she knows, trying to adapt them to my experience.

'Tell me about Kyle,' she says. And I remember a weekend in 2010, when he was eighteen. It was after my breakdown. I was only just about coping.

In 2010, Bruce Hales visited our town. The weekend was hectic with all the entertaining and the endless meetings. But it was that weekend that Kyle, on the cusp of adulthood, had fallen into my arms, broken.

It was a Saturday evening. I was busying myself getting Juliet and Aaron to bed and preparing for the next day. Our four older boys had gone to my sister Chloe and her husband Nick's house. I was tidying up the last of the dishes in the kitchen when my mobile rang. It was Chloe.

'Maria,' she said in a panicky voice, 'you need to get here now. Kyle can't stop crying and is calling out for you. We don't know what's wrong with him.'

I left the children and our guests in Kevin's care before jumping in the car to drive the few miles to my sister's house. There were people everywhere. The sound of piano playing and singing filled the air, as the words of an old hymn rang out. I pushed my way through the crowd and into the kitchen, where I found Chloe.

'Where is he?' I asked.

'He's in the lounge by the piano,' my sister said. 'He wanted to stand by the piano and listen to the hymn, but suddenly he was crying. He keeps saying, 'I want Mum.''

Chloe ushered me into the crowded lounge. It took me a moment to pick Kyle out. His head was bent, and he was resting on Oliver's shoulder for support. Rushing forward, I called his name. Turning his tear-stained face towards me, Kyle collapsed into my arms and, burying his head in my shoulder, he was overcome by fresh deep sobs.

'What on earth is wrong?' I asked, leading him away from the crowd and into the quiet of the utility room beyond the kitchen. At first, he just stayed in my arms sobbing while I held him and stroked his back. After a few minutes, he took a shuddering breath.

'I'm such a sinner and I don't know how to fix it.'

'Why? What on earth have you done that's so bad?'

'I've been talking to a young Brethren girl from France,' he said, struggling to catch his breath. 'She's only fifteen. I've told her that I love her. I know it's wrong of me to be talking to a girl when I'm not old enough to get married and she's so young. Listening to Mr Hales today has made me realise what a sinner I am. Such a terrible sinner. Mum, please help me. I don't know what to do.'

I couldn't answer straight away. I was thankful that his sin was so trivial, but I could see his inner turmoil. Looking back, I can see how frustrated and lonely Kyle must have been, conflicted between following rules and love, but it was my job as a good Brethren mother to help him choose the right path. So, I said what I knew a Brethren mother should say.

'Kyle,' I said, 'we're all sinners who need a saviour. You're no worse than anyone. Today you are broken and today you must put all thoughts of this girl out of your mind. Ask for the Holy Spirit's help.'

Giving me a watery smile, Kyle assured me that he would do just that.

Walking back into the house that day after I had watched Kyle drive away, I knew that this was going to be the start of an avalanche. I hadn't expected my three eldest sons to accept my decision, but for those first days and weeks, I had held onto a hope – a naive hope that all my children would somehow stay with me. But now Kyle leaving had woken me up; woken me up to my realisation that the Brethren would never let them live with me. I knew then that there was nothing I could do to stop the avalanche from falling.

# TWENTY-FIVE

It wasn't long before I found my way to the Ex-Brethren Facebook pages. Despite initial misgivings, I was feeling lonely and, with Kevin no longer living in the family home or able to control me, I now longed to find others who had left – people who would understand what I was going through. I was going to need all the help I could get. As soon as I registered and introduced myself as a new leaver, ex-Brethren men and women from all over the world welcomed me. They asked about my family; they offered practical advice and emotional support. It helped. I 'met' extraordinary survivors on those pages who have since become close friends. Over the years I have drawn great solace from this group. They helped give me some of the strength and reassurance that I needed to move forwards.

The day after Kyle left, I walked into a police station. I told the police officer that I thought I had been abused and that my ex-husband was a danger to my children.

The female officer I talked to was sympathetic. She listened to me tell my garbled story, but she said their station didn't have any expertise with such cases. She referred me to a special abuse unit in another town. I drove thirty miles to speak to officers from that special unit. The woman I spoke to there was also sympathetic, but she said her hands were tied. The law about rape dictated that unless I could prove that I had said 'no' clearly and emphatically in each of the cases I thought were rape, then lawyers wouldn't be able to take my case forward. I knew I couldn't prove that.

I walked away.

I did not pursue my case.

A few days later I tried the social services. They took a statement. They also interviewed the younger children alone. The children told them their father had changed, that he was no longer violent, but I wondered if anyone had directed them in what to say to those in an official capacity. The officers told me their hands were tied. The law was the law. They had to have proof to intervene.

I walked away.

A few days later I went to Women's Aid. I told them my story. They gave me one of the most precious gifts of all: the woman counsellor not only listened to my story but also helped me begin to understand the abuse I had suffered at the hands of my husband and the Brethren. But, she said, given my circumstances, and given the law as it stood then, there was little that Women's Aid could do to protect my vulnerable children from their father and the Brethren.

I felt myself losing hope and energy. When I had spoken to police officers and social workers they had seemed unable to grasp the levels of psychological control that I felt the Brethren system held over its members, or what it was like to lose everything and everyone you had ever known when you either left or were withdrawn from. Worldly people didn't seem able to 'get it'. With hindsight I can see that, at that point, only months after leaving the Brethren, I did not have the power, time, words or the understanding of how abuse and coercive control by a husband works to be able to explain.

What was becoming clearer to me every day was that the only person who could steer my children towards a normal life was me; the only person who could fight the Brethren beliefs, because I knew their ways, talked their talk, understood their moves, was me.

However heartbreaking it was going to be, I'd almost certainly have to let my adult children choose between the Brethren and me. They had to do that for themselves. But I had also come to understand that, because Lincoln, Juliet and Aaron were fifteen, thirteen and eleven years old respectively, I had some legal power. If I was to keep them safe and stop them being returned to the care of Kevin, I was going to have to secure custody. If I secured custody then I could buy myself – and them – some time.

So, as I mourned Kyle's abandonment, haunted by the lights of his car fading into the distance, I made a silent promise: I promised Lincoln, Juliet, Aaron and myself that I would do my utmost to get custody of them.

I kept that promise. The week after Kyle left, I hired a solicitor and started legal proceedings. The local Brethren and my family were ready. They had already employed lawyers and had written up their own agreement. They wanted me to settle the children's custody out of court. I was put under considerable pressure to sign this document, but I stuck to my word and refused.

It took over a year for everything to be finalised through the family courts, but in spring 2014 I was granted full custody of Lincoln, Juliet and Aaron until they reached the age of sixteen. It was an important victory. There were conditions: I had to agree to let the children attend their Brethren school and the Brethren meetings. I also had to let them go to Kevin's every weekend.

I thought long and hard about fighting these terms, but I was afraid that if I forced my youngest children away from the only life and friends they had ever known, it would turn them against me. How, I agonised, was I going to keep them safe while they were staying with Kevin, particularly now that Juliet was a teenager? But the children, I discovered, were already finding ways to protect themselves. They had already arranged that every weekend when they were in Kevin's care, one of their elder brothers should always be present. While that gave me some relief I was also alarmed. They had told social workers that their father had changed, that he wasn't violent, and that they felt safe with him. Yet here they were arranging their own protection from him. How safe *were* they? Would they ever tell me if anything bad happened?

Could I have done more to protect my children?

Could the authorities have done more?

These questions still haunt me.

Police officers and social workers told me again and again in 2013 that their hands were tied. The law put the burden of proof on me. I had to prove that I had refused my abuser sex. But what about the terror and control he had wielded in our home – the threats, the rage, the way he had beaten the children, terrorised me? Did none of these count for anything in the law?

What I didn't know was that people who worked in refuges or supported women suffering domestic violence had been petitioning for a change in the law for decades. Abuse, they insisted, took many forms. It wasn't just physical; it could be psychological and coercive. Such forms of abuse could be deeply violent and damaging too. Two years after I left the Brethren, thanks to the work of these campaigners, the Crown Prosecution Service introduced Section 76 of the Serious Crime Act 2015. It created a new offence of controlling or coercive behaviour in an intimate or family relationship. They called it 'coercive control'. Now the government defined it as:

> an act or a pattern of acts of assault, threats, humiliation and intimidation or other abuse that is used to harm, punish, or frighten their victim.

> Controlling behaviour is a range of acts designed to make a person subordinate and/or dependent by isolating them from sources of support, exploiting their resources and capacities for personal gain, depriving them of the means needed for independence, resistance and escape and regulating their everyday behaviour.

When I read the legal definition of coercive control for the first time, I recognised Kevin's behaviour. That was easy. But, I wanted to shout, my husband was raised to believe that he must be dominant within his own home and that his authority should not be questioned by his family. If I had always felt fearful, had no money of my own and felt that it wasn't safe to confide in anyone, that I couldn't escape, that Kevin had a right to take his conjugal rights – then to some extent was the coercive controller my husband or the environment in which we lived? Where did one end and the other begin?

'What happened to Kevin after you left him?' friends asked me. In the early days after I made the break, I tell them, I had little contact with him. Like so many separated couples we communicated via short emails regarding practical arrangements about the children. I knew from comments that my father and brother had made that Kevin had confessed to the local priests about how he'd treated me and our children, so he would have been living under a very dark cloud and in constant fear of being thrown out if he stepped any further out of line. Now that he had left the family home, he had to rely on the local Brethren to put a roof over his head and on Brethren women to provide him with meals because, as a Brethren man, he had no idea how to cook or run a house. From casual comments my children made, for the first few months apparently he went from house to house, sometimes for weeks at a time. Even when he started to rent his own house in late 2014, he continued to be cooked for by local Brethren women for years. What I didn't know, but might have guessed, was that the Brethren priests were also putting pressure on Kevin to make a further attempt to get me to return to the fold.

In early 2014, while the custody case was still making its way through the courts, Kevin emailed asking for a meeting with me at the family home, alone. I agreed to the meeting on the condition that I wouldn't be under any pressure to return to him or the Brethren.

I was nervous to be meeting Kevin alone after what had happened between us and with the court case ongoing, but I didn't know anyone outside the Brethren well enough yet to ask them to be there with me. I was relieved at first when Kevin arrived with his younger brother Harry as a chaperone. But then I wondered: had Harry come over to protect Kevin from me? Surely it was me who needed the protection?

I ushered Kevin and Harry into the living room. We sat tentatively on the edge of our seats waiting for someone to speak. Suddenly, Kevin stood up awkwardly, walked over to me and knelt at my feet. I felt myself lurch back into my chair away from him. Then, clearing his throat nervously, he said:

'Maria, please listen carefully to what I have to say. I'm sorry for how I treated you for the twenty-five years of our marriage and I'm sorry that I moved out of the family home so soon after you expressed your feelings towards me and the Brethren. I acted in haste.'

What on earth was he saying? Hadn't the priests told him to move out? Before I had a chance to respond, he went on.

'I'm kneeling at your feet to beg for your forgiveness. I want you to reconsider divorcing me. I want you to consider letting me move back into the home, or maybe we could convert the garage into a room for me to live in.'

I couldn't believe what I was hearing. Come back and live here? Had he completely lost his mind? I looked across at Harry to see what his reaction was, but I couldn't see his face as he was staring at the floor in embarrassment. I felt a surge of indignation and anger course through me. Finally, I found my voice.

'Move in!' I exclaimed. 'Kevin, get up off your knees now and don't be so ridiculous. The best thing that you ever did was move out.' I felt my face redden and the pitch of my voice rise as I went on: 'Leave this house immediately. I never want you this close to me again. Please now go away and sign those divorce papers.'

Kevin and Harry stood up. I stormed towards the front door, opening it for them and almost pushing them out. It took him another two years to sign the divorce papers and, over that time, he sent me regular increasingly desperate emails appealing for me to reconsider. I ignored them.

It seemed that once I had found my voice, my strength and my freedom, once I was finally able to say: 'It's finished, I've had enough,' Kevin's strength and power began to shrink and continued to do so year on year. I don't know the details of his life now, but it doesn't surprise me to hear that, though he was never much of a drinker, he has become an alcoholic dependent on the care of others. While he lives among the Brethren, though he has the privilege of seeing our children and grandchildren regularly, he will never escape the stigma and shame of his sins.

# TWENTY-SIX

Just two months after I left the Brethren, and just as I had found the confidence to file for the custody of my three youngest children, I lost the second of my sons, Bradley.

Kyle's decision to leave three weeks earlier had shocked me but nothing prepared me for the degree of Bradley's fury and scorn when he announced his decision to go and live with my brother Edward and his family. Bradley and I had been so close. He'd been the sceptical one. He'd been the one who'd had doubts about the Brethren for years. He had even confided those doubts to me.

Arriving home early from work that day, Bradley had been annoyed to find that I wasn't at home. Lincoln, Juliet and Aaron had gone to visit Brethren friends, so, with time to myself, I had gone to the cinema for the very first time.

By the time I got home, Bradley had worked himself into an angry state and, as soon as I walked through the front door he demanded to know where I had been all afternoon. Not wanting to upset him further by telling him that I'd been to the cinema, I shrugged and asked, 'Why do you need to know?'

'You're not acting like a mum,' he roared. 'You're acting like a teenager. Do you know how stupid you look prancing around like a worldly woman?'

The words stung.

'How dare you talk to me like that,' I said. 'After everything I've done for you.'

'You've done nothing for me!' he raged. 'I'm leaving this house today, Mum, and let me tell you something, if I ever have children, you will never see them!' He stormed into his bedroom and slammed the door. I sat down on the settee, put my head in my hands and wept. What had I done?

Bradley emerged from his bedroom with all his belongings shoved into black bin liners. Before I even had a chance to say goodbye, he left the house, slamming the front door behind him.

I've never had a proper conversation with him since, and I haven't seen him since the summer of 2015 when he and his wife moved away. Bradley has kept his word: I have never met his children. I don't even know how many he has.

My therapist asks me about Bradley. I tell her about how, as a little boy, he loved to take things apart and put them together again. He'd take a padlock apart and examine each part then reassemble it. I tell her about the many people he helped when, in 2008, the Brethren were first allowed computers. He loved anything to do with computers and enjoyed helping the older Brethren like his grandpa to get their heads around it all. I tell her about our shopping sprees together when he was in his late teens and early twenties. Bradley loved nothing more than clothes shopping, I say. Like me he dressed as close to the world as he could get away with. He was like me, I say. He had walked into a meeting once wearing white brogues.

It would have been early 2012 when I took Bradley and his friend Brett to a shopping centre. Brett was a notorious rebel in the eyes of the Brethren. Put him and Bradley together and you were guaranteed a lively time. I loved their company and they seemed to enjoy mine. They didn't care that I followed them around in every shop and laughed at their silly antics. They spent that day flirting with the female sales assistants and trying on outrageous outfits. At lunchtime they insisted we had a three-course meal in a restaurant even though Brethren weren't allowed to go to restaurants. That was the first time I had been to a restaurant. I was trembling when Bradley held the big glass swing doors open for me. I kept looking over my shoulder in case any Brethren might be lurking around the corner, watching us. I had no idea what to order from the menu, but the boys guided me, and their confidence made me realise that this wasn't the first time they had done this. That was one of the things I loved about Bradley: unlike me, he had little fear of breaking the Brethren rules. Kevin and I were forever having to defend him to the priests.

But after eight years of no contact, I tell my therapist I can hardly remember what Bradley looked like. All I have left is a copy of a photo that I found on LinkedIn. I show her the picture.

As I write today, I take the photo down from my windowsill and study it. I look into the eyes of the young man, trying to get a clue as to what is going on in his mind today. He looks overweight. Is he comfort eating like I used to? In my mind's eye, I imagine what it would be like to sit in a room with him once more. What would it feel like to touch my son again, to hear his voice again, to laugh with him, to ask him what he thinks about all kinds of things? But while he stays in the Brethren I will never get that chance. So, all I can do is look at that photo and ask him some questions:

'Bradley, what made you change from your rebellious rule-breaking? Now that you are thirty-two, married and a father, are you living a lie as I did for all those years? Do you ever think about me and wonder if my decision was the right one? Are you spending your life pulled between what is and what could have been? Are you continually pushing all your past doubts to the back of your mind in the hope that you can be a good Brethren husband and man?' And last, but not least, I ask him: 'Bradley, are you happy?'

# TWENTY-SEVEN

In those first months after I left the Brethren, grieving the loss of my two boys, I registered on a dating site. Friends are often surprised by this decision. They can't understand why I might have wanted to find another partner after the way my husband had treated me, nor can they understand how I found the courage to register on a dating site so soon after leaving, while facing so much loss. But the fact is that, apart from my children who remained with me, I was entirely alone in the outside world and very lonely. For me, a dating site was one way to find a romantic companion, someone who might support me in everything I had to face ahead. Now that I had left Kevin, now that I was doing everything in my power to separate myself and my children from the Brethren, I also longed to make up for lost time. I longed to find 'true love'. I wanted a man to love me for me and not just for my body. I longed for a man to put his arms around me without wanting to have sex with me. I longed for affection.

In early summer 2013, quite soon after leaving the Brethren, I went on a date with a man called Max. Lincoln, Juliet and Aaron were with their dad that evening, so I had a night to myself. Max and I had been texting for a few days. We discovered that we lived less than a mile from each other. Max suggested we meet at a local hotel for a meal.

I was excited. Our texts so far had been good. He seemed different to the other men I'd chatted to over the previous few weeks. Most phone conversations I'd had in the early days of online dating seemed to quickly lead to sexual topics, but I wanted more than that. I wanted love and companionship and Max seemed to want the same.

After doing my makeup and hair to the best of my ability, I slipped into a tight-fitting, low-cut cream dress and high stiletto heels. But looking in the mirror, I saw a stranger looking back at me. Who was this person dressed like a worldly woman? I'd never been able to wear a dress like this before and high heels had been impossible. I called a taxi. I had never been in a taxi before. How was I meant to behave? Was I supposed to sit in the front next to the driver or in the back? I climbed into the front, hoping for the best.

Deciding to wait outside the hotel, I paced back and forth nervously, all the while doing my best to balance on my high heels. Thankfully I didn't have to wait long. A taxi pulled up and out stepped Max. I recognised him from his profile photos with his dark, slightly curly hair and broad shoulders.

I took a deep breath and introduced myself.

Following him into the hotel, I couldn't help having a good stare at him. I liked what I saw. He wasn't a lot taller than me; he wore a smart shirt and jeans and obviously knew how to take care of himself. I liked that.

After some stilted conversation, we were handed our menus and now I was filled with another dilemma. How would I know what to order? Everything seemed so confusing. What were scallops? What was a prawn cocktail? Nothing on the starter course sounded familiar so I decided to just have a main. I couldn't go wrong with ordering a steak and chips, I thought. But I was wrong – the waiter asked me how I'd like it cooked.

'Oh, I'm not fussy,' I said. 'However you cook it is fine for me. You'll have to excuse me,' I whispered to Max, as the waiter disappeared. 'I've only ever eaten in a restaurant once before. Until eight weeks ago I was part of a very strict religion, you see, and we weren't allowed to eat in places like this.'

Max put down his wine glass and stared at me incredulously.

'You were in a religion that didn't allow you to eat in a restaurant?'

I laughed awkwardly. Then I told him about many of the other things I'd never done: how I'd never been on holiday; how I'd never watched television or listened to the radio. I told him how I hadn't been allowed to listen to pre-recorded music or go to the cinema. When I told him about my children and how two of them had already left me, he reached across the table and took my hands in his.

Looking back, I'm surprised that Max didn't make his excuses and leave there and then. He must have wondered who on earth this woman was sitting before him. But he stayed; he sat there holding my hands across that little round table while he listened to my jumbled-up, garbled words. Occasionally, when I stopped for a breath, he exclaimed, 'Are you serious?', his eyes growing wide in disbelief.

Then Max told me a little about himself and how he had ended up moving from Manchester for work three years earlier. He talked passionately about his job working for an international medical supplies company. He told me he was the youngest of four children. He had never married and had no children. Both of his parents were Irish. They were strict Roman Catholics who had moved to Manchester before marrying and having children. He was proud to be a Manchester man, he said, but he still held on to his Irish heritage. He loved living in Wellfleet.

After finishing our drinks and meal, Max paid the bill and we set off on the short walk to experience my first ever pub visit. As we walked, Max took my hand in his. A feeling of safety came over me. I liked this man. I felt that I could trust him. The feeling was obviously mutual because, even after I had told him my crazy story, and that I had six children, he hadn't run away. As we neared the pub, Max drew close and asked if he could kiss me. I leant in. We stood in the half-light of the alleyway for some time. I could not remember ever being so happy.

From that night, Max and I began a four-year relationship. As we sat cuddled on his settee one evening in that May, he turned to me and said, 'I've got an idea. Because you've never had the chance to celebrate Christmas, why don't we have a mid-year Christmas in June?'

I felt my eyes well up with tears. 'I would love that. Would you really do that for me?' I asked.

'Of course,' he assured me, kissing my forehead.

And that's exactly what we did. Shortly afterwards, we spent a Saturday afternoon decorating Max's lounge. A week later, I celebrated my first Christmas. Max bought me my first real gold necklace and I bought him cufflinks and aftershave. Even though it wasn't December I still count it as the first Christmas I ever celebrated.

My relationship with Max was totally separate from my life at home with my children. I talked to them about Max and the places we went together, but he never came to my house. Neither of us wanted to confuse the children's lives any more than was necessary or make them turn against me by introducing him to them. They had enough to contend with.

So, every evening, once the children were in bed, Max and I would have a phone call, and then every weekend that the children were with their dad, I would spend at his house. In those early weeks and months, Max's house became my refuge from the Brethren priestly visits, prying eyes and the pressure from my family to try to persuade me to return. I could walk through Max's door on a weekend and cocoon myself in the safety of his life and all the excitement of new experiences. But I avoided talking to Max about what was happening at home because I'd seen how angry he got with the Brethren if I mentioned them. I was scared of losing him, so I told him as little as possible. I went on pretending everything was fine. I was good at that.

But as hard as I tried my pretence wasn't perfect. As I prepared myself for yet another priestly meeting, in my angst and stress I told Max about it. And once I started, I couldn't stop. I told him how each of these visits made me anxious as my uncle would preach to me and tell me how I was on a path to destruction; how the Devil had got into my heart; how after every visit I seemed to take a step backwards, but I didn't want to refuse them because I knew the Brethren elders could use it against me and try to take my remaining children from me. To my astonishment, Max offered to come with me. I think part of him was intrigued. I hesitated to agree at first, but I knew that it would make things uncomfortable for Edward and my Uncle Cuthbert to have a worldly man listening to them admonishing me.

When I rang Edward to tell him I was going to bring a worldly friend to this next meeting, he was taken aback but he stayed calm. He said he'd have to consult. He phoned me back later once he'd conferred with others to say that we'd have to meet at his in-laws' empty bungalow at the bottom of his garden because Brethren rules prevented him from having a worldly man in his own home.

As I rang the bell that evening, I couldn't help but feel brave that I had dared to bring Max along. I hadn't gone so far as to tell Edward that Max and I were in a relationship, because bringing a worldly friend to a priestly visit was risky enough.

Edward was civil. He shook Max's hand. He gave me a light hug. Once we had gone through into the lounge, I took a seat opposite Edward and my uncle. Max took a seat a little further away so he could watch. Nervousness descended upon the room.

Eventually my uncle spoke.

'Well, Maria, it's a bit unusual for you to bring someone along to these sessions and it makes it a little difficult for us to say what we wanted to say.'

Then, turning to Max, he said, 'Anything we say must be kept within these four walls. We will probably speak in a language which you don't really understand.'

Max played nervously with his hands. 'I'm just here as Maria's friend,' he said, 'so be free to say what you want.'

Edward began by gently asking me how I was and how the children were coping. My uncle, unperturbed by Max's presence, started to preach the gospel to me. It felt like he was addressing Max as well as me as he parroted the usual priestly-visit phrases:

'This life you're living is leading to a sink of destruction.'

'Something will happen to you, and you'll be forced to stop in your tracks.'

'Stop now before it's too late.'

'Give your life to Jesus. Give your life to the Brethren.'

Out of the corner of my eye I could see Max's agitation. He clenched his hands. His complexion heightened. If we sat here much longer, I thought, Max was going to say something he might later regret, so I shocked myself by standing up and quickly bringing my uncle's tirade to an end.

'I think you've said enough,' I said. 'I've listened to this stuff all my life and I don't need to listen to it anymore. You know my decision and, unless you want to treat me as part of the family, as an uncle should, then I don't want another meeting with you.'

I never saw my uncle again, apart from a brief glimpse once when he drove past me. After that event Edward either saw me alone or brought his young son-in-law with him. They never preached to me again.

As we left that little bungalow, I gave my brother a hug and thanked him for letting Max come. My uncle rushed towards Max and pushed a Bible into his hands.

'I don't need your Bible,' Max said. 'I was brought up Roman Catholic. I know the Bible.'

'But this is the true translation,' my uncle said. 'I want you to have it. It's a gift from me.'

I could feel my face going red with both embarrassment and anger. Who was he to push this Brethren Bible on Max? Max took the Bible from him. It wasn't worth an argument, and I could tell that he wanted to get out of there as quickly as possible.

# TWENTY-EIGHT

It wasn't just the loss of my two eldest children that hurt in those early weeks and months, but also the loss of my siblings, parents and the whole Brethren community – the only people I had ever known. My dad had taken to emailing me a different verse of scripture every night, but aside from this, the silence was absolute. Although I had known the consequences of my actions, it didn't make the losses any easier to bear. Over the course of the autumn of 2013, despite desperately missing Bradley and Kyle, a stilted kind of peace settled around us again.

Once his dad and younger brothers had left, twenty-five-year-old Oliver, following Brethren rules, took on a new role in the family. He became a father figure and protector to Lincoln, Juliet and Aaron. When he wasn't working in my brother-in-law's business selling machinery to farming contractors up and down the country, he threw himself into helping them with homework, getting them ready for bed, reading them a verse from the Bible and doing his best to smooth out our unusual circumstances.

I was grateful for his help and for the peace that had settled on the house, but I was also nervous. Oliver seemed to feel that he had to shield the younger children from me, as though I might contaminate them in some way, and I was concerned that he was being influenced in this by the Brethren elders. I saw him sit on the corner settee in the lounge and have hushed conversations with Lincoln, Juliet and Aaron. One day he took the children into his bedroom and shut the door. Standing with my ear to the door, listening to what he was saying, I heard him say with a confidence and firmness that one of the local elders had said, 'Mum will come back soon. He says we have to remember how horribly Dad treated her, but she'll be back.'

I went into my bedroom and shut the door so I could think about the words I'd just heard. Part of me was surprised at the touch of sympathy in the local elder's words, but another part of me was angry: angry that he thought he could prophesise what was going to happen; angry that he was giving my children hope that I would return when my mind was made up. As I sat on my bed that day, I was filled with more determination than ever to prove the elder wrong. I would stand by my word. I owed that to my children.

One Saturday morning, when the three younger children are with Kevin for the weekend, I detect a strange atmosphere descend over the house. It's getting on for a year since I left the Brethren, and just over six months since Bradley has been gone. Oliver returns from the Saturday morning meeting and shuts himself away in his bedroom. I have a horrible feeling that something is about to change. I find myself pacing the floor, first going into my bedroom, then into the lounge, before deciding that I have to find out what's happening. I knock on Oliver's bedroom door.

'Ollie, can I come in?'

'Yes,' he mumbles in reply.

On entering, my heart sinks. There is his suitcase laid out on his bed, full of his clothes. He barely even looks at me as he continues to empty his wardrobe. He doesn't utter a word. Part of me feels like I had already lost this boy back on that Sunday evening all those months earlier when I had told him of my decision, but another part of me had been holding onto hope. Hope that he would stay; hope that he wouldn't cut me off as two of his brothers had; hope that my eldest son wouldn't feel torn between the Brethren and me. I put myself between him and his wardrobe, forcing him to look at me.

'Are you leaving?'

Keeping his head bent as though not trusting himself to look at me, he nods.

'But why?' Still, he won't look at me. Eyes lowered, he hesitates before answering, his voice unsteady.

'Mum, you're an amazing mum and a wonderful person, but while you refuse to go to the Lord's Supper with us, I can no longer live here. I'm moving in with Grandpa and Granny today.'

I have no words. I walk towards him and embrace him, putting my arms around his neck. But at my embrace I feel his body tense. He shrugs me away. I take a step back and begin to cry. His words are so bittersweet – he said I was a good mum and a good person – yet he is being torn away from me. My heart is breaking. I don't blame him; he knows no better. And the saddest thing about it all is that it isn't just the Brethren leading him to be this way; it's also my parents, my own mother and father, his grandparents, who are turning my children against me, drip by drip, comment by comment. And more tragic still, they are themselves deluded – deluded into thinking that their daughter has gone to Satan and that their grandchildren have to be rescued from her contaminating and evil influence.

Just two hours later, Oliver picks up his belongings and leaves. As we stand on the doorstep, he puts his arms around me, and says, 'I promise you, Mum, that I will always keep in contact.'

For five years Oliver didn't initiate any contact with me, but he did always answer my emails and my phone calls. In 2018, he stopped picking up the phone.

Today, as I look at the most recent photo I have of Oliver – also secured from LinkedIn – I try to conjure up my son in my mind. I see his face in the picture but I'm struggling to imagine who the man behind it is. Is he still the same Oliver that I knew? Does he still strive to keep the peace, whatever the circumstance, as he always did? Does he still have that calming influence over those near to him the way he had with me? Does he still have that little twitch in his eye? What is he like as a father to his children? What is he like as a husband to his wife? Has he continued to be fully committed to Brethren life or does he have doubts too?

When my therapist asks me to remember the good times I had with Oliver, I remember a particular day. I was going through an extremely difficult time, I tell her. It was the Saturday after that awful night when Kevin had raped me. My children knew nothing of what had happened that night, but at eighteen years old, Oliver seemed to sense that something wasn't right. After the Saturday morning meeting he had come to me and asked if I'd like to go for a long walk with him.

We set off on the winding country road near our house, walking side by side, staying close to each other as we followed the path. It took us past farms, sprawling green fields and trickling streams. We didn't talk much on that five-mile walk but, every so often, we would stop to look at the birds and admire the scenery around us. We kept our conversation light. In Oliver's company, I never felt like I needed to talk; his company was enough. He brought peace to me that day. He gave me a reason to go on, a reason to keep living. That, I tell my therapist, is Oliver.

# TWENTY-NINE

After Oliver left on that Saturday, the dynamics of my relationship with my remaining children changed. Now there was no big brother watching over them they relaxed around me and treated me like their mum again. They didn't seem to see me as the Jezebel that I knew some members of the Brethren – and my own parents and siblings and my three lost sons – were portraying me to be. But I now realise that as soon as they were in the orbit of the Brethren, the drip-drip of judgement and scorn for their mother – their apostate, contaminating, worldly mother – must have continued day after day.

I also look back and try to put myself in their shoes. It must have been hard and confusing. Here were three young teenagers doing their best to juggle two lives with their three elder brothers living elsewhere. They lived a full life within the Brethren. They went to the Brethren school and the daily meetings, and they saw their brothers and their grandparents. Everyone made a fuss of them. Then they had their life with me. I did my best to take them places they had never been, to show them things they had never seen. All the time I did my best to show them that they did have choices in life.

In the winter of 2013 I suggested taking Lincoln, Juliet and Aaron to an indoor skate park for the first time as a treat. They were keen scooter and rollerblade riders. Brethren rules allowed them to scooter and skate in outdoor parks but never inside a sports stadium or hall because they'd be mixing with other young worldly people. This proposal of mine was a big deal for them, and I was shocked by how wholeheartedly they threw themselves into the expedition, despite the risk of being caught. But there were more shocks to come: the night before our planned trip, Juliet came to find me in the kitchen.

'Mum, if we're going to a skate park,' she said, 'I'm going to need trousers. I can't wear a skirt.'

Trousers? I tried not to show my surprise.

'Absolutely you need to wear trousers. Would you like me to choose some for you when I go shopping later?'

'No, I want to choose them myself. Can we go to Primark on the way to the skate park tomorrow?' Doing my best to hide my excitement, I agreed as casually as I could. Neither of us said anything about what the Brethren would say.

The next day was a Saturday and, as soon as the children had returned from the morning meeting, Juliet and I set off to Primark. As we looked through the many rails of jeans and trousers, I couldn't help but marvel at how calm Juliet was being. She wasn't looking over her shoulder as I had done when I had shopped for my first pair of jeans. Wasn't she scared to be seen by other Brethren and get into trouble? Did having me beside her give her confidence and make her feel untouchable? Did this mean she was considering leaving, coming with me fully into a life outside the Brethren? I didn't dare ask for fear of forcing her hand, but I was happy to see that she wasn't scared. I paid for the pair of skinny jeans she had chosen and we made our way back to the car.

We hadn't got far down the road when Juliet, sitting in the passenger seat, started pulling the new jeans up over her hips before removing her Brethren-style skirt. Catching her eye, we smiled at each other.

'They suit you,' I said. 'You've got the perfect figure for skinny jeans.'

She laughed.

When I watched my three children practising their rollerblading and scootering skills on the ramps, hooting with laughter, I felt my heart burst with pride and love. Every time Juliet whizzed past me, I couldn't help but smile at the sight of her in those jeans. What would the Brethren say if they knew?

Aaron and Lincoln kept quiet about the trousers. Whatever they said to each other about what was happening in our house, I knew they would never have told the Brethren. That was an unspoken code between us; we trusted each other. We had already been through so much together. I knew they loved me; I never doubted their love. And now I was beginning to let myself feel some hope that even though I had lost my three eldest sons, my youngest three might stay with me, and they might really choose to live outside the Brethren.

Seeing them relax the Brethren rules at home, I pushed my luck. I bought and installed a television. The Brethren have never been allowed televisions, so buying my first one was a huge milestone for both the children and me.

For the last year I had been watching TV at Max's house. I had learnt that I could choose what I wanted to watch; nobody was forcing me to watch anything. If I thought something was bad, then I didn't need to view it. I also saw that sports, documentaries, reality TV shows and movies could be educational. It helped me understand more of this new world; it helped me gain social skills, which I was so lacking. I wanted Lincoln, Juliet and Aaron to get that education too. I wanted them to know that not everything on TV was evil.

When they came through the door that evening, they found me sitting in front of an episode of *Britain's Got Talent* – not on my laptop with earphones but on a proper screen. I pressed the pause button as I stood up to greet them. I saw their faces turn pale, but I did my best to act normal.

'Well,' I said, 'how was your weekend?'

Making sure not to look at my new acquisition, Juliet snapped: 'Why have you bought a television? You know we aren't allowed television.' They all left the room tutting and shaking their heads.

For the first few weeks, Lincoln, Juliet and Aaron did their best to ignore the TV if I had it on. But as the weeks turned into months, they became more curious. Each evening when they went to the daily meeting, I would use the time to watch it, doing my best to navigate the many options and learning what types of films I enjoyed. When the children came through the door, I would switch the channel to a documentary or reality programme; I knew they weren't ready to watch a film, but I hoped that documentaries and reality programmes would interest them.

At first Juliet would come and sit nervously on the arm of the chair nearest the door as though she might need to make a quick escape. Then, after a few weeks, she moved to perch nervously on the edge of the armchair, resting her head in her hands, her eyes glued to the screen. It wasn't long before she was sitting relaxed next to me, and discussing what we were watching. She loved watching programmes like *Britain's Got Talent* or *The Voice*. Singing was something Juliet loved and was good at. I could see a longing in her eyes as she watched the contestants. Did she dream of being one of them?

Lincoln and Aaron were more cautious. They, like Juliet, would perch themselves on the arm of the chair as though they might need to make a run for it at any minute if any of the Brethren arrived and peered in the window. But those evenings with the curtains drawn and the TV on became precious to me. It was like having my children exclusively in my world without the Brethren. That room was our little haven, and there no one could touch us.

Juliet and I had always shared a love of music, and, soon after I left the Brethren, she started listening to music on my iPhone. She made her own playlist, and as soon as she got into the car in the mornings or after school, she would have her favourite songs blaring through the speakers. Listening to real music for the first time made her want to sing better herself. So, although it was against Brethren rules, I enrolled us both in singing lessons.

Our singing teacher was also the instructor for a choir I joined soon after leaving the Brethren. One afternoon, about a year after we had enrolled for singing lessons, our teacher asked Juliet if she'd like to sing solo in an event that her choir were performing.

I watched Juliet fidgeting uncomfortably. She knew she was good enough to do it, but would she dare? Breaking the Brethren rules by having private singing lessons with her worldly mother was one thing, but singing in public was a whole different scale of risk. She would also have to miss the Brethren daily meeting.

'Yes,' she said at last. 'Yes, I'd love to do that.'

'You *really* want to do it?' I asked.

'Yes. Why not? I might never get another chance,' she said.

I winced to hear her use those words – 'I might never get another chance'. I couldn't bear to think that she considered herself as being on borrowed time because that meant she also thought that, sooner or later, she was going to have to return fully to the Brethren and comply fully with Brethren rules.

Two weeks later, on a Thursday evening, Juliet made up some excuse to her dad for not going to the meeting, and instead she stood up in front of a small choir and sang 'All of Me' by John Legend.

# THIRTY

The following spring I joined a gym and got a personal trainer, both forbidden in the Brethren. I had spent years as an emotional eater without the strength or desire to look after myself properly. Now I wanted to change that. I wanted to get fit and keep in shape. I worked really hard, did well and could feel the benefits. One day in April 2014 I had my usual P.T. training. I sprinted, I did squats, I lifted weights and I felt good. My muscles were toning up, my tummy had flattened a little and I felt generally stronger. However, that evening, after my shower, I stood naked in front of the mirror. I wanted to see the results of all my hard work. As I examined my body in the mirror, instead of seeing toned muscles and a flat tummy, my eyes were drawn to my left breast. It looked strange, and the nipple was inverted. I didn't think much about it. I told myself I'd look it up when I had the chance.

Once I'd put the children to bed I opened my laptop and googled 'inverted nipple'. My search took me immediately to cancer sites. I examined my breast again. It not only looked different now, but it also felt different. I was terrified not so much by the fear of cancer or death or by the fear of pain but by the fear of being judged by the Brethren and by my family. I knew they'd say I'd got cancer because I'd left the Brethren: that God had struck me down as a punishment. I'd heard Brethren brothers and sisters say that about other Brethren who had struggled with cancer, even those who lived in complete observance of Brethren rules: it was seen as a judgement, a warning from God. I thought of the whisperings that would go on at the meetings; the terrible things they would tell my children. Worse still, if I had cancer, then the Brethren would put even more pressure on me to return to fellowship so they could save me before it was too late. Eventually, I drifted off into a fitful sleep, punctuated by nightmares of denunciation and recrimination.

At six-thirty the next morning, I dragged myself out of bed. I got the children up for school as usual and, while they were getting dressed and were safely out of earshot, I phoned the doctor's. I told the receptionist that I had found a lump. She secured an appointment for me for eleven o'clock that morning. As I drove the children to school I kept telling myself to be calm, that everything would be fine.

At the school gates I saw my sister standing in the car park. I needed to confide in someone, needed someone to give me a hug, but though I was terrified, I knew I couldn't trust her. I couldn't bear seeing that judgement flicker across her face. I wasn't ready for that. I realised more than ever that morning just how much my freedom had cost me. I had never felt so alone.

In the doctor's waiting room, guilty thoughts and questions began to swirl around in my head. Was God speaking to me? Are the Brethren right? Was God punishing me for leaving? But in the last year my eyes had begun to open. I was slowly coming out of my brainwashed state. People get cancer, I told myself firmly. Brethren got cancer. It isn't a sign of God's wrath or His judgement; it's just an illness, something biological.

I knew Dr Thomas well. She had been our family doctor for many years. She knew my whole family circle well. I'd been to see her many times while in the Brethren for my mental health, and to ask her to raise my antidepressant dose yet again. She'd never understood Brethren ways – how could she? – but now that I'd left, I'd seen how shocked she was by what I'd told her and by how my family were treating me.

She was a professional. She might have had her private views about the cruelties she saw in the Brethren, particularly as they impacted on her handful of female Brethren patients, but she had to keep her views to herself.

'I'm sorry, Maria,' Dr Thomas said, after examining me, 'but something isn't right here. I'm going to refer you to the hospital.'

I had begun to cry.

She warned me that I might have to wait up to six weeks for an NHS appointment to come through. As soon as it did, she said, I'd be in very safe hands. I had done my Google reading. I knew that six weeks before a diagnosis was too long, quite apart from the terrible, unimaginable agony of waiting, of not knowing, of having to keep the fears to myself. Then I remembered that about a year earlier, Bruce Hales, the Man of God, had ruled that all Brethren should take out private healthcare provided by the business branch of the Brethren, the Universal Business Team (UBT). It was extremely expensive but, as good obedient Brethren, we'd followed the rules and taken out a family policy. As far as I knew, I was still on it. I made a call to the company. Within minutes I had an appointment arranged for the following evening at an independent clinic.

Since I'd discovered the lump the previous evening, I had kept my news to myself. I didn't want to worry Max; I needed more time to take in the news alone. But now I had to tell him. He had to know.

'It's probably nothing to worry about,' he said, trying to reassure me, his voice breaking. I knew I would have said the same if our situations were reversed. But I already knew I had cancer; I could feel it. I couldn't tell Max that my real fears, my deepest fears, were not about the cancer or the treatment that lay ahead, but about what the Brethren would say about me now. There was no explaining that.

Later that afternoon I rang my old Brethren friend Jayne to ask her to come over. I needed her to look after the children while I went to my appointment. Jayne was one of the few Brethren who didn't seem to judge me. She had numerous siblings who'd left the Brethren, so perhaps she had more empathy for those of us who had left. In the quiet of my sitting room I blurted it all out: what I'd discovered and what the doctor had said; my fears for the children. I pleaded with her not to tell anyone until I knew for sure. She held me in her arms and told me she'd pray for me. And yes, of course she'd look after the children and keep my news to herself until I told her otherwise. Her reaction gave me hope that I might find more support and love rather than judgement from within the Brethren.

Max came with me to my appointment that evening. He took my hand and walked with me from room to room through the first consultation and then the mammogram and then the second consultation. He sat in the waiting room while nurses and technicians did a series of further scans. He brought me tea.

'Can you see something?' I asked the stenographer in a choked-up voice, watching her peer in closer to the screen.

'Yes, there's a definite lump or mass on your breast and it appears there are also some lumps under your arm.'

So, there it was.

I had cancer.

I came out from the scanning room and fell sobbing into Max's arms while behind the scenes further specialists leant over test tubes and ran biopsies. In yet another well-appointed room with comfy chairs and potted plants, the consultant explained to us that although they didn't yet know what stage my cancer was at, they did know that it had spread to my lymph nodes. And that, I understood, wasn't good.

'From what we can see on the scans and biopsy results,' he said, 'your cancer appears to be quite aggressive.'

All I could hear was Dad's voice saying, 'Maria, you shouldn't have left the Brethren. This is what happens when you go against God's will.'

'What happens now?' Max said.

'First there'll be the operation,' the consultant said, clicking away on his laptop. 'Then three weeks after that you'll start the chemotherapy. You'll have six treatments every three weeks.'

'You'll need to tell your family,' the nurse said as she ran through the forms. 'You'll need your family's support to get you through this.'

I crumbled. How could I tell her that I didn't really have any family?

'My family has disowned me,' I said, and then seeing both curiosity and shock on her face, I added, 'Because I left the church I was born into.'

'Perhaps this will bring you all back together again,' she said kindly, feeling her way. 'Surely they won't leave you to face this alone?'

I felt the unintended horror of the nurse's words. If the Brethren did help me, if they let my family support me, their primary motive would be to get me back into fellowship. Now that I had cancer, I was vulnerable. But I couldn't *not* tell my family. They had to know.

I spent a sleepless night in Max's bed, waiting for the dawn, glad that I didn't have to face my children yet; glad of the calm before the coming storm.

# THIRTY-ONE

The next morning, when Max had gone out to give me the privacy to tackle my family, I rang my older brother Edward. He'd been the only one of my siblings who hadn't judged me when I'd first left the Brethren. I still remembered the tenderness he had shown me that day we had walked on the beach together.

I sensed surprise and hope in Edward's voice. I knew he was still praying for my return so I cut straight to the chase.

'Edward,' I said, determined not to cry, 'I'm ringing to let you and the family know that I've been diagnosed with aggressive breast cancer. It has already spread to my lymph nodes, so it is quite advanced.'

'Where are you?' he asked. 'If you're at Max's house then give me the address. I'll be there as quickly as I can.'

Edward's kindness and concern, even his preparedness to enter the house of a worldly man to comfort his sister, warmed me, calmed me. It gave me hope. This was family. This was my flesh and blood. This was what I'd been missing for the last year and what I needed in my hour of need.

I told Edward that I didn't have the emotional strength to ring Mum and Dad, so he promised to phone them straight away.

Ten minutes later, my phone rang. It was Mum.

'Oh, you poor girl,' she said. 'Come home. Come and live with us. Come back. We'll take care of you.'

I longed to be cocooned by my parents' love and care but the words 'come back' made me remember that their love would come with conditions.

———

As a Brethren family we rarely showed physical affection to each other, but when I opened the door to Edward a few minutes later, he held me like he never wanted to let go. I could already see that my cancer was giving him renewed hope that I was going to repent and 'return to the fold'. Perhaps he felt that his prayers and those of my family were being answered. I too longed for reconciliation, but not on these terrible terms.

'Where has everyone been for the last year?' I sobbed, burying my head in Edward's chest.

'Don't worry,' he said. 'We'll never leave you again. We'll be here for you now. You'll see.'

I wanted to believe that Edward's protestations of loyalty and love were unconditional, and in another world, they would have been, but he was Brethren. All I could hope for was that they would help me through this immediate trial for as long as they were allowed to.

Later that day I visited my parents. It was the first time I'd been inside their house – the house where I had spent so much of my life – for almost a year. Both hugged me. Mum and I cried together. I told her everything I knew, what had happened so far and what was going to happen: the operation, the chemotherapy, the spells in hospital. We discussed how I was going to break the news to my children. We agreed that I should tell Lincoln, Juliet and Aaron first. I would bring them to Mum and Dad's house after school and tell them there. Then, later that evening, Oliver, Bradley and Kyle would come over and I could tell them too. That way, Mum said, we'd all be together.

Dad picked Lincoln, Juliet and Aaron up from school that day and brought them to my parents' house as agreed. I could see from their faces that they were already worried; they knew that I'd been banned from entering my parents' house, so something big – or bad – must have happened. I gave them reassuring hugs as Dad led us all into his study.

'I've been diagnosed with breast cancer,' I said, trying my best not to go round the houses, but to get the cruel truth straight out into the open. 'It has spread to my lymph nodes.' It sounded as if I was talking about someone else.

'Oh, Mum,' they exclaimed in unison.

Like many fourteen-year-old girls, Juliet didn't show much emotion or affection, but over the last year she'd become much closer to me. As she stood in Dad's study that afternoon, we held each other and cried.

'The consultant is confident that I can survive this,' I said, 'but I'm going to have to have an operation and then there'll be treatment. It is going to be tough on us all.'

Now that his father and his three older brothers had left the family home, Lincoln, at fifteen, despite being naturally shy, considered himself the man of the house. In the last year he seemed to have changed from a young teenager into a young man.

'We'll help you through, Mum,' he said, standing as tall as he could. 'We'll all be here for you. Remember that the consultant said you can survive this. So, you will.'

Lincoln stood by his word. Through the months of my treatment, he was there for me night and day. From that first day he insisted that he and I keep our bedroom doors open, so if I needed him at night, I could just call. Aaron, too, was so sweet and understanding. Every evening before going to bed, he'd say, 'If you're lonely in the night just come and get in my bed beside me.' And there were nights when I did just that. I'd climb into his single bed next to him and hold him tight. There were other times when he and Juliet would both get into my bed and we'd hold each other, drawing comfort and strength from each other's warmth. Those days brought the four of us closer still. Those memories will stay with me forever.

As my three older sons arrived at my parents' house that day, I could see hope etched on each of their faces. I knew that since I had left the Brethren a year earlier, they would have been praying constantly that I'd return to fellowship. Being summoned to my parents' house to meet with me could mean only one thing: their prayers had been answered. I had seen the error of my ways. And now I was about to dash all their hopes.

As everyone settled, I took in the familiarity of my parents' lounge. This is where I belonged – with my family, surrounded by my children, the ones I loved above anyone in this world. But we were not alone. The same seven framed portraits of the Men of God hung on the walls above our heads. I could feel the eyes of each of those men on me as I sat facing my older sons, each one of them eager to hear that I was about to return to Brethren life. Cruelty seemed to follow cruelty. I could see the judgement in the eyes of those men.

I shuddered, but at that moment I also realised how far I'd come from these negative, judgemental Brethren beliefs. I took a deep breath, squared my shoulders and looked directly at my sons.

'Please don't judge me when I say what I've got to say,' I began.

'Mum,' Oliver said, clearly expecting me to start my announcement by making the usual declaration of contrition, 'just say it. We won't judge.'

'I've got cancer,' I began again, my voice breaking up this time. 'I have aggressive breast cancer and it has spread.' All three young men, my grown boys, leapt from their seats and came to me in an instant. They took me into their arms.

Kyle, the emotional, affectionate one, sobbed. 'I'm here for you, Mum,' he whispered into my ear. 'You'll get through this.'

At that moment, sitting on my sofa with my sons hugging me tight, all I felt was unconditional love – love not tainted by differences of beliefs; love untainted by judgement; pure unconditional love from children for a suffering mother.

# THIRTY-TWO

The following months were taken up with operations to remove my breast and lymph nodes, chemotherapy and radiotherapy treatment. I did my best to make life at home with Lincoln, Aaron and Juliet as normal as possible. My parents and Max helped with the shopping, separately, of course. I hadn't yet been able to face introducing them to my worldly boyfriend. On the weekends, when the children were at their dad's, Max and I went out to restaurants and bars when I felt able. I still wanted to make the most of my newfound freedom; I wasn't going to let cancer stop me. Lincoln, Juliet and Aaron helped out at home too and were always there for emotional support.

The Brethren elders had given my family permission to support me through my illness only because I had still not been officially withdrawn from, but their contact with me had strict limits. Mum helped in any way that she could, but she refused to come into my house because my home was 'unclean'. Dad and my siblings helped with the children, taking them to school or picking them up if I wasn't able, but they too would never enter my house.

Between May and July of that year I lost all my hair due to the chemotherapy treatment. At the clinic I saw many other women who had lost their hair too, but, unlike them, I chose to wear a wig rather than a headscarf. The thought of wearing a headscarf again made me shudder. It brought back too many terrible memories.

When I travelled to the appointed hospital for my chemotherapy treatment, I was supposed to have someone

243

accompany me and to drive me there and back. Dad volunteered. We both enjoyed the hour-long journeys to and from the clinic. We generally kept the conversation light and to a minimum to avoid any potential conflict. But one day, wanting to provoke a discussion, I took a risk and plunged in.

'Why do all religions think they are "the one"?' I asked. I watched Dad's hands tighten on the steering wheel before he began to parrot a stream of Brethren phrases:

'It's part of the mystery. There is only one true way: Christ and the assembly. We are the bride of Christ . . . God in His sovereignty put each of us in the assembly, we can't question that . . . Many of these denominations which claim they are "the one", are, as you call them, religions, but we, the Brethren, aren't a religion, we're simple Christians who've had the privilege of being chosen sovereignly by God to be in and follow the only true light. There is only one man who can take us through and that's our beloved brother Mr Hales.'

As he talked about how he felt sad that people hadn't the privilege or the light that he had, and then about how Catholicism and Protestantism had gone so badly wrong, it struck me, perhaps for the first time, that my father sincerely believed everything he was saying. He'd known nothing else and wanted to know nothing else. My father was an intelligent man, a smart businessman, but he had spent his entire life in a deluded state, under the control of a man-made organisation. Nothing I said would ever make him see differently.

I know my dad honestly believed – and probably still does – that I took the path to damnation when I left the Brethren. I know he felt compelled to save me from that terrible fate.

'Maria,' he said to me once, 'I am watching you about to step off a cliff. It's my job to do all I can to save you.'

My poor deluded father. How I wished I could save *him*.

Other Brethren members from outside the family were also permitted to show their support during the weeks of my operation and treatment. Sometimes there would be a knock at the door and a Brethren sister would be standing there with a shepherd's pie or a crock-pot of stew. Another afternoon I had a visit from an old Brethren friend called Alison who'd had breast cancer two years before. She did her best to avoid looking at the large television that took up one corner of the room. She perched on the edge of the settee, as if ready to make a hasty escape if need be. We talked easily about our cancer journeys. We talked about our children, her family and different Brethren members: who was pregnant, who had a new baby or who wasn't well.

Then, out of the blue, Alison said, 'Maria, I want to pray with you. Please will you kneel with me while I pray?'

I was taken off guard, but because she had come a long way I didn't think it was fair to refuse. So, there we were: two women kneeling in prayer in my sitting room. Praying was no longer part of my life and, as I knelt to pray that day, dressed in my worldly clothes, jewellery and makeup, it felt all wrong. Alison reached into her bag and pulled out two tissues. She neatly placed one on her head, and one on mine, before taking my hand in hers and praying.

'Lord Jesus,' she prayed, 'help Maria through her cancer, give her strength. Help her in her faith. Help her come back to the light and feel your arms around her. Help her feel the Brethren's arms around her. In thy name, Lord Jesus, amen.'

As I said the word 'amen' I wished I could feel something, but I felt only embarrassment at kneeling there with a tissue on my head, and resentment that Alison had sprung this on me. I'd left religion and religion had left me. I wanted no part of this life anymore. I could survive cancer without the Brethren's prayers. I felt a strength within me that I knew could get me through. I'd stepped outside of that life and into another; I could never go back.

# THIRTY-THREE

By October I had completed my chemotherapy treatment. I was scheduled to start a five-week course of radiotherapy the following Monday. I was looking forward to the weekend. Max and I would most likely go out on Saturday night when the children were with their dad. We'd spend time with friends to celebrate the end of my chemo.

By six o'clock that evening, Lincoln, Juliet, Aaron and I had enjoyed a meal together – a fish pie that Mum had cooked and given me for the freezer. The three of us had talked about school and what was planned for the weekend. Once we'd finished our meal the children tidied up the kitchen while I watched the news.

Suddenly my phone rang. It was Dad. His voice was serious. 'Edward and I would like to call round to see you for a few minutes before meeting time.'

'Sure,' I said, puzzled at what would be serious enough for them to step over the threshold of my home. What could be so important that it couldn't wait until tomorrow?

Ten minutes later there was a loud knock on the door. Dad and Edward followed me into the living room. I could see immediately that they were on Brethren business – they had that look about them. I gestured for them to sit down but they shook their heads. Edward plunged in.

'We've called to tell you that your matters will be discussed at the meeting this evening.'

'The Brethren feel we need to reassess your position,' Dad added.

'What do you mean by "reassess my position?"' I asked, panic in my voice. It meant that my 'case' was about to be discussed in detail in public at the Brethren 'care' meeting, the meeting that made disciplinary decisions. And I knew what was likely to happen. Almost certainly the men at the meeting would decide that I had to be formally 'withdrawn from'. I didn't need this; I was weak and depleted after my chemotherapy treatment, and I was starting radiotherapy on the following Monday – every day for five weeks.

'We can't say what it means yet,' Dad replied. 'It's felt that we need to bring it to the Brethren to see what they feel.'

'Bring it to the Brethren' meant that a decision had already been made. And as elders of the local meeting, Dad and Edward already knew what that decision was. After discussing my case in detail at their meeting that evening, they would then tell the Brethren what other senior leaders had decided.

'Do whatever you think you need to do,' I said angrily as they let themselves out my front door.

Juliet came into the living room. She'd clearly overheard what Dad and Edward had said. 'Mum,' she said, 'I'm not going to the meeting tonight. I don't want to sit there and listen to them talk about you and everything you're meant to have done.'

She was right. No child should have to witness the public humiliation and denunciation of their mother. I was glad to know that Juliet understood that, at least.

When their dad came to pick them up for the meeting that evening, Aaron was the only one who got in his car. Once he'd left, Juliet, Lincoln and I watched a documentary about paramedics. It took our minds off what was happening at the meeting that night.

'I'd love to become a paramedic,' Juliet said as we watched the trainees learning how to do CPR, 'or join the army.'

I smiled.

'Juliet,' I said, 'if you want to do either of those jobs, you won't be able to stay with the Brethren. For a start you'd need to get training or go to university and you know that the Brethren wouldn't allow that.'

She sighed. 'Do you think they'd let me be a forklift driver? I'd hate to be stuck in an office like all the other Brethren girls.'

'No, Juliet,' I said, trying not to laugh, 'I don't think you'd be allowed to be a forklift driver if you stay in the Brethren. You'd have to wear trousers and that's not going to be allowed, is it?'

There was still some reason for hope for my daughter while she harboured such ambitions, while she was missing meetings, watching documentaries with me. Perhaps, I wondered, Juliet was starting to see the possibility of a life lived outside the Brethren.

Dad and Edward brought Aaron home from the evening meeting at nine o'clock. Without even looking at me, Aaron took himself up to his bedroom and shut the door. I gestured for Dad and Edward to come into the living room again and shut the door. It was the end of the day, and I was tired. Why did they have to come now to deliver their judgement? Couldn't they see that I was too exhausted and broken? Sitting myself down on the settee, I rubbed my hand over my bald head and braced myself. They both still refused to sit.

'So,' I said, unable to keep a weary sarcasm from my voice, 'what did the Brethren decide?'

Dad answered in the coldest of voices I have ever heard him use.

'The Brethren,' he said, 'have decided that they can no longer walk with you.'

For months before my cancer, I had longed to hear those words, to end the countless meetings. But now? I knew this judgement meant that I'd be cut off once again from my family and they wouldn't be permitted to see me let alone help me. After all these months in which I had come to depend on their support, in which they had professed their undying love, this sudden withdrawal and the cruel timing of it was a brutal blow.

'Why?' I asked, feeling hot tears of injustice beginning to well up inside me.

Edward couldn't look at me. He kept his eyes on the floor as he spoke. 'The Brethren,' he said, 'feel that as you no longer want to attend the Lord's Supper we can no longer associate ourselves with you.'

I stood up in my anger but had to quickly sit back down. I was too weak to stand.

'Why now? Why do this now when you know I'm starting my radiotherapy treatment next week? I haven't been to the Lord's Supper for over eighteen months. Why cut me off now?'

Dad shook his head as they both walked towards the door. As he opened the door, he turned back one last time and, looking at me coldly, he said, 'We're sorry that it's come to this, Maria. It's all so sad but you've chosen *this* life, so you have to face the consequences.'

'How dare you!' I shouted at their retreating backs as they walked down the drive. 'How dare my own father and brother come into my house and be so cold-hearted as to withdraw from me while I am at my very weakest!'

But they did not turn back. I watched their cars disappear into the night.

The children stayed in their bedrooms for the rest of the evening. I knew they were upset. They knew this meant that though they were allowed to continue living with me – I had custody of them until they were sixteen – they'd have to live as separately from me as possible. And when they were among the Brethren they'd have to live with the shame of living with a mother who had been withdrawn from.

It was Monday, the first day of my radiotherapy treatment. I took the hour-long journey to the hospital alone for the first time. As I was travelling back home, my phone rang. I pulled into a lay-by to answer it. It was Mum.

'Where are you?' she said in a tearful voice.

'On my way home from the hospital,' I replied. 'Why?'

'Oh, Maria,' she said, 'I love you.' Then she put the phone down. It was the last time my mother ever called me.

Later that afternoon, when I picked the children up from school, no one, not even my sister, dared look me in the eye.

I was an outcast now. I was a leper. I was unclean. No longer one of them.

By the time we got home from school I was exhausted, but I needed to make the children their meal. I cooked them roast chicken, roast potatoes and vegetables. I was looking forward to sitting down with them and hearing about their weekend; it would be a comfort and a distraction. The children sat at the table while I served up their dinner and then I joined them. They seemed tense, hesitant. Then, as I began to eat, Aaron said, 'Mum, we can't eat with you anymore. Could you eat in the other room?'

I couldn't believe my ears. It took me a minute to take in what Aaron had just asked me to do. I wanted to scream in anger. How was this OK? Leave my own table? Tears pricked my eyes, angry tears, but I didn't move. All three of them looked at me expectantly. As hot tears rolled down my cheeks I gave them a watery smile and slowly shook my head. I would not leave the table. I would not let the Brethren's rules continue to control my life. I could see Aaron's lip quiver at my response but, gaining his composure, with plate in hand, he stood to leave the table while nudging Juliet and Lincoln to do the same.

Obediently, Juliet and Lincoln picked up their plates and, with Aaron close on their heels, they all went into the living room to eat their meal. I sat alone in the empty kitchen, unable to eat at all.

My youngest children never shared a meal with me at my table again. I know I shouldn't have been angry with Aaron as he was acting on what he'd been told to do by the Brethren. But I am still incredulous that a thirteen-year-old boy could have been instructed to say these words to his own mother while she was undergoing treatment for cancer.

Now that I had been withdrawn from, there were other changes. Now when Kevin picked the children up to take them to the meeting, he came an hour earlier. When I asked Juliet why, she said that they had been told to go from my house to Granny and Grandpa's house before the meeting in order to 'get clean'.

'Our house is unclean, Mum,' she said, shrugging defensively. 'It's just what they've told us to do now. We can't take the uncleanness into the meeting.'

I turned away, biting my lip. I didn't want to make things any harder for her by voicing my outrage.

# THIRTY-FOUR

By the end of the year I had completed all my chemotherapy and radiotherapy. My body was pronounced cancer-free. Now all I had to do was gain my strength for my breast reconstruction the following year.

I continued to have cancer check-ups through the winter and into the spring of 2015. Mr Davis, my surgeon, talked me through the different options for the reconstruction surgery. He was keen for me to have a newer sort of surgery, requiring travel to Ipswich. I decided to go with it, and booked for June 2015. All I had to do now was get my strength back and return to as normal a family life with Lincoln, Juliet and Aaron as Brethren rules allowed.

Max and I made a plan. He and I would drive to Ipswich for my operation, which was scheduled for the following day. We booked a beautiful holiday lodge on the Norfolk coast where we would stay for my recovery once I'd been discharged. Max would care for me until I was fit enough to make the journey back home. Now all we had to do was wait.

Since I'd been withdrawn from, I'd had very little contact with any of my family apart from my three children who were still living with me. The only contact I'd had was from my dad, who sent me a scripture quote every night via email. Occasionally he would inquire about my health, but I never visited my parents and they never visited me.

Although my family had cut me off again, I felt that it was only fair and right to let them know about my upcoming operation. Three weeks before the scheduled date, I sent Dad an email. To my surprise, he phoned me immediately. He wanted to know why I was going to Ipswich for the operation and who was going to care for me while I was there. I explained how the specialist surgeon worked there; that they didn't offer this special kind of procedure in my home town. I assured him that my care, once I'd been discharged, was all organised. We were renting a lodge. Max would take care of me.

There was much 'hmming' and 'ahhing' on the other end of the line. I could sense that Dad wasn't happy. He finished the call abruptly and said that he'd speak to me again before we set off.

Two weeks before my scheduled operation I got another call from Dad. He hardly gave me time to say hello before launching into what he had to say.

'We aren't confident that you will be properly cared for while staying in a holiday lodge,' he said, 'so we've spoken to some Brethren from Ipswich who have a separate annexe on their house. We think it would be better if you stayed there. Your sister Claire will come and look after you.'

I was so taken aback that it took me a while to answer. My parents hadn't spoken to me in over six months and now here they were trying to organise my convalescent care. Was the plan to get me into this Brethren annexe when I was in a weak and vulnerable state and keep me there so they could put renewed pressure me to return? I was furious.

'No, Dad,' I said. 'I'm quite happy with the arrangements I've made with Max and I'm perfectly confident that I will be well cared for. Thanks for thinking of me though,' I added before putting the phone down.

He rang me back a few seconds later; he was pleading this time, which made me even more certain that a new plan had been formulated that he was under orders to execute.

'Please, Maria,' he said, 'just think about it. You've missed your family and we've missed you. We just want to help you.'

It was true, I did miss them, and I did long for my family's care at this time, but I knew I couldn't trust their motives or the motives of the people who were making the orders behind them, so I kept to my resolve, despite my father and other family members trying to persuade me several more times by phone over the next few days.

Then, one afternoon, just a couple of days before Max and I were due to travel to Ipswich, Dad rang me again.

'Your mum, Claire and I are going to travel over to Ipswich,' he said, 'so that we can be at the hospital on the day of your operation.'

'OK,' I said, warily, 'but why? You've had nothing to do with me for months and now you want to come and be near me during an operation. I don't understand, Dad, and if I'm honest, I'm not sure I want that.'

'We feel it's right that we should be there while you go through such a big operation,' he said. 'We want to be praying for you.'

I decided I'd go along with it and make the most of any contact with my mother, father and sister that I might have left. I knew I'd have to keep strong and stand my ground though, but I was confident that I would be safe in the hospital and with Max by my side. What harm could they do?

The big day arrived. I was scared about this operation. It was a lot bigger than my mastectomy. Dad phoned the evening before to say that he, Mum and my sister would like to meet me at the hospital on the Sunday morning before I went in. I agreed. I longed to see them, even if it was only for a few minutes.

Dad strode into the hospital foyer with his usual aura of authority, dressed in his Sunday best, with Mum and Claire following closely on his heels, dressed in their padded-out silk headscarves and their conservative skirts and tops. They had clearly come straight from the 6 a.m. Lord's Supper in Ipswich. How odd they all looked to me now.

When I introduced them to Max, my dad reached out to shake his hand. Mum and Claire kept silent behind him, heads bowed. I wanted to show them what a nice person Max was, but once Dad had shaken his hand, they ignored him. Thanking them for coming, I said my goodbyes before making my way to the ward with Max.

'We'll see you later,' Mum called after me.

See me later? That wasn't what I had agreed to. They were supposed to be here just to pray while I underwent my operation.

'Maria, it's time to wake up,' the nurse announced in my ear.

Forcing my eyes open, I felt a pain searing across my stomach. I howled. The nurse handed me a device with a button explaining that the button would release morphine straight into my veins. I pressed it and gratefully felt myself drift back into a drug-induced sleep.

When I opened my eyes again, I was back in the ward. I could hear familiar voices around me, but my eyes seemed to keep closing of their own accord. I listened for Max's voice. I mumbled his name. Someone came to my bedside and leant over me.

'Maria, it's Mum. Can you hear me?'

Struggling to open my eyes, I asked, 'Where am I? Why are you here, Mum? Where's Max?'

'You're back in your private ward and Max is waiting in the corridor,' Mum said. 'We wanted to be here for you when you woke up.'

I was confused. Why was Mum here? She hadn't come this close to me physically since I'd left the Brethren over two years before. Gradually I was able to keep my eyes open. Now I could see Dad and Claire standing close to my bed. Dad had his arm around Mum, and she was crying.

'We're here for you, Maria,' she whispered tearfully. 'We want to help you.'

I wanted to ask her why they were there, to ask where Max was, but I was too weak and in too much pain to do anything but nod. 'We're here for you, Maria.' They'd said those same words a year ago and then had cut me off again. I reached for the morphine button. I pressed it hard. Mum kissed me on my forehead as I fell back into sleep.

'Don't worry about anything for now,' she said. 'Just get some sleep.'

For the next few hours, I drifted in and out of sleep. At one point when I woke I was thankful to see the familiar shape of Max in the chair next to me. I felt safe with him there. I reached out and took his hand in mine before drifting off again.

When morning came the nurses helped me to get out of bed so that I didn't develop clots. I had drains and tubes attached to me, but I was grateful to get myself upright. The sooner I got moving, the sooner I'd get well and be out of there. As soon as I was comfortable in my chair, I saw Dad, Mum and Claire peeping their heads around the ward door, smiling encouragingly. Why were they still here? On the one hand, it felt good to have them beside me, but on the other, it felt disturbing. Then Dad made one of his announcements.

'Claire's going to stay in Ipswich for a few days so she can be with you as much as possible while you're in the hospital. She'll come and be with you every day to keep you company,' he said in a 'don't question me' tone.

'I just want to be here to keep you company,' Claire said.

'Please don't put any more pressure on me to go back to the Brethren,' I said. 'And I want to be able to see Max. You can't stop me seeing Max.'

'I promise,' Claire said.

I liked Claire but I didn't quite trust her. Since I'd left the Brethren, she had done everything she could to persuade me to return. She had tried getting cross with me. She had tried showering me with affection. She had tried reasoning with me. I felt sorry for her. I know she missed me, and I reminded myself that she was just following Brethren orders. So, as I lay in that hospital bed, my mind still addled by morphine, I decided to do my best to trust her. I was too exhausted and weak to argue.

When it was time for Mum and Dad to leave, Mum leant over and whispered in my ear, 'Please come back, we miss you so much.'

I kissed them both goodbye.

In the days that followed my operation, Claire came to the hospital every day. She sat in the corner of my ward, knitting or chatting if I was awake and felt able to talk. I would fall asleep to the clicking of her knitting needles as she sat watching over me. It was a strange time for both of us, but we had many good conversations. She stuck to her promise and didn't preach to me or even mention my returning to the Brethren. We talked about our children, our parents, our childhood, my old Brethren friends and past memories. An affection kindled between us again.

Kevin phoned every day, asking how I was. It was strange, as I hadn't had any proper contact with him since I'd been withdrawn from. I knew he was acting under instruction. I tried to accept whatever contact any of my family made, still hoping for a reconciliation on my terms for the sake of Lincoln, Juliet and Aaron, and for any future life we might salvage together, but initially I was still suspicious. Max hadn't been able to visit nearly as much as he would have liked. It had been awkward for him to visit during the day with Claire there all the time. He came in the evenings instead when she left to attend a daily Brethren meeting.

One day, my younger sister Chloe appeared in the doorway during visiting hours accompanied by Oliver's wife Jessica, my daughter-in-law. I barely knew Jessica because she had married Oliver after I had left the Brethren. I was speechless.

'It's lovely to see you, Mum,' Jessica said.

Mum? I didn't know this girl. I'd only met her a couple of times before I'd left the Brethren. Chloe came and stood beside me; her face was serious.

'Maria, please tell me what I can do to make things right. Tell me what I've done wrong and I'll make it right. Just come back. We need you. Your children need you.'

'Chloe,' I said, struggling to find the strength to speak, 'I am here. I haven't gone anywhere. You can talk to me anytime you want. I need my children, and I need you too. You have chosen to cut me out of your life, not the other way round.' Chloe was crying now. Jessica was crying too.

I thanked Chloe for making the journey to see me. I thanked her for bringing Jessica too. I told her I was sorry that I'd upset her, but I was also sorry that she couldn't accept me for who I was. As we gave each other a hug, she whispered in my ear, 'Goodbye, Maria, please think about what I've said.'

Jessica came over to my bedside, leant over, hugged me tight and gave me a kiss on my cheek.

'Look after that husband of yours,' I said.

'I will,' she replied. 'He misses you.'

'I miss him too,' I said. 'Tell him I miss him so much.'

As I watched them walk out of the ward, I lay back on my pillow full of a new hope that my family might finally accept me for who I was. Perhaps the Brethren had changed their minds about me. But another part of me also suspected that all these visits, all these elaborate displays of affection from my family members, may have been part of a strategic ploy to try and get me to return.

I spent four days in hospital before being transferred to a private clinic for a further three days. It was time for Claire to return home. She drove me to the private clinic and stayed while I got settled in. I was feeling stronger now, but I knew I was going to miss my sister. As I settled myself in the comfy armchair in my little private ward, Claire took a seat by the window.

'So,' she said, 'now that we've shown you how much we love you, will you come back to the Brethren and to your family?'

I took a sharp breath. I should have been prepared for this final ultimatum, but over the previous days I had let myself believe that my family's love and kindness towards me was unconditional. Claire's blunt question shattered that hope.

'I won't return to the Brethren,' I said. 'You know that. How many times do I have to say it? I'm here for all of you, I love all of you, I need all of you, but I won't return to the Brethren.' And then something within her seemed to snap.

'Maria,' she said, her voice quickly rising to a shout of exasperation and contempt, 'you really are the most selfish person I've ever known. You sit there with your short hair, trousers, jewellery and makeup and ask us to accept you! You're obviously mentally unstable. Don't you realise that you're killing us all with your behaviour? Your children are emotionally damaged. Come to the Lord Jesus and He will save you!' She paused, trying to contain her rage. 'I still believe you'll go to heaven, Maria, but it won't be the heaven that the Brethren are going to and that scares me.'

I was dumbstruck. Why was my sister berating me for having short hair? I had no hair! Chemotherapy had seen to that. Why was she accusing me of being mentally unstable? Brethren rules and my abusive husband might have pushed me to the edge but now that I had left, I was sounder in my mind than I had ever been. Couldn't she see that? But I also knew that Claire was furious because, despite sitting by my bedside for several days, as I suspected she must have been told to do, she had failed to persuade me back into fellowship. She'd have to go back and tell my family and the Brethren elders that she had failed. There would be shame in that.

Claire stood up, shoved her knitting into her bag and, turning her back on me, made for the door.

'Claire,' I said, my heart breaking now that I could see what this had all been about, 'thank you for all the lovely conversations that we've had this week. Thank you for keeping me company. I'm sorry that I can't give you the answer that you want. Now, please go.'

Without a sound or a backward glance, she left the ward. I rang her that evening to make sure she got home safely but from that day until now I've never had a conversation with my sister again.

Once I had got over the shock of Claire's tirade and the confirmation that my family's visits and protestations of love had all been part of a strategy to win me back, I thought I'd seen the end of their visits, but they hadn't quite given up yet. On that Saturday I was in my private ward watching a movie on the television when a nurse popped her head around the door.

'There's someone here to see you,' she announced cheerily as Kyle, my third son, walked through the doorway.

'Kyle!' I exclaimed, heaving myself up from my chair, hobbling to him and hugging him tightly. 'What are *you* doing here?'

'Mum, I wanted to come and see you. I've got some news for you that I wanted to tell you in person,' he told me with a huge grin. I couldn't believe that he'd come all this way just to see me. I couldn't help but be touched.

'It's so good to see you, son,' I said, trying not to hold on to him too tightly. 'What's your news?'

'I'm getting married!'

'You are?' I exclaimed. 'Who to?'

'Emily Baker,' he answered.

I knew Emily. She was the daughter of one of my closest friends while I had been in the Brethren. I was glad that it was someone I knew, but shocked that no one, not even Claire, had chosen to tell me.

'That's so exciting!' I said. 'When is the wedding?'

'We're still waiting for an answer from Mr Hales,' he said. 'You know how it is.'

I did. I remembered.

'You've got a house?' I said, wondering how he'd found the money.

'Yes, I'm in the process of buying one.'

'I hope you found something reasonably cheap,' I added, remembering how the Brethren encourage young people into big mortgages.

'It wasn't as cheap as I would have liked,' Kyle replied, 'And it needs work done on it, but it's a good family home, so we'll be able to live there for a long time.'

I patted his arm and said simply, 'That's good. Well done.'

I couldn't help worrying how he was going to take on a big mortgage at only twenty-four years old, but I wasn't going to talk about that. I hadn't seen or spoken to Kyle since I'd been withdrawn from, and there was so much I wanted to ask him, but before I got the chance to ask him any further questions, he announced that it was time for him to get a taxi back to the station.

He seemed eager to leave but I understood. He would have been acting under instruction and, once he'd told me his news, he wasn't allowed to prolong his conversation with me. He hugged me and kissed me goodbye on my cheek. Kyle had always been the most affectionate of my children. Oh, how

I missed this show of love and affection. I held him tight and kissed him in return.

I said goodbye. I had no idea when or how or if I'd ever see him again.

'Please let me know your wedding date once you've got the go-ahead,' I called after him.

'I will,' he assured me. 'Goodbye, Mum, and get well soon,' he called as he disappeared down the corridor.

Soon after Kyle left, while I was still sitting taking in his news, my phone rang. It was Kevin again. For two years now he had been fighting the divorce I had filed for, so even though we'd been separated for over two years, he was still technically my husband. He'd rung me every day since my operation. I didn't want to talk to him – I had nothing to say to him, but I answered my phone.

'I'm just ringing to see how you're feeling today,' he said, going through the motions again. It was time to put a stop to this charade, I thought. It was time to put a stop to all of it. I'd had enough.

'Look, Kevin,' I said, 'I'm not sure why you keep phoning me. You know how I feel about you. You know I don't want you to be in my life, so why do you keep ringing me?'

'I want to show you that I still love you, Maria,' he said, dropping the pretence. 'I think you're making a big mistake and you'll regret getting a divorce. Please rethink what you're doing.'

Bile rose in my throat. This man was my abuser, yet here he was ringing me up and pleading with me not only to return to the Brethren, but to return to him to save him from the divorce that would shame him in Brethren eyes. I did not want this man anywhere near me again. No doubt he'd been told by the priests to try one last time.

'Kevin,' I said, 'please just leave me alone. I don't have any feelings for you. You know what you've done. You're the one person who I never ever want anything to do with again. Don't phone me again. Goodbye.'

I slept soundly that night and, when I woke, I had a new sense of purpose. It was a Sunday in early summer 2015, and today I would be discharged from the hospital. I would spend a week in a beautiful lodge on the Norfolk coast. I'd spend the week being looked after by Max. I'd pamper myself and relax in a hot tub, I'd watch television, I'd read a novel, I'd visit pubs and I'd eat out in restaurants. I'd do all the things I'd never been allowed to do while in the Brethren and I wouldn't feel guilty. I'd feel liberated and free.

# THIRTY-FIVE

A few weeks after my operation, Lincoln, Juliet and Aaron, now all in their mid-teens, went away with Kevin as usual. The court had ordered that they spend two weeks with their dad during the summer holidays. He usually took them to visit his family in the South. I had no reason to be concerned, but the day before they were due home, I got a phone call from Kevin asking if it would be possible for them to stay another week. I was uneasy but I didn't want to spoil the children's fun, so I agreed.

Before the children went away that summer, I had made a decision – one I hadn't mentioned to them. I had decided to get a puppy. I'd wanted a dog for as long as I could remember, but since the 1960s pets had been forbidden in the Brethren as the Man of the God at that time had ruled that having a pet made Brethren distracted from the Lord's work, but a distraction was exactly what I needed. I found the weeks without the children almost unbearable; the emptiness of the house, the silence and the loneliness sent me into a state of anxiety. I would sit in the living room trying to watch television or read a book but would end up pacing the floor. What if I lost Lincoln, Juliet and Aaron? How would I cope? A puppy would keep me company when the children weren't around, and I was sure they would enjoy it too. So, while the children were away, I bought an eight-week-old Bichon Frise, a little ball of white fluff. I called him Bailie. He brought new light to my life.

The day before the children were due home after their three weeks away, I started to panic about their reaction.

Would they be angry with me for bringing something else into our home that was forbidden by the Brethren? But as I watched Bailie running from room to room, playing at my feet and cuddling up in my arms, I was sure that as soon as they saw him, they'd fall in love with him as I had done.

I was overjoyed to see them home and ran to the door to greet them with Bailie close on my heels. Juliet was first to come through the door. She looked drawn and pale. But before I could hug her and ask her if she was OK, she spotted the puppy. Dropping her bag on the floor, she stared at the little bundle of fur at my heels before stepping back in surprise.

'Are you serious? A dog? You know we aren't allowed pets. Why have you done this?'

Before I could answer, Juliet grabbed her bag and suitcase and pushed past Bailie and me, storming off into her bedroom and slamming the door. The boys didn't look so bothered, but Aaron shook his head, tutted and said, 'Probably wasn't a good idea to get a dog, Mum.'

Juliet stayed in her bedroom all that afternoon, refusing to talk to me. I heard her on the phone telling someone about the dog. I was shocked at how angry she sounded. Eventually, she came down into the kitchen, where I was busy preparing our meal.

'Well,' I said, mashing the potatoes, pretending everything was fine, 'did you have a good time away? What did you get up to?'

Leaning herself against the big cream dresser in the corner of the kitchen, she said angrily, 'Mum, if you don't get rid of that dog, I will have to leave this house immediately.'

I was shocked by the extent of her anger. She hadn't reacted this way when I'd installed the television. I tried to reason with her.

'Oh, come on. Bailie will keep me company when you're away with your dad. He won't do anyone any harm. Look at him, he's just a puppy.'

But Juliet wouldn't back down.

'No, Mum, I mean what I say. It's me or the dog,' she said, as she stomped out of the kitchen.

What had happened to her in these last few weeks?

Later that evening, when she came home from the meeting, she called me into her bedroom. As I sat down on her bed next to her, I could see that she'd been crying. As I tried to put my arm around her, she shrugged me away.

'Mum,' she said, 'while I was away with Dad, I stayed with Stephen and Joanne Hill.' Stephen and Joanne had been close friends of ours when we'd lived down south. They were a family of eight like us. I knew Juliet enjoyed their girls' company.

'One evening I got really upset, so Stephen and Joanne sat me down and we talked. I told them all the bad things I've done. I confessed all my sins to them. I told them about having a Brethren boyfriend and about watching television with you. Mum, I realised that I've been an awful person.'

I stopped her, trying to protest against what she was saying. But she wasn't listening.

'No, Mum. I've sinned so badly but I've asked Jesus for forgiveness. He's forgiven me and now I won't be that person anymore. I'm going to commit my life to Him and the Brethren. Please don't try and change my mind, and I mean what I say about that dog. Please get rid of it or I will have to move out.'

Juliet had changed.

I managed to find a new home for Bailie that week and handed him over. Though giving him up was painful, I couldn't risk losing my children for a dog.

In a matter of months after my operation, my parents came to see me.

'Maria,' Dad said, 'we have come to see you today because we feel that you haven't listened to God speaking to you through your cancer and, for that reason, we want no more social interaction with you.'

'Dad,' I said, 'did you act out of love for your daughter when you came to my hospital bedside, or did you only do it because you thought that I'd return to the Brethren?'

'Everything we did,' he said, without any hesitation or shame, 'everything we did back in the summer was in the hope of you returning to the Brethren.'

I had heard enough. I stood up. I gave Mum a hug and a kiss and then I said, 'Please leave my house now.'

They both stood up and left. Apart from a short conversation with Dad in March 2018, I have never had a face-to-face conversation with either of my parents again. I have never even seen my mum again. I miss her and I know she misses me too. We were more than mother and daughter, we were friends.

Every year I send my parents birthday messages. I send them emails of love on Father's Day and Mother's Day. Sometimes I get a short reply of acknowledgement, but mostly I hear nothing.

As the months dragged on, Juliet never returned to her previous self. She was civil to me, but she kept her distance. She would occasionally take a peek at the television, but it was never the same after that fateful trip down south. Aaron and Lincoln seemed to follow her example by keeping their distance from me as much as possible. I got a full-time job as a manager in a clothing store to help support myself, so the three of them spent more and more time with their Brethren friends.

Looking back, I ask myself, could I have done more to save my remaining children from the indoctrination? Should I have taken them away from the Brethren school? Should I have stopped them from attending the daily meetings? I believed I had been giving them a choice. I wanted them to see – through me – that you can live happily outside of the Brethren. I knew that if I'd forced them to stop leading the only life they thought possible they'd have turned against me much sooner. I was also so busy trying to navigate my way through this strange new world and surviving my cancer treatment. Yes, I was still functioning as a mum to Lincoln, Juliet and Aaron, but I was also doing all I could to fit into a new life outside. It wasn't an easy time for any of us but especially not for the children. No young teenager should have to make the choices they had to make.

Summer turned to winter and then to spring. On St Patrick's Day in March 2016 Juliet came to me to ask if she and her brothers could spend the day with a Brethren family.

I happily agreed to them having a day out with their friends, but I asked them to make sure to be home that evening by nine o'clock.

As the children were out for the day, I rang Max and proposed that we go out to celebrate St Patrick's Day. Putting on my green glad rags, I headed out to the local pub to meet him. Max and I enjoyed a few happy hours together before I took the short walk home in time for the children's return.

On arriving home, I busy myself in the kitchen by making school lunches for the following day. Something is making me nervous. I try to settle in the lounge and watch some television, but I find myself constantly looking at my watch. Nine o'clock comes and goes; I try not to worry. They'll be back soon, I tell myself.

At 9.15 I can't wait any longer. I ring Juliet. She doesn't pick up. I ring both of her brothers. They don't pick up either. Now I'm worried. I try phoning Kevin. He doesn't pick up. As it approaches ten o'clock, I am certain something is wrong. I send an email to Kevin in the hope that he'll have the decency to reply. Five minutes later my phone rings.

It's Kevin.

'Juliet has decided not to come home tonight,' he says matter-of-factly. 'She's going to stay with the Hollands for a few days. Also,' he adds, 'if it's OK with you, so too will Aaron and Lincoln.'

My heart sinks. I am certain that this day has been set up as a way of getting my children away from me. I am enraged but I try to keep my voice calm as I tell him that I want them all home immediately. Kevin replies with almost a gloat in his voice.

'Lincoln and Juliet are both over sixteen now so they can decide what they want for themselves, and they have decided they don't want to come home tonight.'

Now I'm really angry.

'Get Aaron home immediately,' I say. 'You know that by law he must live with me, so get him back here right now.'

Kevin puts the phone down. I pace the house, continually ringing his mobile, but it goes to voicemail every time. What am I going to do? How can they be allowed to do this? I find myself in the front living room, pacing, staring out the window, hoping to see Kevin's car come up the drive. Suddenly, headlights light up the room. I run out the front door just as Aaron is climbing out of the car. Putting my arms around him, I hold him close. I weep in relief that he's come home; I weep because Lincoln and Juliet haven't. I yell at Kevin.

'How dare you do this! How dare you do this behind my back! I'm their mother! You should have warned me. We could have talked. This isn't right.'

I slam the car door.

Aaron stands next to me with his head bent as though he's ashamed. I put my arm around his shoulders and we walk back into the empty house. As he looks up at me, I see tears in his eyes, and I realise how hard this is for him. He's going to miss the others so much, especially Juliet. All of us have relied on each other so much. We each need each other. Neither of us says a word. I kiss him on his forehead before he goes upstairs to bed.

I climb into Juliet's bed and cry myself into a fitful sleep – a sleep filled with the scent of my daughter; sleep filled with guilt, fear, anger and sadness.

From that day, and for weeks afterwards, I slept in Juliet's bedroom every night. I felt closer to her there, as I'd hug her pillow and drink in the fading scent of her. It was like my daughter had died. But she was still alive.

For the next few days I was inconsolable. I rang Dad and pleaded with them to do something so that at least Juliet would come home, but he just kept repeating that it was her decision. I tried to reason with him: couldn't he see that she was sixteen years old and far too young to make such a life-changing decision? I rang Oliver and pleaded with him too, but the answer was the same.

'Mum, it's Juliet's decision and you need to respect it.'

And what of Lincoln? If my family weren't encouraging my daughter to come home, they certainly wouldn't be attempting to persuade Lincoln to return to his mother. Having turned sixteen a year previously, he was now being ushered into the preaching role as a young Brethren brother, despite his reserved personality. Oliver confirmed this when I asked about Lincoln's intentions. All I could glean was second-hand information, filtered through my eldest son.

I was at my wits' end, trying my best to keep myself together for Aaron but falling apart inside. While Aaron was at Kevin's I drove around the country roads like some sort of maniac. I pulled the car onto the grass verge and screamed, banging my head against the steering wheel. Should I have ended my life that day in January 2013 after all? The end of the pier loomed large in my mind. I could almost feel the freezing water engulfing me. Then through my pain I heard a voice: *Maria, you chose life. You can change your life. Keep strong. Keep strong for Aaron. Keep strong for you and all that you have to live for.*

I sat up straight, dried my tears, started the engine and steered the car away from the verge. I had chosen life. I was going to live it.

Three days after Juliet decided not to come back she returned to collect her belongings. She came into the house with eyes downcast and, like Aaron, she seemed ashamed of what she was doing. I begged her to stay but she just shook her head.

'Mum, I'm sorry,' she said, and it sounded to me like she had rehearsed her speech. 'I love you, but I can't take the pressure anymore. I can't live here any longer. It's too hard trying to live two lives, and I've chosen the Brethren. As has Lincoln. He'll be coming soon to get his things as well. But Mum, I'll never stop contact with you.'

Putting our arms around each other, we held each other tight, both of us crying as our hearts broke for each other. Then she pulled away from me and insisted it was time for her to leave. Walking towards the front door, she turned back briefly before saying those words again, 'Mum, I'll always stay in contact with you.' I whispered a tearful 'thank you' and then she was gone.

Almost a week later, a sheepish Lincoln arrived to do what his four older brothers and his sister had already chosen to do – to take his clothes and belongings and depart the home he now found to be in such stark contradiction to his beliefs. His mother was now a 'worldly', and, as such, was contaminating the 'purity' of the Brethren way of life.

He had always been the quietest of my children, not having the swagger or the rebelliousness of Bradley, or his love of clothes and the trappings of the good life. Lincoln, out of all of my sons, was perhaps the one most likely to choose a devout path. It still didn't make his leaving any easier, though. I pleaded with him to reconsider, at least for Aaron's sake. Could he not see another life choice for himself?

No, Mum,' he said, quietly but decidedly. 'I was waiting to see what decision Juliet would make. We've talked about it so much, every day while we've been staying at the Hollands. We know this is hurting you, but you have chosen this worldly life outside of our family and we cannot go along with it. I'm sorry. It was actually Juliet leaving that made up my mind for me. I know what she's doing is the right choice, and I must follow her in that decision. And I hope one day that you will get right with the Lord once more, Mum.'

As we parted on the doorstep, I had the weird sense that it was like talking to a young Edward, my older brother. Lincoln was following the family tradition of joining a hierarchy of devout Brethren brothers, never to take off the blinkers that would ensure his life was comprised of narrow choices based on scripture and the Brethren leaders' rules. Why couldn't he see he had the whole world to explore as a young man, if only he wanted to? I would have supported him in anything he wanted to do. My heart was already broken; to feel that all my children were surrendering their futures, and possibly squandering their potential, was like twisting the knife.

For six weeks Juliet and I talked every day by email or phone – and then she stopped responding. Aaron was heartbroken in those first weeks after Juliet and Lincoln left home. He wasn't eating properly and seemed to be pulling away from me. As I was in a full-time job, he would often go to his Brethren friends after school.

One day after work, my brother-in-law, Shaun, came to drop Aaron off and asked if he could have a chat. I welcomed him into my home with a sinking feeling. I guessed what this chat was going to be about. Shaun wouldn't come further than my hallway to say what he wanted to say.

He stood with his hand resting on Aaron's shoulder as he faced me and said, 'Chloe and I are wondering if it would be possible for Aaron to stay with us for a while. He's so lonely without Juliet and Lincoln and, with you at work, it would make things easier for you and for him.'

I looked at Aaron to see his reaction to this suggestion. His eyes seemed to be pleading with me to say yes. My heart went out to him as I thought about what this would mean for us both. I let out an almost defeated sigh. I had no fight left in me.

'OK, I'm happy for him to stay with you as long as I have full access to see or contact him any time I want.' I watched Aaron's eyes light up. I could see he longed to go. Shaun smiled and patted Aaron's shoulder.

'Sure,' he said, casually. 'That's no problem. You're welcome to pick him up from ours to take him out any time you like.'

As Aaron ran upstairs to pack, I was filled with grief yet again. My last child was leaving me and, although I knew I'd see him when I wanted for a while at least, I knew that I'd finally lost the battle to save any of my children from the Brethren.

For more than a year I had constant contact with Aaron. In the summer we would sit on the sea wall eating ice creams; in the winter we would sit in my car eating portions of steaming hot chips. But if I ever suggested he come to the house, he always refused. Had he been told to stay away?

In September 2017 Aaron stopped answering my phone calls and emails. When I pleaded with my sister Chloe for information, she told me that he'd moved in with Kevin. I've sent him birthday cards and letters, but he never responds.

Also that year, Kevin finally signed the divorce papers. We put the family house on the market. Once it had sold I had enough money to buy a small semi-detached house in the area. Finally I was financially free of Brethren control. Somehow, I hoped I'd learn to live with the heartaches and losses.

I also said goodbye to Max around this time. We were still great companions and best friends, but I needed more than that. For me it was time to move on. I'd never had to break up with someone before and, looking back, I'm sure I could have been gentler in my approach. But in those early years after leaving the Brethren I was driven by a sense of great urgency. I felt that I was living on borrowed time and feared that this newfound freedom might soon be taken from me. I knew I couldn't settle for anything less than the deep romantic attachment that I had always dreamt of. I was restless, determined to find what I was looking for – whatever it was – somehow, somewhere. But I will be forever grateful to Max. I know that my integration into this new impossibly complex and unknown world would not have been possible without his kindness.

In early 2017 I also received my very last letter from Juliet. It was confusing and upsetting. On the one hand she wrote that she loved me and wished she could have a proper, real and caring mum again. On the other hand she was saying that she wasn't able to speak to me as she'd decided to dedicate her life to Christ and the Brethren, and she had to take a stand against those who were 'against' the Brethren. She closed it by saying that she 'might' be able to meet and talk to me at some point in the future if I needed to speak to her about 'something important'. As I sat in Juliet's bedroom on her bed that day reading her words, I wept. How many more tears would I cry?

What strikes me as I read Juliet's letter again is how much contradiction there is in her words. I ask myself: did my seventeen-year-old daughter write these words? What was *really* going through her head as she wrote them? What does she *really* think deep in her heart? As I reread the words, 'I still need you, Mum, because you're the one that knows me best', I can't help agreeing with her. Yes, I *am* the one who knows her best.

The Juliet I knew was witty. She was fun. She was always a bit rebellious for the Brethren: she loved her downhill biking, her skating – many things that the Brethren frowned upon. The Juliet I knew was adventurous and ambitious. I remember the light and excitement in her eyes when she told me she wanted to join the army or be a paramedic. Juliet also had low self-esteem and could be shy in social settings, but she was academic and had come out of school with three A-levels. I am proud to call her my daughter.

My study is decorated with photos of my children that I've found on LinkedIn, and I refuse to give up hope; hope that one day at least one of my beautiful children will have their eyes opened just as I did. When that time comes, I am ready to welcome them back into my home. This is one of the reasons why I have written this book: in the hope that sometime, in some universe, they might find their way to reading it and understand how much I love them and mourn them.

My therapist asks me: do you want to carry your children with you? She is still using her bereavement therapy training to help me heal from what has happened, but she is struggling. She doesn't know how to deal with six deaths at once, and where the 'deaths' are those of people still living.

I tell her that I definitely want to carry my children with me.

So, she says again: 'Tell me about them; tell me who they are; tell me what you miss; how you feel.'

I struggle at first – of course I do. How do I remember their individual smells, their unique personalities, their births, their child selves, their adolescent selves, the things that made me laugh, the things that made me cry about all of them, without falling apart, without descending into a kind of hell? But I tell her that I want to do this, I need to do this, I need to carry them with me, even if I will never see them again.

As time has gone on, I have been continuing the sessions with my therapist. In one recent session she said something profound to me; something that is helping me to look at the loss of my children in a healthier way; something that is helping me see that I might eventually let go of the guilt.

She said, 'Maria, look at this time of your life as a new stage of motherhood. You're in a stage where you are being totally honest with yourself and your children. You're no longer living a lie, so really you were showing love to them by leaving. You were showing by example that there is a choice to live outside of the Brethren. This love might be tearing you and your children apart but at least they know that they can trust you. Look at this time as a temporary separation and never give up hope.'

# THIRTY-SIX

In early 2018 I reached a very low part of my life. I had recently been made redundant and my mental health was suffering at the loss of my children, my family and my Brethren friends. Living in a small town meant that I was constantly seeing them, and it hurt when I passed them in the street and they refused to even acknowledge me. By 2018 three of my children were married and I knew that grandchildren were being born, yet I couldn't meet them. And then I had an encounter that tipped me right over the edge.

Pushing open the heavy swing door of the local chemist shop, I walk down the centre aisle towards the prescription counter. Halfway down, I see the familiar figure of a young woman ahead of me. Her head is bent; she is busy looking at the products on a shelf. Quickening my step towards her, I instinctively call out, 'Juliet!' Her head jolts up at the sound of her name and, before I can reach her, looking flustered, she immediately rushes into the next aisle to get away from me. I continue to follow her regardless, calling out her name as I go. We go up and down the aisles like cat and mouse until I finally catch up with her and we come face to face. It has been almost two years since I have spoken to my daughter. As I put my hands on each side of her arms, gripping them firmly, not wanting her to escape, I look her up and down, wanting to take in every bit of this young woman. She glances around nervously, and I can see fear in her eyes; I realise she is scared of being seen talking to me. She is scared that a Brethren member might walk into the chemist at any moment and see her talking to her unclean mother.

I think of the fear I had felt as a young woman if I saw an ex-Brethren man or woman approaching me in the street. It was terrifying. I couldn't look at them for fear they'd somehow contaminate me. So I understand Juliet's fear, but she is my daughter, and I can't let her go just yet. I have so much I want to ask her. Has she got a job? How did she do in her exams? Is she happy? How are Lincoln and Aaron? But right now I just want to give her a hug. I go to hug her, but she recoils.

As she moves away from me, I whisper, 'I will always love you, Juliet.'

At that moment a sales assistant calls out, 'Prescription for Juliet White.' And that is her cue to make her escape. She runs to the counter, snatches the parcel from the assistant and then she is gone. The door slams shut.

I feel my knees buckle. I drop to the floor. Hunching forward, I put my head in my hands. I feel myself break. My friend Diane, who works in the chemist, rushes to my side and helps me to my feet. She leads me to the pharmacist's area at the back of the store. She puts her arms around me. She holds me tight. I am not crying now. I am howling – wild howls. I am gasping to catch my breath. I am mortified that I've broken down in this way in such a public place, but I am thankful that most of the assistants know my story. They surround me with comforting words and encouragement. Drying my tears, I thank them and Diane profusely for being so kind and then I bolt for the door.

Sitting alone later that evening, in the little home I have so lovingly renovated and made my own now that Max and I have gone our separate ways, I am overcome by an extreme sadness and loneliness. As I sit there listening to the loud tick of the clock in the silence, tears choke me. Again I ask myself whether I should have chosen death instead of life on that cold winter's day five years earlier. What had all of this struggle been for? No one would even know or care if I died here alone.

Heaving a shuddering sigh, I wipe my tears away, pick up my phone and log on to Facebook. Usually, I hate displaying my feelings on the Facebook Ex-Brethren page, but in my desperation, I type the words, 'I need to get away from all this heartache'. Within minutes, the ex-Brethren community reaches out to me. My phone pings with scores of messages of support and encouragement.

Then I receive a phone call from Alex, an ex-Brethren friend in New Zealand. He asks me what is wrong. Between tears, I blurt everything out. I tell him about what happened earlier that day when I met Juliet. I tell him about how lonely I am; how I have left my partner Max, how I've recently lost my job, and that everything seems to be stacked against me. I tell him of how my sons are now married and having children. I tell him about how the Brethren won't allow me to meet my grandchildren; about how I get snubbed in the street if I bump into any Brethren I used to know. He listens silently until I finish unloading all my burdens on him.

'OK,' he says, 'why don't you get on a plane and get yourself to New Zealand? There's a huge ex-Brethren community here and we'll all make sure you are cared for.'

I laugh through my tears. 'You're joking, right?'

'No. I'm serious, Maria,' he says. 'Just think about it.'

I thank him so much for his call and promise to think about his suggestion.

I did think about it. In fact, I stayed awake most of that night thinking about it, and by morning my mind was made up. I would go to New Zealand and take myself as far away from my children, my family and my old friends as I could. Maybe I would even end up living in New Zealand.

Three weeks later I packed my suitcases, locked up the house and made the long journey to the other side of the world. A new chapter in my life had begun. I spent six months travelling on the North Island of New Zealand, meeting and enjoying the company and care of the ex-Brethren community there. Then I decided to do some exploring on my own on the South Island. I took a job as a live-in au pair on a farm outside a small town, caring for two little girls while their parents were busy looking after the cattle and land. I was hoping that caring for other people's children might help me to fill the longing that I had to see my own children and grandchildren.

A few weeks later, in my free time in the evenings, I was scrolling through Tinder, hoping to find a connection with a man in the area. I was feeling lonely. Everything was so foreign to me. I'd never ventured so far from home or out of my comfort zone before. A profile caught my attention. It read:

'Hi. I'm Farmer Julian. I recently arrived from the UK to work in New Zealand. I'm 6' tall, still have my own hair, teeth, and all other necessary faculties [wink emoji]. Some might describe me as ruggedly handsome. I'm looking for a lovely lady to connect and have some fun with.'

I liked the sound of this guy. He sounded like fun and, looking through his pictures, I liked his face. He had a look of genuineness about him, and the fact that he was from the UK made me want to reach out. It would be fun and a comfort to chat to someone from the homeland, so I 'swiped right'. I jumped with excitement when my phone immediately pinged saying, 'You've got a match!' We wasted no time in making contact and were soon exchanging phone numbers so we could arrange a date to meet.

In September 2018 I met Julian Clarke for the first time, in an almost deserted restaurant on the other side of the world. He was easy company. We forgot ourselves instantly as we began to talk. I laughed more that evening than I had laughed in a long time. There was lots of flirting and banter on that first date as we sat in that dimly lit dining room with its worn red carpet and dark wood panelling. There was serious talk too as we wanted to learn more about each other.

Julian had come to New Zealand soon after his twenty-six-year marriage had come to an end. His roots were in Cheshire, but he'd always wanted to try farming, so he had secured a summer farming job on the Isle of Man, which led to another job in New Zealand. This gave him the opportunity he wanted to continue in farming, but also to get away from his life in the UK for a while and a chance to find himself again.

Julian had arrived in New Zealand to start his new job in a small town on the South Island. Six months later I had arrived only thirty miles away from where he was based.

Somehow, it felt that the two of us, both exiled from our homes in the UK and looking for a new start, were destined to meet each other.

That night Julian told me how he'd spent years longing to go back to the farming life he'd loved as a boy. How he'd been left almost destitute after his divorce. I told him a little of my story and why I had found myself making the long journey to New Zealand. Although Julian was shocked, he was interested. He asked me questions about my children. He leant across the table and took my hands in his as I talked. I could see honesty and compassion in his dark-brown eyes. As we looked into each other's eyes that evening I got a sense that even if we didn't end up as lovers, we would always be friends.

As we got to know each other in New Zealand, we were two lost souls in a faraway country who had found each other just when we needed each other most. When I wasn't working or travelling, I spent time in the little shack provided by his employers. It was the oddest place you can imagine – not much more than a glorified shed with its timber structure cladded with whitewashed tongue-and-groove boards. When you stepped inside through the rickety front door, you found yourself in an open-plan living area with a small settee against one wall, and a pine table with matching chairs against the other. A small television unit sat in the corner with the smallest TV I had ever seen. The kitchen reminded me of something from the 1960s, with its old-fashioned cooker, Formica cupboards and worktops. Two doors led off the living area – one led to a small double bedroom with a worn brown carpet, a built-in cupboard in one corner and a double bed pushed tight against the wall in the other, while the other door led into a small walk-in shower room. It may have been old-fashioned and quirky, but it served us well. It became our haven of comfort and home.

Julian would come home exhausted from a hard day out in his spray truck after working all hours. He would tell me stories about his day: how he'd had to spray a field that was on such a steep hill he was scared the truck wouldn't make it; stories of getting the truck stuck in a marshy patch of land; how once he had flown with his boss in a helicopter to spray an inaccessible field. Even though he was often physically shattered, he always made time for me when I was there. And I would share my nannying stories with him: of the mischief the children I cared for would get into; how little Elsie had climbed into my bed at six o'clock one morning for cuddles; of feeding the lambs on the farm; stories about all the amazing sights I'd seen on the days I went out exploring.

One night, Julian asked me about Kevin. We were sitting cuddled up on the worn black leather settee, his arm around my shoulders as I nestled my head against his chest. He wanted to know about the abuse I had hinted at suffering at the hands of my husband. I told him how many Brethren men treated their women as subservient, but that Kevin was worse than most. I told him how he demanded sex from me when and where he wanted it, sometimes up to three times a day. I told him about the awful night I was raped by my husband when I was awoken at 3 a.m.; about how Kevin had placed his hand over my nose and mouth while he raped me. I told him about the time Kevin insisted on having sex with me while our six-year-old daughter was awake in the bed beside us. As I talked, I glanced up at Julian and I saw him shaking his head in disbelief. Tears rolled down his face and onto my hair.

That evening, Julian assured me that what had happened to me was not normal; others had been kind, but he was the first to truly listen and show me such compassion and empathy while I told my stories of Brethren life. And no man had ever encouraged me more – encouraged me to keep going, telling me how strong I was, helping me discover my worth. Other men I'd dated had either got angry from my story and not wanted to talk about it or had advised me to get over it and move on. Julian was different. And in return, when he was having a tough day missing his children and family, I would comfort him and help to keep him going on his journey.

The best memories I have are the days when the sound of our laughter echoed through that little shack, as we playfully teased and bantered with each other; as Julian showed me what passionate lovemaking was about. How his gentle caresses and touches lit a fire within me that I'd never known before. We spent many evenings cuddled up together watching old movies on Julian's laptop propped up on a chair in the corner of that dingy little sitting room. He was the first person to take the time to introduce me to so many old classics. We watched *Dirty Dancing*, *Sister Act*, *Schindler's List* and *Pretty Woman*. I laughed my way through old comedies like *Groundhog Day*, *The Full Monty* and *Ferris Bueller's Day Off*.

On a balmy spring Sunday, just a month after we had met, I decided it was time I treated Julian to some of my home cooking. I decided on a traditional Sunday roast of lamb, roast potatoes, roast vegetables, and I even added Yorkshire puddings, for a taste of home. Julian came home tired and dirty from his day of spraying fields. While he had his shower, I busied myself laying the table, doing my best to make it look romantic with the limited resources there were available in that basic little house. I folded pieces of kitchen roll neatly into triangles, displaying them in the two wine glasses. I set out the odd pieces of cutlery as best I could. I even found an old candle at the back of one of the cupboards and, by dripping some hot wax onto a plate, I was able to prop it up to display it as a centrepiece on the worn pine table. I stood back and admired my handiwork. Although not perfect it added some warmth and romance to the room. I was pleased with my efforts and was looking forward to serving this man who was fast becoming my lover and closest friend.

As Julian comes out of the shower, all cleaned up, he is pleasantly surprised by the cosy scene before him. While I busy myself over the old electric cooker, he comes up behind me. Putting his arms around my waist, he gently kisses the side of my neck. His touch excites me. This is the gentleness and romance that I've spent my life longing for. This was what had been missing in my marriage. I teasingly shoo him away, flapping a tea towel at him. He picks up another tea towel and starts what we call a tea towel war. We chase each other around that tiny kitchen, flirting, flicking the tea towels at each other and laughing. I eventually manage to stop him from chasing me. Taking both his hands in mine, I lead him to his place at the table.

I begin to serve the food. Firstly, I pile Julian's plate high with lamb, vegetables, roast potatoes, Yorkshires and lots of gravy and set it before him. He looks puzzled when he sees me go back to the kitchen area to serve my own.

'Why did you serve me first?' he asks, looking perplexed.

Now I'm puzzled. I always serve the man first. That's how I've been taught: men first and women second. In all my married life and my relationships, since I have left the Brethren, no one has ever questioned it.

'That's just what I do,' I tell him, as I continue to pile food onto my plate.

He gets up from the table and comes to stand behind me. Putting his hands on my waist, he turns me to face him and, with a kiss on my forehead, he says affectionately, 'In future, you will serve both our plates before bringing them to the table. I'm your equal and you should always treat me as such.'

As I take my place at the table, blinking back tears, I reach over and squeeze his hand as I whisper, 'Thank you.'

On 22 February 2019, Julian and I arrived back in the UK. He had secured a job close to the Lake District to be near his family while I had found myself a live-in nanny job near London. As we now lived so far apart we saw much less of each other and, eventually, reluctantly, agreed to go our separate ways. But I don't think either of us ever thought that our journey was over, and, in June 2020, we met up again. In September of the same year I gave up my job in London and moved back up north to live with Julian.

# THIRTY-SEVEN

By April 2021 I have been living with Julian for nine months in a pretty, rented house. I am happy. I have two nannying jobs. We spend our weekends with friends and exploring the beautiful countryside around us, visiting Julian's family in the Lake District when we can. As the day draws to a close, I sit down at my desk in my study and open my laptop to write.

April of this year sees Aaron's twentieth birthday. My children's birthdays are always hard – I am still grieving. It's been four years since I last saw Aaron. What does he look like now? He was only sixteen the last time I saw him. He was a late bloomer, so he looked younger than his years back then. He's now a man. Is he tall? Does he look like me? Is he happy?

Today I went to work as normal, but all day my mind has been consumed by thoughts of Aaron. What is he doing today? Where does he work? Is he thinking about me? Even a photo might give me some insight into the man he has become. When I think of him in my mind's eye, I'm still seeing the teenager who left me four years ago, his face furrowed, torn between his love for me and the rules of the Brethren.

If only the Brethren were allowed Facebook or Instagram, then I could maybe find a photo of him. But the only social media they are allowed is LinkedIn. It's a business platform, and for the Brethren business success is important. Over the years I've often searched on LinkedIn for photos of my children. It has been the only way for me to get an update on what they look like and who they work for. It's always a pleasant surprise when I find an updated photo. I study their faces and try to see what their lives might be like now. I zoom in close to their eyes and try to read what might be going on in their minds. I've managed to find photos of all my children now except for Aaron. I've searched many times for my youngest son, but to no avail. Would I even recognise him? He'll be the one who's changed the most.

Getting home from work at around two o'clock in the afternoon, I get myself a coffee, sit down and search Linked-In again. I type in 'Aaron White'. There's a match! I'm excited but scared at the same time. What if it's another Aaron White and not him? Can I bear the disappointment? Going into the profile, I find a photo of a handsome young man, but I don't recognise him. My heart sinks. But scanning the connections again, I see all the Brethren names. This young man also works for my brother-in-law. This *is* my Aaron.

I look at the photo again, in shock. This can't be him – this young man looking back at me bears no resemblance to the boy I knew. I zoom in to study his eyes. Aaron is the only one of my children who has blue eyes like me. Then I see it: he's got my eyes. This *is* my son; this *is* my boy. Bringing my face up so close to the screen that I can see my own reflection for a moment, I stare hard into his eyes. The image blurs with my tears. This is Aaron staring back at me, yet, if I'd passed him in the street, I wouldn't have recognised him. Twenty years ago I gave birth to this boy and now, because of some man-made rule, I've no way of seeing him in the flesh. My only hope of ever seeing or speaking to him again is if he leaves the Brethren.

I take a breath. I remember to be thankful. Although it has been bittersweet seeing my son's face today for the first time in four years, I'm so thankful that I have seen the man he has become on his birthday. I can keep looking at that photo; I can print it out with the others, frame it, keep imagining the person he has become; keep looking into those blue eyes and hope that he hasn't forgotten me, his mum. I will never give up hope that one day he will also part ways from the Plymouth Brethren Christian Church and we can be reunited.

# THIRTY-EIGHT

Shortly after Aaron's birthday, in April 2021, I sold my house in Wellfleet. After my visit to New Zealand, I knew that I could never return to live in Wellfleet; there was too much heartache to ever be able to call it my home again.

Julian and I hired a van to get us up there and remove the stuff I wanted to bring back with me. I wasn't looking forward to this visit as there were so many memories and people I loved still living there, but I needed to sign legal papers and pack up all my belongings that I had left behind in 2018. I knew that this would probably be the last time I visited my home town.

Part of me was excited. Part of me was nervous. Would I see my children? If I saw any Brethren in the street – my parents, my sisters and brothers – would they acknowledge me? I wanted to make the most of this trip and use the time to show Julian the place I had called home for many years. We decided it was best to wait until I saw how I was feeling before I decided if I should visit my children or not. I did my best to relax and get a good night's sleep the night before. I knew I'd need energy for the emotional and physical challenges ahead.

We set off really early and Julian drove while I looked out the window. As we got closer to our destination, the sea flanked us on one side, and on the other was the familiar landscape I'd grown up in. My sisters both lived close by. How I'd have loved to have been able to drop in on them like a normal family. I remember the many hours I had spent in my sisters' homes, all the times I travelled from Wellfleet on a Sunday to attend the Brethren meetings, and the many Brethren homes I'd gone to for Sunday lunch. Different people flitted through my mind as we made our way north. I was, I realised, remembering the good times. I was shutting out the bad times: the rules and regulations; the life of control; the life of fear; the life of an unhappy and brutal marriage; the life of abuse. I didn't want to remember those times. Those memories were too painful.

It was still early as we drove into the familiar surroundings. Before we went to the estate agents, so I could pick up the house key, we decided to go to the local supermarket to get some provisions. As we walked back to the van, we passed a queue of traffic. I recognised the driver of a vehicle staring at me. It was a Brethren brother. He was scowling at me. This person had once been my friend; this person had spent many hours in my home, and I in his, yet here he was looking at me as if I was evil. I smiled at him and nodded in acknowledgement. But he immediately turned his head away. The traffic moved and he was gone.

As I put the key in the front door of my home, I couldn't help but feel apprehensive. This little home had been my pride and joy. This was the home I had made into a refuge after leaving the Brethren. Julian stood beside me, reassuring me, telling me that everything would be OK, telling me that I could do this. I told myself that I'd been through worse, and this needed to be done.

On entering the house, the cold hit us. My tenant had moved out six weeks previously. The house smelled musty and damp. It didn't feel like my little home anymore. We set about cleaning each room to make it feel more familiar. I lit the wood burner to make it smell more homely.

Putting my arms around Julian, I said, 'Let's make the most of this weekend and pretend that life is normal.'

'Your home is beautiful,' he said, his hand on the small of my back, 'you should be proud of what you achieved here.'

The next day, a Saturday, we spent all morning emptying my garden shed. Most of what we found there was only fit for the skip, but I wanted to find the family photo albums I'd stored there when I'd first moved in. I wasn't sure if I was ready to look at them just yet. But when we found the cardboard boxes they had almost disintegrated with the damp. Most of the photos inside the albums were so damaged that the faces were no longer recognisable. I pulled out an album of Juliet as a baby and flipped through each photo only to find that her face was smudged and faded beyond recognition. There were only one or two photos that could be saved. Putting my head in my hands I cried. All of my life within the Brethren had been recorded in those albums. Maybe, I told myself, it was meant to be. Maybe I needed to put it all behind me and throw all those memories in the bin. After all, I'd never be able to reminisce and laugh over those photo albums with my children and grandchildren like a normal family.

I got up off the damp wooden floor of that shed and made the decision that even though my children had cut me out of their lives, I had to make one last attempt to reach out and make contact.

As Julian picked the soggy boxes up off the floor, I put my hand on his arm and said, 'Today I want to knock on Oliver's door and see if he'll see me.'

Julian turned and gave me a kiss. 'It's your choice, you know,' he said, 'but I think you're doing what's right.'

It's midday by the time we've packed up the contents of the shed and decide to call it a day. I want to show Julian some of the nice restaurants in town, so we book a table for lunch. As Covid restrictions are still in place, we need to take a table outside. I choose one of my favourite restaurants on a busy corner in the centre of Wellfleet. I have always liked sitting outside this restaurant because I can watch the people and the cars go by. While we wait for our food and drink, I realise that I'm staring at every person and car that goes past in the hope of catching a glimpse of my children, a glimpse of my parents, or maybe my siblings.

A car stops in traffic right beside our table. Looking at the driver, I can see he looks familiar and he's staring back at me. It's my Uncle Cuthbert! He looks so much older. Without thinking, I wave and smile. The corners of his mouth twitch before he turns his head away.

We finish our lunch and then make the short drive to Oliver's house. I take the driver's seat and, as I make the familiar journey to my eldest son's home, I realise that my hands are shaking. Why am I shaking? This is my firstborn, my son, the boy I carried in my womb. Why am I scared of my own son? I try to stay optimistic. Maybe he and his wife will welcome Julian and me into their home and let me meet their two sons, my grandchildren.

As we both step out of the van, Julian takes my hand and squeezes it reassuringly as we walk towards the driveway. It's not a long driveway and, as we walk the short distance, I can see a child's face at one of the windows. I smile and lift my hand tentatively in a wave as I realise that I'm looking into the face of my young grandson. I can see the little boy calling to his dad, 'Daddy, there's someone at the door.'

I want to run to him and take him up in my arms to tell him that I am his granny but suddenly he's gone from the window. I lift the silver knocker on the black front door, give it a gentle knock and wait. Silence. I look back at the window where I had seen the boy's face but it's as if he had never been there. I peer in. The room is empty. It's as if no one is home. Did I imagine that little face there? No, I know I didn't imagine it. Julian and I both saw him. I knock at the door again, harder this time. Still there is just silence.

Going to the other windows at the front of the house, I stare inside. I see a box of Lego emptied out on a big dining table in one room, baby toys on the floor of another, but there's no sign of life – nothing. They must all be hiding in a back room.

I want to hammer the door down and tell Oliver that it's me – it's Mum. I want to yell at him and tell him that I'm still the same person who loves him as always. I want to run into his home and hug him and his little family. I want to tell him that it's not fair that his children have never met their granny. But I know it's pointless; I know I can't force them to open the door. Instead, I turn and walk back down the drive towards the van. I feel Julian put his arm around my slumped shoulders.

As I start the engine and drive slowly away, I can't help looking back at the windows of my son's house, longing to see the child's face just one last time. I want to see the young woman who married my son – a young woman I barely know. But the windows are empty.

We drive away. I have no idea where I'm going – I just drive. Julian reaches across and takes my hand as I change gear. That's when the deep heart-wrenching sobs begin. I can't control them. My vision is blurred. I see a car park and pull in. I turn off the engine. Slumped over the steering wheel, I sob as though my heart will break. Julian knows that there are no words, so he just puts a comforting arm around me as I weep. I weep for my children, I weep for my grandchildren, I weep for my children's spouses, I weep for my parents, I weep for my whole family. I am defeated. Why did I even try to reach out to them?

Finally, when my tears subside, I lift my head and gather myself as I have learnt to do so many times. I won't let them defeat me. I must never give up hope. But once we are back at my packed-up house, I'm consumed with a desire to run. I want to get away from this place. I've no life here now. I need to put Wellfleet behind me and make a new life with Julian back in Cheshire. Monday can't come soon enough, when I will get on the road and make my way back to my new home.

December 2021, a few days before Christmas. Everyone I know is preparing for their family gatherings, working out where to put up visitors, wrapping presents for their children or grandchildren. I'm trying to keep myself busy.

I get home from work and sit down with Julian to watch television. The adverts are full of pictures of big families sitting around tables, eating Christmas dinners together, laughing together, playing games together.

My phone pings with a Facebook friend request. Checking out the person who has sent it, I notice that she has several mutual ex-Brethren friends, so I assume she is another of the recent leavers who contact me because I'm a recent leaver too. As I scroll through her Facebook page, I notice one of her recent posts is a quote: 'One of the hardest things you will ever have to do, my dear,' she has written, 'is to grieve the loss of a person who is still alive.'

The quote stirs tears. I too must live with the grief of losing my six children.

I accept her friend request. Maybe I can help her. I send her a message asking if she's a recent leaver. She and I start a back-and-forth conversation, finding out more about each other and how we managed to leave the Brethren. It's not long until we realise we have a common connection: she knows Aaron! She goes on to tell me that Aaron was interested in her daughter and she was their 'go-between'. Now I can't type fast enough. I want to know everything. It's like I suddenly have this little insight into his world. What she tells me next makes my heart skip a beat. She tells me how Aaron talked about me, and how much he still loves me and misses me. I feel tears running down my face as I watch her next message load. She tells me about how, up until she left, Aaron would reach out to her for support because his dad is an alcoholic. She tells me how he's struggling to cope as he watches his dad slowly killing himself. This news about Kevin's alcoholism shocks me at first but then I realise this is probably his only way of coping with the stigma and shame that he lives under.

I push those thoughts from my mind, as all I want to hear is what Aaron has said about me. I know how untrusting new leavers are of us ex-Brethren, so I'm pleased when she shares Aaron's words. He has told her that he loves me; that I would sleep in his bed for comfort when I had cancer; that I'd always been his best friend but the relationship was 'just torn' as he couldn't live with me 'being against Mr Hales', the Man of God.

My tears are really flowing now. What does he mean: 'just torn'? Does he mean he feels torn between Mr Hales and me? Does he mean that we've been torn apart? Who is torn and who is doing the tearing?

Seeing my tears, Julian turns off the TV and asks what's wrong. I show him the messages. He puts his arms around me and holds me as I cry. There are no words. It's bittersweet. It's so good to hear that Aaron still loves me, but so sad that he can't reach me because he is trapped within that organisation.

'Where is the love?' I ask.

Remembering the work I've done with my therapist, I hear myself talking to Aaron in my mind just as I had talked to Juliet the day I found out she had married.

'Oh, Aaron,' I say. 'I wish, my son, that I could put my arms around you right now and hold you tight, but you are right, it is just torn. Our feelings are torn, our emotions are torn, our lives are torn. We have been torn apart. I can't change that. But I can promise you that I will carry you and your siblings in my heart always. I will keep on talking to you. I will keep finding your faces on LinkedIn. And one day, should you choose a different life for yourself, I'll be waiting.'

I continue to send my children birthday cards every year, and with every year that goes by I'm sad for another year lost but I will never give up hope. Maybe one day one of my children will come knocking on *my* door. And I'll always be ready.

# EPILOGUE

It's now March 2022, and as Julian and I climb into bed together in our little home, we cuddle up close to each other and do what we've done every night since our relationship began: we say our gratitudes. Three gratitudes each is the rule. Tonight, it's my turn to go first.

'I'm grateful for you,' I say.

Julian thanks me before saying his gratitude: 'I'm grateful that we have great companionship.'

'Well, I'm grateful that I keep you on your toes,' I say, laughing.

He comes back at me quickly, saying with a wink and a smile, 'Well, I'm grateful for good sex.'

Giving him a playful nudge, I say my third gratitude, 'I'm grateful for all that you've taught me.'

He hugs me close in the crook of his arm and says, 'And I'm so grateful and so proud to have you next to me.'

As I close my eyes and drift off to sleep, I am grateful for all that I've gained since that day on the end of the pier. I have found a loving relationship with a respectful, caring, passionate man. A man who shares his children, his family and friends with me. A man who has also suffered but who is interested in what I have to say. A man who holds me when I wake from a bad dream in the middle of the night, who makes me laugh, who shows me films, who disagrees carefully with me and without shouting. I've gained relationships with people who love me unconditionally. People who support me; people who help me to keep going on this new path that I've chosen to walk – people I can call true.

I know how much I have lost because of my choice to break away from the Brethren. I know how much has been taken away, how much has been torn apart, how torn I have been, how torn my children have been made to feel – yet I will also be forever grateful that I chose this life. That I chose freedom.

# ACKNOWLEDGEMENTS

I am incredibly grateful to all those who contributed to the creation of my memoir. Your wisdom and support have been instrumental in bringing this project to life. Thank you for believing in me and for being a part of this journey.